SIX NOVELISTS LOOK
AT SOCIETY

By the Same Author

Literary Commentary
The Art of Ernest Hemingway
George Orwell
Arthur Koestler
Aldous Huxley
Graham Greene
Tomorrow Revealed

Fiction
Cat on Hot Bricks
Rain and the River
A Land Fit For Eros (with J.B. Pick)

Literary History
Sex in Literature: I, Introductory Survey
Sex in Literature: II, The Classical Experience.
Sex in Literature: III, The Medieval Experience

SIX NOVELISTS LOOK AT SOCIETY

An Enquiry into the Social Views of

Elizabeth Bowen,
L. P. Hartley, Rosamund Lehman,
Christopher Isherwood, Nancy Mitford, C. P. Snow

by
JOHN ATKINS

John Calder
LONDON

First published in Great Britain 1977
by John Calder (Publishers) Ltd
18 Brewer Street, London W1R 4AS
© John Atkins, 1977.

ISBN 0 7145 3535 4 Casebound

Typeset in 10 on 11pt Times Roman by The Blackburn Times Press,
Northgate, Blackburn.

Printed by M. & A. Thomson Litho Ltd., East Kilbride, Scotland.

CONTENTS

FOREWORD

In this study I am interested in social aspects before anything else. All the rest is subordinate. This has involved a great deal of critical selection, for the novel in its nature is a comprehensive form. Nevertheless, critics have always contrasted the social with the political and both with the personal. Irving Howe has remarked that the social novel of the nineteenth century marked the consolidation of individual action, as found in eighteenth century picaresque, into the political triumph of the merchant class (*Politics and the Novel,* New York, 1957). A typical hero was involved in testing himself and his values against the remnants of aristocratic resistance and the gross symbols of the commercial world that offended his sensibility. In our own day novelists have continued to emphasize the war on commercial vulgarity, and the merchant class has been consistently ridiculed. They have also enlisted a neo-aristocracy and spurious aristocratic sentiment in support. But the notion of testing the hero is obsolete. The hero himself is obsolete. In the nineteenth century the social novel declined into conventional mediocrity, as in some of Trollope, or fractured in different directions such as private sensibility, public affairs and politics. A veritable social novel pre-supposes social stability and Jane Austen is the ideal. A veritable political novel is concerned with the idea of society rather than its workings.

Now I am not concerned with anything that can be called *the* social novel but with a group of novelists who flourished between the wars, (and, in some cases, still write) and who reflect certain social attitudes, preoccupations and realities. I doubt if any of them would be referred to as a 'social novelist' in a university seminar, yet each of them has something apt to say on social matters. My aims in seeking out what they have to say have been threefold: to discover what social milieu each writes about, and what he neglects; to elicit their critiques of English society (and not German society, as might be done with Isherwood, or French as with Mitford); and to look for signs of positive alternatives, although this is certainly not the novelist's job, whatever weekly reviewers may think about it. I have also had to resist the temptation to pursue other matters, e.g., the personal life with Elizabeth Bowen or individual morality with L.P. Hartley, although in some cases these may be more characteristic concerns of the author than the social.

The social aspect of the modern novel has not been favoured by many modern critics. V.S. Pritchett has been an exception to this rule. In an article written for *Partisan Review,* October 1948 ('The Future of English Fiction'), he said: '. . . our most talented novelists retired into the private gardens of their sensibility and left the world outside to their inferiors'. This comes as something of a shock to one who remembers the thirties as an age of extreme social concern, among novelists as among other thinking people. Pritchett obviously feels that the novel is a middle-class vehicle (this in itself is a social criterion), our youngest literary form, born with modern capitalism and saturated with individualism and liberal culture. 'Is the novel tied to the fate of capitalism and the liberal view of life?' he asks, thus appearing to pre-empt his answer. But would there be much scope for a social novel under socialism? May not official myths come to mean more than private histories? Elsewhere Pritchett has noticed that one class has always seemed comical to another. As it is the middle class that has done the writing it follows that the working class is represented as a lot of comedians more frequently than the middle class, though retired admirals have had their share. The truth is, as I shall emphasize further on, our classes are not monolithic. If numerical supremacy leads to taking the mickey, what about the female menace?

I have chosen novelists of roughly the same generation, but with a temporal spread. They all began their writing careers between the wars. I have indicated when their first work of fiction appeared at the beginning of each chapter. All were still living when I began writing but three, L.P. Hartley, Elizabeth Bowen and Nancy Mitford, died during the course of my writing.[1] The particular six I have chosen are, of course, arbitrary, but they are names one was likely to come across when reading literary reviews of the period 1930 to 1960, either as authors or as subjects of criticism. Naturally, there could have been others—the six could have become a dozen, say, or I could have replaced some of my present number with Joyce Cary or Evelyn Waugh, Ivy Compton-Burnett or Anthony Powell, Graham Greene or Pamela Hansford Johnson. On occasion, especially in my final chapter, I have stepped outside the six and briefly referred to other writers, notably Waugh and Orwell, because they have illustrated a point better than any of my selected novelists could do. I don't think the results would have been very different if I had varied the names. These form a recognizable group (though certainly not all subscribing to the same philosophy), they stand for a recognizable period and they all reflect, in their varying ways, a recognizable way of life. There is no pretence at sociological objectivity either on my part or on that of my subjects, but when one of the latter pleases a reader he has been acclaimed as accurate or perceptive. He may have been both these

1. And a fourth, Rosamund Lehmann, has produced a new novel just as we go to press. *A Sea-Grape Tree* can be no more than noted.

things but he is also liable (or should I say certain?) to be partial. We often forget that although it is impossible to please all the people all the time it is very easy to please some of the people some of the time.

One last word. While preparing this study I had to read several works by G.D.H. Cole. In one of them he complains that events move so quickly these days he was always in danger of being out-of-date by the time he reached publication. Such time-lags are unavoidable, he says, 'nor is it my fault that books take nowadays a long time to produce.' Apparently the speed of modern life has passed publishing by (I have read that one of the first Brontë books was published within a month of the original reception of the manuscript—that can only happen these days when you are writing about the Middle East). But I was once reprimanded by a reviewer for not including in my study a book that appeared after I went to press. It is probable that one of my three living authors will bring out a new novel before I can get this into print and flatly contradict something I have stated with some certainty.

I

The English Social Scene, 1920-1970

This is a study of the work of six novelists whose writing careers extend, by and large, from 1920 to 1970. Three of them are still living (as I write) and, we may believe and hope, still writing. Nevertheless, the bulk of their work and the significant part of their work, was done in the period mentioned. Here and there I have quoted from a post-1970 work, but only to emphasize a point made in the earlier writing. As I am concerned with their social attitudes, it seems sensible to provide an account of the background against which they worked. This is the subject of my first chapter. But I wish it to be understood that I am solely concerned with the fifty years between 1920 and 1970. It is necessary to assert this because the years since 1970 have been so troubled that generalizations have become impossible. We simply don't know where we are going. The England of today is already a very different place from the England my six novelists were acquainted with.

The Division of Wealth

The maldistribution of wealth in modern Britain is too well-known to need any detailed description in a book of this kind. In 1920 England had come out of a war which had hurt her more than she knew. The period under discussion was bifurcated by a second world war. The two halves were as different, socially, as two countries situated in different parts of the world.

For a quick look at the England of the thirties we could do worse than read J.B. Priestley's *English Journey,* first published in 1934 and considered sufficiently interesting to be re-issued in 1949. Priestley managed to convey the picture of a society utterly complacent in one

1. This book has been found sufficiently valuable as a social document to be re-issued yet again as a Penguin Book (1977).

section of its corporate body and utterly despairing in the other. The maldistribution of wealth had polarized and the result, in human terms, was such that a young person reading about it today must find it hard to credit. We who witnessed it also found it hard to credit but were bitterly aware that those who controlled society appeared to find the situation bearable. In those days Jarrow was a by-word: the City that Died. There was no escape from the prevailing misery, wrote Priestley, wherever you went. The only comparisons that might be made were between one wretched street and another possibly less wretched. One out of every two shops appeared to be permanently closed. Men did not work, they just hung about, not in scores but in hundreds and thousands. They 'wore the drawn masks of prisoners of war.' Prisoners they were. Some said of the class war, and it was difficult to avoid such glib explanations.

The worst sights were to be seen in the North. Priestley, with his dramatic skill, delineated vivid little vignettes and contrasted them. In Blackburn he heard of a housemaid called Alice. Her mistress, noticing that her boots were worn out and wishing to be kind, asked her what size she took. This was a question Alice simply could not answer. She had never had a pair of new boots and knew nothing about sizes. Her boot size had always been that of the last possessor. Her father, mother and brother were all out of work. 'Their club pay ceases at the end of this year', Priestley wrote, 'but their real life ceased some time ago,' Now on the same day as he was told about Alice a fine big mill was put up for auction. It had cost a hundred thousand pounds some twenty years before yet there was not a single bid. Nobody had any money to buy or rent mills any more. The entire district had been sliding towards bankruptcy for years. There was plenty of wealth in the country but you had to look somewhere else for it.

Psychologically such a situation causes great tension. Naturally there is envy by the poor for the rich, but far more complex states of mind are evolved. For example, at about the time Priestley was writing it was announced that some miners had been seen drinking champagne. The type of person who considered this shocking was not averse to drinking champagne himself, but he could not bear the idea of a miner drinking it because miners were supposed to be poor and therefore could not afford it. But if they were drinking it they could afford it and therefore they were not poor. Such reasoning would not be accepted in academic circles or by economists, nor would psychologists defend it, but politicians and students of opinion have to take note of it. Priestley's reaction was extremely sensible but there were few in that guilt-ridden era to share it.

> A man who has been working for seven hours at a coal face, crouching in a horribly cramped space about half a mile underground, has a right, if anyone has, to choose his own tipple; and I for one would be delighted if I knew that miners could afford to drink champagne and were drinking it. Horatio Bottomley and his friends, we are told, drank champagne all day for years and nobody protested, though Bottomley and his kind never filled anyone's coal scuttle, only emptied it, and probably never honestly earned for themselves a bottle of stout, let alone cases and cases of champagne.

Today I have no doubt that a few miners with eccentric tastes do drink champagne, although the majority would prefer not to—in fact, when they charter planes to Italy they take their beer with them, having an attitude to Abroad very similar to that of a character in one of Nancy Mitford's early novels. But times change, no-one objects to miners drinking champagne today. This is because they are relatively well paid and you should only kick a man when he's down.

The bitterness between the rich and the poor during the thirties was immense and growing. If Hitler had waited another five years he might not have raised up that celebrated English solidarity which finally defeated him. The poison would surely have done its work in a few more years. There was a tremendous sense of being cheated among the population at large. It didn't come immediately because there was a misleading trade boom after the end of hostilities and then, when times really became bad, it took time to sink in as it always does. Those intellectuals, for example, who wanted a more permissive society before the war were disappointed when the walls of Jericho did not fall down. The society they wanted has arrived now and they are quite as responsible as the pop-singers, but they do not get the credit because the time-scale of social change is not yet understood. It was for this reason that men did not really start complaining about fighting the war for nothing until a good ten or twelve years after they were demobilized. Priestley mentions a re-union battalion dinner he attended. Of course, many of the men could not afford tickets so it was arranged that they should have free admission, but still many of them could not come: they had no clothes. This, quite rightly, was the cue for Priestley's indignation. These men had gone out with Kitchener's New Army, they had stood in mud and water, scrambled through the barbed wire and come back as official heroes wanting to pick up their ordinary lives again—'and now, in 1933, they could not even join us in a tavern because they had not decent coats to their backs.'

When his book was re-issued in 1949 Priestley wrote an Intro- duction for it in which he drew attention to the fact that the England of the depressed areas and the dole had vanished. There is still a great deal of ugliness and mistakes are still being made, but one can no longer feel that England is a country to be ashamed of. (The enormous gulf that exists between pre-war and post-war England is one of the major impressions to strike Isherwood on his return to this country: see chapter five.) Although the economic condition of the country was supposedly improving during the nineteen thirties, and although parts of the country were supposedly prosperous, from twenty to thirty per cent of the working classes were still living in 1939 below the Rowntree minimum *even outside the depressed areas.* (Rown- tree had used a minimum standard of nutrition laid down by the British Medical Association, and it made no concessions to luxury.) By the end of the second war, however:

> . . . we are not the blind donkeys we were in 1933, when there were materials to spare and men aching for work and yet we could not plough up and make fertile all our wasted acres, could not re-build the old factories and install new plant in our essential industries . . . whatever mistakes we may be making now, we no longer waste men, women and children as we were doing when I wrote this book, in the England of the depressed areas and the dole.

At the time one wondered how much the British working class could stand. Some foreign observers felt they were unbearably docile. The British social structure was probably saved by the cheapness of imports, especially food, between the wars. Food producers had vast stocks during the depression which they had to sell off. Food in a sense always constituted a buyer's market because the seller could not hold it too long. The extraordinary thing is that, if we ignore for the moment the two million or so unemployed, and a few more mil- lions on short time (we shouldn't ignore them, but society managed it pretty blithely at the time) the standard of living actually rose during this period in Britain! Mercifully cheap food for the poor meant also cheap food for the better-off and more money for luxuries. Between 1929 and 1933, years that bounded one of the worst economic crises in modern history, real wages rose by ten per cent. The difficulty was to get the wages. But the world slump caused much less hardship in Britain than in most other countries. The imperial situation acted as a buffer.

Things are better now, as Priestley remarked and as everybody who is old enough to remember would never deny.[1] When poverty was such a hideous fact, one of the major preoccupations of economists was the assessing of calory needs, poverty lines and such standards. Bowley's poverty line represented a much more depressed standard of living than the Rowntree human needs standard, but even so at least fifteen per cent of the population fell below it during the decade. Writing in 1956, G.D.H. Cole declared that this type of absolute privation had virtually ceased to exist as a serious social problem, though there were still many households that could not measure up to the more generous Rowntree standard (The Post-War Condition of Britain). But we would be unwise to be unduly optimistic. There is a group of economists, of whom Richard M. Titmuss is the best known, who suspect that income inequality has been increasing since 1949 whilst the ownership of wealth, which is far more highly concentrated in the United Kingdom than in the United States, has probably become still more unequal in recent years. In terms of family ownership, the growing inequality has become even more striking. In the Introduction to the 1964 re-issue of Tawney's Equality, Titmuss refers to an analysis by Professor Townsend and Dr Abel-Smith of national surveys of income and expenditure carried out by the Ministry of Labour in 1953-4 and 1960. These show that there had been a sharp increase in the proportion of the population living at or around the official definition of subsistence, accompanied by a rise in the incidence of malnutrition. 'The indications are that at least a quarter and probably a third of the people of Britain live in households which fail to attain all the desirable levels of dietary intake. And, contrary to what is often believed, the numbers in this situation seem to have increased since the mid-fifties.'

So we ought not to be complacent. There may well be a distinction, of course, between poverty and malnutrition. The latter may be the consequence of the former, or of nutritional ignorance. If we can feel that the worst extremes of poverty have now been abolished, we cannot feel so optimistic about the distribution of our national wealth. H.F. Lydall and D.G. Tipping, in the Bulletin of the Oxford Institute of Statistics, vol. 23, no. 1, Feb. 1961, showed that the most striking fact about British society was still the way in which the ownership of net capital was concentrated in a few hands. One per cent of the

1. By 'now' I mean 1970, the terminal date of my social observations. Since 1970 another economic slump has appeared, but the despair that accompanied the earlier one is absent. Socially, this is of the greatest significance.

population owned 42% in 1951-6 and 5% owned 67.5%. These stark figures should be sufficient to cause a feeling of uneasiness, but even they are under-estimates, for they exclude pension funds and trusts, which have grown enormously in recent years, and they do not take account of the increasing tendency for large owners of property to distribute their wealth among their families, to send it abroad, and transform it in other ways.

Inequality in the ownership of wealth has increased more rapidly in Britain than in the United States since 1949. Titmuss says that the British system of taxation is almost unique in the Western world in its generous treatment of wealth-holders in respect of settlements, trusts, gifts and other arrangements for redistributing and rearranging income and wealth. This was reflected in the remarkable fact that in the mid-fifties it was in the young adult age group (20-24) that the concentration of wealth in relatively few hands was most marked. Even in 1938, in his Preface to a new edition of *Equality,* Tawney had referred to the situation with a stinging irony:

> Institutions which enable a tiny class, amounting to less than two per cent of the population of Great Britain, to take year by year nearly one quarter of the nation's annual output of wealth may appeal to the emotions of wonder, reverence and awe. One cannot argue with the choice of a soul; and, if men like that kind of dog, that is the kind of dog they like.

It is remarkable, says Titmuss, how long years of economic depression, a civilians' war, rationing, "fair shares for all", "penal" rates of taxation and estate duty, and the Welfare State have made so little impression on the great fortunes.[1]

Extreme inequality not only offends one's sense of justice, and even the aesthetic sense, but also imposes severe social penalties, which Tawney summarized thus. There is a perpetual misdirection of limited resources to production or upkeep of costly futilities, instead of for better food, houses and schools. For lack of simple necessities, the human energies which are the source of all wealth (how often this is forgotten!) are, in the case of the majority, systematically under-developed from birth to maturity. A jungle of vested interests has been created which resists attempts to reconstruct on more rational lines a system inherited from before 1914. And it results in a class struggle which, though not always obtrusive, is always active under the

1. 'Penal' taxation has taken its toll of small businesses and the self-employed. The big fish have the resources to escape the net.

surface, and is fatal to the mobilization of cooperative effort.

Tawney in 1938. The situation has improved today, though according to Titmuss there is no firm ground for optimism. But during the greater part of the period under review this judgment of Tawney's was applicable. This was the dominant socio-economic situation for those who could see it.

The Class Structure

Trying to define class, and moreover, to back your definition with live illustrations, is guaranteed to develop one's nervous tension. The *Encyclopaedia Britannica* grapples bravely with the problem. A class, it says, is an aggregate of persons, within a society, possessing approximately the same status. The class system, or the system of stratification of a society, is the system of classes in their internal and external relationships. It is the set of relationships constituted by the granting of deference to individuals, roles and institutions in the light of their place in the system of power, property, occupation and other factors. A man is judged in accordance with the judging person's perception of his income and wealth, his occupation, his level of achievement within his occupation, his standard of living (including the location of his residence), his ethnic characteristics, his kinship connections, his educational level, his relationship to the main centres of the exercise of power in the society as a whole and in the particular institutions in which he functions, such as business firms, churches, universities, armies, government departments, etc., and his associates, formal and informal. This is a static definition; the complexity is increased greatly when one considers the fringes of these social areas (always of special interest to novelists, as it is in these areas that drama and tension are most likely to develop). The denial of claims of deference to the *parvenu,* for instance, because he is too new, or too crude, or too rich, or too contaminated with foreign connections, is a fertile source of alienation in society and a powerful factor in the promotion of change.

As an example of the kind of complexity involved, take that very English conception, the 'gentleman'. There used to be a tradition that 'a gentleman doesn't indulge in trade'. Today they have to to survive, but there is a hint that they still undervalue trade and try to don the gentleman's mantle on the golf course or the country estate as soon as they can. 'Not since Marie Antoinette milked cows in the Trianon has there been a ruling class in Europe with such an urge to play the peasant', comments Michael Shanks in *The Stagnant Society,* 1961.

'. . . I have always felt it to be a national tragedy that the centre of government and finance is in London and not in Birmingham.' One result of this situation is the attitude adopted to the time of starting work. This is an important status symbol in modern Britain. The later one starts, the greater one's social esteem, which is plainly the relic of a more leisurely age. Industrial workers clock in half an hour or an hour before the clerical staff. Really important people do not start work until the morning is half over. Our industrial society still tries to run itself on vaguely pastoral lines in some respects.

Any possibility of a neatly categorized class system is rapidly becoming a thing of the past. Those convenient divisions into upper, middle and working are no longer of any value. Orwell recognized this and began to contort his thinking with fantastic hybrids such as the upper-lower-middle. If you want to make any kind of academic distinctions these days you will be concerned with meticulous details and careful shading, to reveal minute differences of internal décor and tricks of speech: where you place the telly, the shade of the wallpaper, the type of breakfast food—it is factors such as these that distinguish the demi-semi-middle from the lower-demi-semi in the social scale. 'These nuances are becoming a temporary obsession, hardly flattering to our national intelligence or common sense', writes Shanks, and those who see the so-called posh Sunday papers regularly must agree.

The most refreshing, because condemnatory, approach to this ramshackle system based on emotional spasms and prejudices, has come from Tawney and Orwell. The former wrote in *Equality:* 'The destiny of the individual is decided, to an extent which is somewhat less, indeed, than in the past, but which remains revolting, not by his personal quality, but by his place in the social system, by his position as a member of this stratum or that.' In his Epilogue, 1938-50, an additional chapter specially written for the 1952 edition, Tawney said that our educational system teaches the fatal lesson that character and intelligence count for less than money and that the majority of children were to be educated, from infancy onwards, as second-class citizens. I personally recognize the truth of this. As an adolescent I used to rage against the very idea of character, which seemed to me to be a confidence trick taught by my superiors. Later, when I learnt how men behave, I recognized its importance, but it was a lesson that had to be learnt against the social grain and with the tide of hypocrisy. Orwell stressed the unreality of our class system in addition to its injustice. 'The peculiarity of English class distinctions is not that they are unjust—for after all, wealth and poverty exist side by side in almost all countries—but that they are anachronistic. They do not exactly correspond to economic distinctions, and what is essentially an industrial and capitalist country is haunted by the ghost of a caste system.' (*The English People*, 1947).

Class war, a phrase which becomes more and more meaningless as the system becomes more complex, has not really existed in any significant sense during the period under review. Marxists like to speak of an 'underlying' class war, but underlying wars are not part of the vocabulary of reasonable men. There was a time when the classes felt warlike towards each other, but that was when the distinctions were so obvious they did not have to be pinned down by references to wall-paper and modes of address. Priestley caught a glimpse of this situation when he talked to a Catholic medieval craftsman in the Cotswolds, who loathed the modern world. 'He disliked all our ways. He asked me to share his contempt for the new urban mob, the products of industrial towns and free education at council schools and cheap books and so on and so forth; but as I consider myself one of these very people, I had to decline.' Such opinions are so subjective they have no value for us here—this man thought of townees as a bunch of monkeys compared with fine, upstanding peasants, whereas for Priestley they had more intelligence, courage, chivalry and humour than any peasant. Yet a writer like Waugh would have agreed with the craftsman.

Despite many exceptions and qualifications, the old class divisions of Britain are declining. (See Raymond Postgate, 'Class in Britain and Abroad', *Class*, a symposium edited by Richard Mabey, 1967.) Although the wealth of the population remains absurdly maldistributed, the old privileges of wealth which once dominated society are passing away. Public opinion is becoming too fierce to accept them. But a new set of privileges, based on occupation, is replacing them. Every occupation has its perks but they vary immensely in quality and quantity: they range from the free pencils available to the teacher through the cheap canteen lunches of the factory worker, the free tickets of the railway worker and the huge discounts on fares offered to airline employees to the expense allowance of the company director. Because British society has evolved for centuries without any definite breaks, the classes and the castes and the privileged groups rub shoulders with each other and jostle one another amusingly at such ceremonies as the coronation. (See T.H. Pear, *English Social Differences*, 1955.)

However, despite all these qualifications and shades of difference, people still talk of classes and most of them feel they belong to a class —though the one they think they belong to does not always coincide with the one to which a sociologist would assign them. Some students of society have tried to overcome the difficulty by speaking of class models which are acknowledged by different groups of people. It is really a matter of dimension: you adopt the model which embodies the notion of social stratification you consider the more significant. Here is one such writer, Frank Parkin:

> The working class model envisages the social system as divided roughly into two main categories- those who exercise power and authority, and those who are subjected to it; society consists of 'them' and 'us', and there is little social traffic between the two. In line with this, the ethic of success and individual achievement has scant relevance; collectivism and solidarity are the dominant concepts, whilst the possibilities for personal advancement are strongly devalued. In contrast to this the middle class model of stratification assumes not a sharp dichotomy, but a graduated hierarchy of authority and opportunity. Society is seen as a ladder which the talented and ambitious can climb; conflicts are not inherent in the social structure but can be avoided by sensible management and goodwill on all sides.
>
> *Middle Class Radicalism*, 1968.

So the working class, or large parts of it, still think they're exploited and ordered about. In financial terms, however, they are getting more important. The share of wage-earners in the Gross National Product rose sharply between 1938 and 1946 (G.D.H. Cole, *The Post-War Condition of Britain*, 1956). Comparing 1938 with 1954 we find that wages rose from 37.9 to 42.4% of the total of personal incomes; salaries rose at the same time from 17.9 to 21.3%. In fact, wages, salaries and forces' pay combined rose from 59.6 to 70.2%. So earned incomes have been rising steadily since the war, which leads to another complication—as people earn more they get the idea that they are rising up the class scale, even though they may be standing still, in relative terms. In 1952, for example, Gallup Poll discovered that 49% of the sample claimed to be middle class, compared with 46% who thought they belonged to the working class. Admitted that Britain has a larger middle class than most countries, yet it still does not outnumber the working class on any acceptable basis of evaluation. Cole, in his *Post-War Condition*, suggested that the 'middle classes' formed something between 22 and 30% of all occupied heads of households, while the 'working classes' accounted for from 69 to 78%. This assessment was purely economic, and it is difficult to see how any other definite figure could be arrived at.

It is really the middle classes that cause the trouble—they are traditionally more fluid, more ambitious and more subject to the demands of fashion.[1] It has become normal to speak of a group of middle classes rather than one solid middle class, as one can still, without departing too far from a sense of reality, speak of a solid working class. Cole in fact enumerated twelve middle classes, ranging from heads of private businesses and active partners and directors in business, through salaried administrators, professional men, higher and middle grades of the Civil Service, big and middle shopkeepers, large and middle farmers, unoccupied rentiers, full-time students, clerks and typists, nurses and primary schoolteachers, shop assistants to ('just possibly') lower supervisory grades in industry, transport, etc. Even Michael Shanks's Stagnant Society is mobile enough to make any statement concerning class of doubtful value after the passage of a few years. Basic industries, such as coal-mining and railways, textiles and shipbuilding, decline. A decline in the importance of manual workers is accompanied by the growth in importance of service trades and white-collar workers. The United States lead the way, it has come to be accepted that what is happening there now will happen here tomorrow. In Britain about 40% of workers are employed in manufacturing, compared with 25% in the United States. The ratio of staff to production workers in British manufacturing rose from 16% to over 20% between 1948 and 1957. In I.C.I. the number of staff workers rose by 45% in a ten year period, manual workers by only 2%. Increasing prosperity not only causes people to rethink their social status, but also creates a bigger demand for services.

When writing about class one is conscious all the time of the necessity to clear one's mind of clichés such as class-war, opposed camps of capital and labour, and similar simplicities. The conflicting camps of the Marxists have been broken up into strata: shareholders and managers, skilled and unskilled workers, each with a hierarchy of grades. It is doubtful if the bourgeoisie and proletariat still exist in the traditional way. There are no longer uniform blocks of identically situated and oriented people. The terms are still used, unfortunately, but they have little connection with social reality. Ralf Dahrendorf writes that people now tend to look at society in a different way: no longer in terms of division and antagonism, but by judging the situation from the point of view of a happy co-operative whole (*Class and Class Conflict in Industrial Society,* 1959). Sociologists

1. Fashion really depends on spare wealth. A prosperous working class automatically becomes fashion-conscious.

who insist on cleavages and conflict merely stir up troubles that have been overcome. It is not true that all the disagreements have been overcome, but that people should believe it is a sociologically important fact.

The lower groups (the subjected) still speak of 'them' and 'us'. ' 'Them' is the world of the bosses, whether those bosses are private individuals or, as is increasingly the case today, public officials' (Richard Hoggart, *Uses of Literacy*) 1957. Such a dichotomy is long established and is one of the few that seems to persist without any signs of weakening. One does not look to the Marxist analyst to explain it (if you did, you would get a dusty answer). It is the only clear-cut antagonism left in an enormously complex social structure.

Working Class Attitudes

There are few signs that Them and Us intend to disappear from the social scene in the foreseeable future. The reason is simple: the dichotomy is keenly felt, far more so than the traditional antagonisms of academic economists and sociologists. The basic attitude is one of loyalty to one's mates and hostility and suspicion towards all outsiders. The workers have always gained their advances by group solidarity; they are not as attracted by the idea of individual initiative as the middle classes. Along with the solidarity goes intolerance of those who do not conform. This can be a disturbing feature of working class communities, where a dissenter is regarded as a traitor or a 'blackleg'.

The McLernon case of 1955 illustrated this. The shop stewards discovered that the flow of work at a Rolls Royce factory in Scotland no longer justified overtime. In order to preserve overtime they started a go-slow. McLernon, a connecting-rod polisher, refused to do this. The stewards urged the union to dismiss him and then urged the management to sack him on the grounds that they only employed union men. They refused. To the middle class McLernon was a hero, the only man with common sense and the courage of his convictions. To his workmates he was a blackleg, a selfish man who put his personal feelings before the interests of his fellows.

But there is also a deeper and more intimate quality fostered by working class life that distinguishes it from the middle class ambience. This is most clearly noticeable in the works of D.H. Lawrence. It often happens that the most characteristic aspects of a class or group are so intangible that it is virtually impossible for the ordinary person to do more than feel them; to express them or body them forth in any mean-

ingful way is beyond our powers. Thus Lawrence has taught those of
us who are outsiders truths about working class life which, without
him, we could not even have approached in the imagination. To the
middle class observer, a childhood such as Lawrence's is not likely to
bestow tranquillity or security or even, in the ordinary sense,
happiness. Raymond Williams tells us what it in fact does for the
child. 'It gave what to Lawrence was more important than these
things: the sense of close quick relationship, which came to matter
more than anything else. This was the positive result of the life of the
family in a small house, where there were no such devices of
separation of children and parents as the sending-away to school, or
the handing-over to servants, or the relegation to nursery or playroom'
(Culture and Society, 1780-1950). Those who do not know the life
stress its noisier aspects—rows are in the open, there is no privacy in
crisis, there is mutual blame and anger when the margin of material
security is insufficient. But the whole situation is part of a continuous
life which makes for a complete attachment. Lawrence learnt from
this experience that sense of the continuous flow and recoil of sympathy
which was the essential process of living. What he learned was by
contrasts, reinforced by the accident that he lived on a kind of frontier,
within sight of two different yet related Englands: the industrial and
the agricultural. 'In the family and out of it, in the Breach and at
Haggs Farm, he learned on his own senses the crisis of industrial
England', writes Williams.

One other aspect of working class feeling saddens many people.
This is the undoubted bourgeoisification of the English working class
which at times reaches such intensity that I for one feel 'working class'
is an unfair description and that 'middle class manqué' would be more
accurate. The working class ideal, of happy united family sitting
snugly round the hearth, possessing little but their own trust and
comradeship, has declined in the face of bourgeois material values and
the associated concern with status. It was one of the unhappy conclusions Orwell reached in *The Road to Wigan Pier*. He describes how
he stayed with a Trade Union official in Manchester. The family were
what are sentimentally described as 'decent working class'; they wore
clogs in childhood; the atmosphere of the home was entirely white-
collar. 'I am struck again by the fact that as soon as a working man
gets an official post in the Trade Union or goes into Labour politics,
he becomes middle class whether he will or no, i.e., by fighting against
the bourgeoisie he becomes bougeois.' Aldous Huxley points out in
one of his essays that by devoting too much time and energy to fighting evil (for example), one is compelled to concentrate on evil and
eventually takes on some of the colouring of evil.

Perhaps the peculiar situation of the British working class, in being the providers and valets of the world's most successful and, for a time, richest bourgeoisie has had its effect. It has been a privileged working class, which in itself gives it a semi-bourgeois nature. This has been recognized abroad for many decades, and even today the peasants of Asia have little respect for their New Left international brothers who are able to devote so much time to esoteric argument which does nothing to increase the food-flow. Between the wars Britain depended on the rest of the world for food and raw materials. Only one-third of her food was produced at home. Coal, even manufactured goods, began to be imported. This conditioned the whole situation of the nation. Britain needed either peace or supremacy at sea. The alternatives were ruin or starvation. Cole and Postgate, writing in *The Common People*, 1956, claimed that everybody knew this. They may not have been able to express the equation with the neatness of a trained economist, but in their subconscious minds they understood the situation. It affected the entire view of life of the British people. It explained the hold of imperialism, even on the minds of those who rationally rejected it, and it explained the Labour Party's difficulty in formulating a socialist policy towards the Empire. Thanks to the 'invisible exports', which appeared to be closely connected with Britain's imperial position, she was still a great creditor country. A large proportion of British foreign investments was in the Empire. The tenacity of British Imperialism can be traced not only to capitalist greed or political power-seeking but also to a general awareness of what made life just that little bit more bearable in these islands.

Aristocrats and Aspirants

Orwell saw modern capitalism as organized selfishness. 'England is the most class-ridden country under the sun. It is a land of snobbery and privilege, ruled largely by the old and silly' *(The Lion and the Unicorn, 1940)*. British capitalism had its back to the wall and seemed quite incapable of adapting itself to the new situation. As we know, the patient recovered but Orwell had good grounds for his pessimism. In his *War-Time Diary* he quotes a letter written by Lady Oxford to the *Daily Telegraph:* 'Since most London houses are deserted there is little entertaining . . . in any case, most people have to part with their cooks and live in hotels.' Orwell's comment was: 'Apparently nothing will ever teach these people that the other 99% of the population exists' (3 June 1940) And on 27 June he said that L.H. Myers ('who knows or at least has met all these people') told him that 'with individual exceptions like Churchill the entire British aristocracy is utterly corrupt and lacking in the most ordinary patriotism, caring in fact for nothing except preserving their own standards of life'.

Most of us are probably sick of hearing about the hold of the Public Schools on British life, but boredom does not remove that fact. Tawney threw a spotlight on the situation in his *Equality* and Richard Titmuss went to some pains to show us, in his Introduction to the 1964 edition, that there had been little change. He did admit that there had been a slight decline in public school influence among the bishops, but judges and bank directors were hardly affected. Nearly one-third of 133 directors of the five banks in 1961 had been educated at Eton. He called them 'debtors to the rest of society'. Since the 1920s the Etonian hold over the Conservative party has dramatically increased. Mr Heath is a suburban decoy. The proportion of all British fourteen-year olds who are at Charterhouse, Eton, Harrow, Marlborough, Rugby and Winchester is too small to show statistically—or at least diagramatically, which is a bye-product of statistics. Yet the proportion from these schools in the Conservative cabinet of 1963 was two-thirds. We may feel bored by this but unless we are utterly servile in spirit we must feel both angry and ashamed as well.

On the whole the children of the well-to-do middle class elements receive a better education than the rest. This is sometimes expressed in rather curious ways. For example, a few years ago a comparison was made of the average mathematics performance of thirteen year-old children from twelve developed countries. The children of the English professional groups had a higher average score than those of any group from any other country—but their blue-collar counterparts ranked only seventh among all blue-collar groups. Considerable effort is made to correct the educational imbalance, but the fault is a radical one. 'The Civil Service Commissioners lean over backwards to avoid favouring public school boys', writes Anthony Sampson (*Anatomy of Britain*, 1962). Apparently they write a letter of congratulation to every grammar school headmaster who produces a successful candidate, and they were very excited when they collared their first successful candidate from a comprehensive school in 1960. But in fact the area of privilege has merely been displaced, not destroyed altogether. The Civil Service is not a public school preserve but a depot for Oxbridge products.

Along with the educational divisions go the associated ones of what T.H. Pear calls 'speech melody' *(English Social Differences)*. The home and school background, sometimes working in harmony, sometimes in uneasy alliance, produce a way of speaking that marks the man long before he picks up a pen to write a thesis. Social differences, writes Pear, are emphasized by 'the way in which the voice goes up and down.' Those many candidates who have been recommended for a post or turned down after a brief interview, with no reasons given for either decision, have been usually judged on speech melody. But this is one of the areas of social behaviour that is finally breaking up. In fact, there has recently been a craze among the well-to-do for plebeian speech, almost entirely confined to the young—it is a nuance that Nancy Mitford plays with energetically in one of her novels. Television has been the catalysing agent; during the days of radio the BBC accent represented large estates and money in the bank, although many who used it were frequently aspirants rather than tenants. Television (especially ITV) has developed the popular touch. Stuart Hall, in a contribution to *Class* (ed. Richard Mabey, 1967) entitled 'Class and the Mass Media', put it like this:

> Whether in news reports, trailers for programmes and studio announcements, documentary or discussion, ITV seemed able to bring into broadcasting a range of voices free of the accent of established power which still clung to the BBC. In this respect ITV, though structurally independent of the commercial contracting companies, performed a minor miracle in television. Speech and accent, like prose in the press, carry in our society their own class connotations. In sum ITV, whatever its faults, errors and abuses (and they were and are manifold) did manage to suggest how limited an affair broadcasting had become in the hands of the BBC monopoly, how much of an abstraction from the ranges of voice and experience present in our society an evening with the BBC could turn out to be.

But TV is a socially mobile medium. The rest of society tends to lag behind. I have stated that the Civil Service Commissioners try hard not to be swayed by a public school background, but it is much more difficult for them to ignore the insidious promptings of the right speech-melody. Thus they try to go beyond the public schools by dipping into the grammar school element at Oxbridge. Redbrick still lags far behind. Between 1957 and 1963 the administrative class recruited 260 graduates from Oxbridge and only 9 from Redbrick. Sir Alexander Carr-Saunders, who once interviewed for the Civil Service, explained how it happened to Anthony Sampson: 'Everyone on the board was prejudiced in favour of the Redbrick candidates: yet they always ended up choosing Oxbridge men. You see, they speak the *same language*.' (Quoted by John Windsor, 'Oxbridge and Redbrick: the Great Divide', *Class,* ed. Mabey.)

Another area that has recently witnessed social change is trade. Early in this century no gentleman would soil his hands with trade. It was customary to speak contemptuously of those who did participate. Today business men like Sir Miles Thomas are members of White's; the most extreme example of the trend is to be found in the stately homes which are beginning to resemble Lidos. Press barons are still considered rather different from their fellow peers, but no-one would be too proud to associate with newspaper ownership, however yellow. In the period under review *The Times* has made a fairly successful effort to persuade its readers that the business of politics and government is essentially a matter for 'people like us', members of the club. Individual men of power may make gross mistakes but in general the class to which they belong will find the remedy. But parallel with this runs the immensely successful *Daily Mirror* which does not pretend to be near the traditional seats of power but claims, quite explicitly, that its mass readership can bring effective pressure to bear on the 'people like us'—who are, rather quaintly, 'them' to the *Mirror* reader.

The upper classes have suffered most of all through the decline of domestic service. In 1951 only 1.2% of all private households in Great Britain included one or more domestic servants, and only 0.1% had more than one servant. In 1931, 4.8% of private households included one or more domestic servants, and 1.1% more than one. (Cole, *Post-War Condition of Britain,* 1956) Statistics can be very disappointing and at first sight there does not appear to be any change of magnitude —but we must remember that we are speaking of a very small section of the total population. The interesting thing is not that nearly one in twenty of English households employed a servant in 1931 but that twenty years later the figure had fallen to slightly over one in a hundred.

One of the marks of upper-class behaviour is the desire for privacy. This is ensured by servants. Lack of servants has probably caused a greater change in the quality of upper-class life than any other factor; no comparable change in quality has taken place in the working class, despite greater prosperity, cars and beach huts. Even after the second of the World Wars there were families and individuals (Lady Oxford was surely one) who imagined that life would be resumed at the placid country-house level in an Edwardian afterglow. It was difficult for such people to appreciate the merits of planning, nationalization and the Welfare State. But in this type of conservatism they were not alone. The British Medical Association and the Law Society have regretted the march of time; the trade unions have been suspicious of it, despite the corporate power they have achieved, because traditional relationships are threatened.

When we talk of class feeling, class hatred and that sad misnomer, class war, we notice a difference in direction. Even during the worst times of nineteenth century exploitation and poverty, it was only a minority of the working class who indulged in these emotions. Today there is perhaps more intense class feeling in existence, but it is to be found among the 'superior' classes who detest the social gains of their 'inferiors'. 'Let anyone who doubts this pay a few visits to superior watering-places, such as Brighton or Bournemouth, whose hotels are full of snobbish persons bitterly resentful of high taxation and the 'pampering' of the poor through the social services', writes G.D.H. Cole in *The Post-War Condition of Britain*, 1956—and the feeling still persists. Nor need you go to Bournemouth—a drink in a thousand saloon bars will serve. On the contrary, one rarely hears 'hymns of hate' at Labour or Trade Union meetings, which are sober, well-conducted affairs, on the whole hoping to be mistaken for their 'betters'.

In his vision of the future, *The Rise of the Meritocracy*, 1958, Michael Young asserts that the general mood of the British people has never been egalitarian. This is broadly true, and it is not hard to discover why. Most British workers are hopeful of entering the middle-class, just as many members of the middle-class look forward to the day when they will qualify as aristocrats, though the term is no longer used. It is extraordinary that Britain remained rural-minded long after it pioneered the Industrial Revolution and 80% of its population were collected together in towns. 'The soil grows castes; the machine makes classes', says Young. This explains the paradox noted by Orwell and others. Large numbers of children inherited power and position as well as wealth. An informal kind of ancestor-worship prevailed. The aristocracy became a father-figure in the collective unconscious. Top management tried to give the impression of gentlemen of private means and that, by an unwritten law, meant a country mansion, acres and horses. By tacit agreement little attempt was made to distinguish the true from the false or (to be kinder) the later from the earlier. It was characteristic of Waugh that he always did.

The criterion of success could be stated bluntly: 'it's not what you know but who you know that counts', and this put Redbrick firmly in its place. Tremendous efforts were made to maintain social position. 'Downward mobility' was uncommon because family pride would not allow it. Bad eggs could be sent to the colonies, or they could become remittance men in the South of France; no superior family could allow divorce to blot its escutcheon. Children were bought places at private schools which they would never have acquired on merits. Combined pressure of home and school produced a person whose dullness was hidden by a patina, and who could be eased into a cosy corner of one of the less exacting professions, such as law or stockbroking. Few people will publicly attack the idea of merit for promotion, but merit was not considered measurable in the past (if you succeeded in your exams you could be faulted on character). Now seniority could be measured, and seniority could be equated with wisdom. 'Merit' was often little more than a disguise for nepotism. Many a young chap has landed a valuable job because an uncle has said, 'I've got a nephew, he's absolutely brilliant . . .'

The British have known instinctively that if you want to change things it is best to go about it slowly. This has often been cited as an example of British political maturity, and I think with reason. The extraordinary contrast between French and British development since 1750 should provide sufficient evidence. It is hard to think of a country where a violent revolution has done more than provide a spurt of development, which has very rapidly deteriorated into near-stagnation. Evolution seems to work quite as quickly as revolution, and at far less cost. It is better to nibble at the establishment than to take up arms against it. The industrial magnates nibbled very success-fully at the aristocracy, and the workers are treating middle-class England as a piece of highly succulent cheese.

Class Assimilation

In 1934 Priestley said there were three Englands: Old England, Nine-teenth Century England, and the new post-war England. The latter, however, belonged more to the Twentieth Century than to England herself. America was the birthplace. It was already an England of arterial and by-pass roads, filling stations and factories like exhibition halls, giant cinemas and dance halls with cafés, bungalows with tiny garages, cocktail bars, Woolworths, motor-coaches, wireless, hiking, factory girls looking like actresses, greyhound racing and dirt tracks, swimming pools and cigarette coupons. The tone was set by large-scale, mass production and cut prices. Woolworths was the symbol: nothing more than sixpence. In this sector of England there was almost equality of opportunity, because at that time there were many who did not want to enter it; those who did, did so on agreed terms. 'It is an England, at last, without privilege', wrote Priestley, and added, 'Modern England is rapidly Blackpooling itself.'

This judgment was exaggerated, true in essence rather than in deed. Since Priestley's book was written there has been a new social surge in favour of new kinds of privilege, based on mystiques and cults rather than economics. 'I cannot help feeling that this new England is lacking in character, in zest, gusto, flavour, bite, drive, originality, and that this is a serious weakness. Monotonous but easy work and a liberal supply of cheap luxuries might between them create a set of people entirely without ambition or any real desire to think and act for themselves . . .' This was acute observation at the time. The emergent middle class culture of the thirties was brash yet insipid. It would be wrong to equate it with what has happened since. Many of the attributes which Priestley declared to be lacking have been restored, but the new pop-and-teen culture is not easily assessed. It frequently announces its hatred of hierarchy and indifference to gradations, yet its heroes relish possessions and would price themselves out of any sane market—but then, they know this one isn't sane. But at least the war caused a jolt. The new society is no longer colourless and imitative, there is a creative stir and an awareness of more than creature comforts. The 'modern' youth of between-the-wars were an uninspiring lot, represented by the office worker in a safe job who had managed to get an MG sports car, and imitated the rich to the best of his ability: roadhouses, occasional weekends in London (meaning the Windmill), even in Paris (meaning the Folies Bergères), tennis clubs and calling things 'ripping'.

What happened during the war? Traditional England received such a blow that inevitably things could never be the same again. But there was one event which was noticed by many observers, an event so rare that it had the taint of the miraculous about it. For a period something like national unity was achieved. I am using the term not in the sense of the normal political cliché but to indicate something far more significant, far more encouraging, even nobler. After 10 May 1940, when the very independence of England was in danger, unity somehow became a reality. 'It is for once not untrue to say that few in any class failed to do their utmost for the community', wrote Cole and Postgate in *The Common People*. Self-interest actually took second place to community interest. Even the capitalists, whose patriotism tends to become dubious when financial interest is put under strain (during the second Labour Government many capitalists behaved with a disgraceful lack of patriotic self-respect), cooperated. Profits were severely restricted, factories were forcibly concentrated, enormous sums were paid in taxation, Government direction of policy and production were implicitly obeyed. Strict and fairly competent rationing of clothing and food, with sumptuary regulations in restaurants, was observed with little evasion—at least, in the early days, when the danger was greatest. Even the billeting of evacuees, a direct invasion of the privacy which had always meant so much to the well-to-do, was in most cases accepted. The war, which was called total, affected British life totally. Because all classes suffered and, as far as was possible in an inegalitarian society, suffered equally, there was a general acceptance and an agreement to pull together. The same writers make this comment upon the effect of the war:

> The second World War shook the foundations of British society much more than the first. The strain on man-power and the call for industrial adaptation were much greater: evacuation and the development of war industry required much more migration and disturbance of family life: bombing from the air was on a quite different scale, in both its physical and its psychological effects. A higher proportion of the national income was absorbed by the war effort; and the realisation of overseas investments in order to pay for war supplies cut more deeply into Great Britain's position as a creditor country. All classes, rich and poor alike, of both sexes and of all ages, were drawn much more completely into the struggle.

This socially blissful condition could not last. Britain was still a class-ridden country. Classes had not been abolished, they had only agreed to co-operate. When the war was over and the classes began to withdraw from their embrace, each left its mark on the other. This may have been superficial, but it is doubtful if in class matters what is to be seen on the surface can ever be completely divorced from more significant implications. For example, it is often impossible to tell merely by looking at a man or a woman or even by hearing them talk what class they belong to. There has been a remarkable assimilation, especially in clothing but also in speech and everyday behaviour. First of all radio permitted working class people to pick up middle class accents, and later television gave object lessons in how everyone behaved—and it was possible for the poor to ape the rich with some conviction and, what might have seemed laughable a generation earlier, for the rich to ape the poor. G.D.H. Cole, in his *Post-War Condition of Britain,* compared our contemporary situation with that of fifty or sixty years ago—almost the span of Elizabeth Bowen's writing career. The class structure remained essentially the same. At the beginning of the century there were still to be seen children in rags, living in widespread squalor. The unskilled workers were manifestly ill-clad and underfed. Skilled workers were widely separated from the middle classes by differences of manners, speech, clothing and behaviour. The differences still existed but they were to a large extent hidden from public view. Cohesion of the class structure was beginning to crumble.

Democratic Decline

This is no place to go deeply into what we mean by democracy. It may seem irresponsible of me to take my cue from a writer who is usually considered anti-democratic. I mean D.H. Lawrence—but then Lawrence probably qualifies as the most misunderstood and most misrepresented of all modern English writers. He expressed himself on the subject, without contradicting his utterances elsewhere, in 'Nottingham and the Mining Country', to be found in his *Selected Essays*. As we might expect from Lawrence, his view of democracy was a lot more organic and a lot less institutional than the familiar textbook one.

> So, we know the first great purpose of Democracy: that each man shall be spontaneously himself—each man himself, each woman herself, without any question of equality or inequality entering in at all; and that no man shall try to determine the being of any other man, or of any other woman.

At first sight this may seem a long way removed from what we usually understand by the term, but in fact political democracy is meaningless unless it is rooted in certain strong individual qualities. Political democracy flourished (to a certain extent—it has never flourished anywhere like the green bay tree) in England because these qualities on the whole existed and released tolerant influences throughout the social body. Some of the most generous social movements have failed because at heart they denied this requirement, wrote Raymond Williams in *Culture and Society, 1780-1950*. 'No man shall try to determine the being of any other man, or of any other woman': no matter whether this determination be done in the name of production or service, the glory of the race or good citizenship, it is evil.

In the same essay Lawrence says that 'we have frustrated that instinct of community which would make us unite in pride and dignity in the biggest gesture of the citizen, not the cottager.' This instinct of community was immensely strong in Lawrence but is usually overlooked. He attacked the industrial society of England, not because it offered community to the individual, but because it frustrated it. He argued that it was stronger than the sexual instinct, and thus its repression caused correspondingly more upheaval in the psyche. The fuss over *Lady Chatterley's Lover* and other events in Lawrence's career have obscured the true nature of his work. If anyone could read *Lady Chatterley* from scratch, that is, without being aware of the assault it made on sexual convention, he would almost certainly be more impressed by what it says about industrial society than about the sexual relationship. Clearly his 'instinct of community' is deeper than his sexual instinct in this novel. Those who attack it do so because they are disappointed with its sexual revelation and miss the statement on industrial society. The same is true, though not to such a marked extent, of *The Rainbow*,

Lawrence was writing just before my six novelists began their careers. The implications of what he had to say were immense, but right at the heart of his criticism was the conviction that people were being bullied (half-heartedly, it is true) into some kind of democratic behaviour from outside. This was the explicit situation. The implicit situation was quite the reverse: the kind of community that democracy demands was never even given a chance to establish itself.

Just before Lawrence universal education had been introduced. Here again the results were not what had been hoped for. There seems to be a tragic irony in all progressive programmes—so very often they produce the exact opposite of what their founders seek. Education was to bring in the golden age. In fact, true education is a most difficult target to hit, and certainly the Board Schools and new Secondary Schools were in no position to provide it. Instead they shoved the population on to a transitional stage in which the characteristic virtues and attitudes of the illiterate (qualities which, according to Lawrence, were absolutely indispensable for any real social improvement) were lost without being replaced by those of the genuinely literate. What was happening in England was merely an early variant of a familiar situation in the Middle East and Africa of today. Trouble was and still is caused by 'students' (usually schoolboys) whom European administrators would cite as evidence of educational failure. In fact, they merely illustrate the truth that you cannot become educated without first becoming half-educated. But if in the process you lose certain valuable qualities you previously possessed, you may end with a situation worse than you started with.

This is discussion of democracy at the hidden psychological level. But where such tensions exist, they will certainly be reflected on the surface. When one reads accounts of life in England between, say, 1870 and 1900 and compares it with that of our own time, one cannot feel that the democratic spirit has grown during the later period, despite the emancipation of women, the extension of news media, and the undoubted advance in formal education. The techniques have pro-liferated and the soul has gone out of the machine. There was more democratic health in the Mechanics' Institutes than in TV by the fire-side. But the process started several decades ago and we cannot blame youth. In fact, it may be that the young have felt dimly that our democracy has grown false and that their protest is in direct succes-sion to Lawrence's. But I wouldn't be dogmatic. There is no evidence that the young are really alarmed by a failure in democracy. It may be, however, that what they feel in their bones (I suppose Lawrence would have said guts) has not yet got into their heads.

The decline was visible on the surface by the time the first World War broke out. The great Liberal administrations were ones of which we can still feel proud. They believed in government by persuasion and not by force, and in the duty of magistrates to be tolerant and of minorities, when they were tolerated, to give way. They believed in parliamentary institutions, in representative government and in the party system as a means of canalizing and, in the last resort, com-promising political differences. Politics could work on the basis of this set of beliefs as long as no body of persons large enough or influential enough to resist the ordinary police methods of coercion wanted with real passion something which they could not hope to win in a reason-able time or to retain, if they had it already, by parliamentary means. During the years leading up to the first war several important groups found Parliament standing in their way. They felt too seriously about their claims to be limited by the traditional rules of the game. Before the impact of these forces the old liberal ideas were seen to be helpless. In fact, something was happening in Britain that was to happen all over the world in the course of a few decades, and on a much larger and more terrifying scale: parliaments were coming up against problems which could not be solved by traditional parliamentary methods.

Three forces emerged, and in each case their policy was affected by the new mood that had crept into the minds of the population, aided by their conviction that now they were educated and were capable of solving any of the problems that faced them. The suffragists, the trade unions and the Irish were all goaded by broken promises and a feeling that peaceful means had failed and would have to be replaced. The Tories were so set on bringing the Liberal government down they would stop at nothing. In other words, one of the two great parties had ceased to play the parliamentary game and was ready to appeal to force, even against the verdict of the electorate. A complete nexus of forces, ranging from the dissipation of the old working class family unit to the mental naivety of a population that believed it had been trained to take decisions on a national scale, combined to sap the vigour of democracy. And the process has continued. More and more one comes across such judgments as the following by Erich Fromm (*The Sane Society*, 1955): 'The voting process in the great democracies has more and more the character of a plebiscite, in which the voter cannot do much more than register agreement or disagreement with powerful political machines, to one of which he surrenders his political will.' This is certainly not democracy. It had never been intended by Bagehot or John Stuart Mill; Ruskin, the idol of the thoughtful working man who would never have dreamed of calling himself an 'intellectual', would have been shocked; Matthew Arnold had had intimations.

The sickness of democracy infects the organs of society. It would be possible to show how frequently employee participation, talked about so widely in our own time, has declined in various sectors. One example will have to suffice. I take it from an obscure area of our society, company pension schemes. In the following table column A shows the number of schemes that had elected employee representatives, column B the number of schemes that nominated employee representatives, and column C the number of schemes that had none at all.

Period	*Schemes*	*A*	*B*	*C*
1900-09	2	2	0	0
1910-19	4	3	1	0
1920-29	13	3	5	5
1930-39	16	4	6	6
1940-49	16	3	4	9
1950-59	24	4	4	16
1960-64	13	2	0	11

(Figures taken from "Pensions in Secret" by Tony Lynes, *New Society*, 16 January, 1969)

Alienation

Before the last war the main problem was seen to be economic; the failure of distribution. Since the war it is seen to be psychological: alienation. Of course, this generalization does not apply to every society all over the world, but it is largely true of our own. It contains an interesting paradox. It represents a triumph for Marx, not in the field where he was an expert but in the one where he was an amateur. The Marxian analysis of the economic situation is no longer relevant and only interests those who have not the intelligence to understand or have a vested interest in a particular kind of revolution. But every year shows the accuracy of Marx's theory of alienation. Incidentally, this was what Lawrence was writing about.

Tawney drew attention to the perversion of values that marks our time. Both the aristocratic spirit, which emphasizes subordination and the respect of the lower for the upper classes, and is now dead, and the plutocratic or commercial spirit, which insists on the right of every individual to acquire wealth and by it to gain consideration for himself and power over his fellows, and is very much alive, pervert the sense of values. 'It is to cause men, in the language of the Old Testament, "to go a-whoring after strange gods", which means, in the circumstances of today, staring upwards, eyes goggling and mouths agape, at the antics of a third-rate Elysium, and tormenting their unhappy souls, or what, in such conditions, is left of them, with the hope of wriggling into it' *(Equality)*. The English must abolish their respect for riches and they must respect each other for what they are, not for what they own. At times Tawney sounds like a Lawrence who has had a training in economics. He calls reverence for riches the hereditary disease of the English nation, the *lues Anglicana*. The working class movements denounce capitalism but do not realize that the system is maintained not only by capitalists but also by those among them who would be capitalists if they could. Injustices survive not only because the rich exploit the poor but also because, in their hearts, too many of the poor admire the rich and would be quite prepared to exploit each other if given the chance.

The alienation of the worker from his society, from his job, from his family and eventually from himself has given rise to a number of suggested remedies, of which the socialist one is perhaps the best known. But it is not only Left-wingers who deplore the situation. There is a large number of critics, ranging from neo-medievalists through *laissez-faire* revivalists to social creditors who are all firmly convinced that the existing system is hopeless. There must be very few people today who are sufficiently complacent to believe that there is nothing wrong with our society. There are quite a large number, however, mainly among the business community who feel that there is nothing radically wrong, and that all would be well if only there were less interference from academic economists, long-haired youths and journalists in search of a story. One has to extend tolerance and even admiration to so sincere a critic as F.A. Hayek who believes that the socialists have undermined a viable system by their carping:

> We cannot blame our young men when they prefer the safe, salaried position to the risk of enterprise after they have heard from their earliest youth the former described as the superior, more unselfish and disinterested occupation. The younger generation of today has grown up in a world in which in school and press the spirit of commercial enterprise has been represented as disreputable and the making of profit as immoral, where to employ a hundred people is represented as exploitation but to command the same number as honourable. (*The Road to Serfdom*, 1944)

Hayek occasionally approaches Orwell in his ability to unmask hypocrisy. He knows what Orwell knew, that among all the programmes that have been put forward for the advancement of the human race, liberalism and socialism surpass all the others on moral grounds; and then, regrettably, that perverted socialism is a much nastier thing than perverted liberalism. Hayek reminds us that all the things we are taught to condemn as 'nineteenth century illusions' are moral values: liberty and independence, truth and intellectual honesty, peace and democracy, and respect for the individual qua man instead of merely as a member of an organized group. He asks what are the fixed poles that are now regarded as sacrosanct. 'They are no longer the liberty of the individual, his freedom of movement, and scarcely that of speech. They are the protected standards of this or that group, their "right" to exclude others from providing their fellow-men with what they need.'

The legendary legion of wicked landlords has been replaced or is being replaced all over the world. Good. But by what are they being replaced? Here's the rub, for it brings little benefit to the human race if wicked landlords are replaced by a shadow-organization called 'the community', which wields unprecedented power, and is in fact a complex of committees and officials. In all administration there should be two criteria always before the lawmakers: that no individual should excessively benefit from a public act and that no individual should excessively suffer. J. Parry Lewis, writing in *New Society* (15 August 1968) gives instances of how the one guiding line will normally be followed and the other frequently ignored.

> In deciding upon a piece of redevelopment this community, actuated by motives which may extend from genuine concern for 'public welfare' to nothing more than a desire to erect a monu-

ment to their own era of power, takes action which always affects many people adversely. Even when the proposal goes to appeal, it is eventually assessed largely in terms of the public good and those who lose are written off as necessary victims of progress. ('Redevelopment and the Small Business'.)

In Stalinist Russia 'those who lose' numbered millions.

State bureaucrats have in fact taken over the functions of the entrepreneur, and it is absolutely false to claim that they are inevitably better masters. The fiction, of course, is that they are not masters at all but servants,[1] a fiction which in many cases can only be maintained by those who have never had to grapple with the state apparatus in a matter involving personal rights which do not fall into an accepted communal category. Max Weber saw it all long ago when he wrote of 'monopolistic appropriation of privileged opportunities and also prohibitions of certain modes of acquisition.' The Man from the Ministry is among us, and his power is increasing. He can reward by giving financial incentives and backing, confer status such as membership of the House of Lords or of a government committee, and punish by taking over or refusing permission to develop. In England he still retains a faintly absurd bowler-hatted image. Elsewhere he is a commissar or a party executive. One should also bear in mind that this type of bureaucracy is not only found in the state apparatus. The companies and combines are like states within states. Anthony Sampson said that to visit the headquarters of a big industrial corporation is like visiting a foreign country and 'talking to their managers one is aware of a complex, self-enclosed microcosm, held together with oil, soap or steel' *(Anatomy of Britain)*. The same power exists and is used—the power to reward or punish, to give or withhold.

The political analysis of the socialists has been valuable in one sense: it explained how capitalism would pass away, and we are watching it pass away more understandingly than might have been the case. But the complementary part of the analysis, the inevitability of socialism, is by no means so assured. The small stockholders, with whom Marx concerned himself so much, have lost interest in their investments, except as a source of income—and a highly taxed one at

1. A joke current in communist countries. A visitor takes a room in a hotel, and is awakened by a procession of people going past his window early in the morning. He asks for an explanation, and is told that these are the masses going to work. He gets back into bed but is awakened again an hour later, this time by a procession of motor cars. These, he is told, are the servants of the masses going to work.

that. Thus they are only a minor source of income for most people who hold them, and these people hardly ever bother about them except when they (or more likely, a representative who has thrust himself forward) wish to exploit their nuisance value. The modern criticism of capitalism has passed beyond rationality because it is usually criticism of a non-existent state, though it may have existed a hundred years ago. No-one has put this aspect of the contemporary economic scene better than Joseph A. Schumpeter in his *Capitalism, Socialism and Democracy*. I quote from the third English edition, 1949.

> From the fact that the criticism of the capitalist order proceeds from a critical attitude of mind, i.e., from an attitude which spurns allegiance to extra-rational values, it does not follow that rational refutation will be accepted. Such refutation may wear the rational garb of attack but can never reach the extra-rational driving power that always lurks behind it ... Just as the call for utilitarian credentials has never been addressed to kings, lords and popes in a judicial frame of mind that would accept the possibility of a satisfactory answer, so capitalism stands its trial before judges who have the sentence of death in their pockets. They are going to pass it, whatever the defence they may hear ...

The typical bourgeois is rapidly losing faith in his own creed. This is verified by the manner in which he behaves when facing direct attack; he talks or pleads, or hires people to do it for him; he snatches at every chance of compromise; he is always ready to give in; he never puts up a fight under the flag of his own ideals and interests. Capitalism is a stone that is being worn away by the drip of propaganda, not by the 'logic of history'. This is a remarkable victory for the socialists, for history is full of examples of small groups who have stood by their guns successfully. The only conclusion we can come to is that the bourgeois order no longer makes sense even to the bourgeoisie itself and that, when all is said and nothing is done, it does not really care. So we come back to the position of the small stockholders.

Yet, says Schumpeter, this class harbours human material of first-rate quality. He even claims that the model individual in the bourgeoisie is superior in his intellectual and volitional attitudes to the model individual in any other class of industrial society. The social molecules that rise and fall within a class, and sometimes beyond the boundaries of a class, are families rather than individuals. Thus these movements are measured in generations.

In the preface to the third English edition Schumpeter says that the ethos of capitalism in England has gone. In a chapter written in 1938 he pointed out that there has been such a slackening of entrepreneurial effort since the beginning of the century that state leadership and state control in certain important industries (for example, the production of electric power) was not only approved but demanded by *all* parties.[1] The English have by now become what he calls 'state-broken'. English workmen are well organized and usually responsibly led. An experienced bureaucracy of acceptable cultural and moral standards could be trusted to assimilate the new elements required for the extension of state power and influence. In the 1949 preface he says there are no longer any people left in England who are 'rich after taxes'. He pronounced an obituary for capitalism in a speech made in December, 1949, 'The March Into Socialism': capitalist civilization was passing away; 'let us rejoice or else lament the fact as much as anyone of us likes; but do not let us shut our eyes to it.'

Some of this cannot be accepted. Professor Titmuss, for instance, would not agree that there are no 'rich after taxes'. On the whole, Schumpeter was describing a trend and, as is normal in such an exercise, he exaggerates. But I think we can accept his main argument, that capitalism is passing away with very little fight. The new situation, however, does not appear to be much more beneficial to the rank and file of humanity than the old one, although I think we have to make one exception: throughout the world people are, to a considerable extent, better off in material things. This has been a notable achievement—but the greater the gain the more the losses, both real and putative, are thrown into relief. People find themselves dwarfed by monolithic state apparatuses, giant corporations, vastly complex industrial processes, even the organization of their recreations—in other words, they are subject to what we have agreed to call alienation.

The notion of alienation may have pre-dated mass movements but today it is those who belong to mass movements who have suffered its effects most keenly. They are in society but not of it. It is a condition in which men are psychologically and socially divorced from society as a result of a lack of ties linking them to the wider community. They are unable to relate themselves in meaningful and satisfying ways to the social system and are therefore highly susceptible to the appeals of mass movements, particularly those with a messianic flavour and strong moralistic appeal, and a tendency towards direct action. This

1. There are signs now that this is being reversed, but—after 1970.

provides a sense of purpose and a significance to life by creating a feeling that they are helping to change the course of history.

Alienation is a measure of the individual's powerlessness in mass society, a sense of personal helplessness in face of powerful political forces which appear remote from and unresponsive to individual demands and needs. Ralph Schoenman wrote in *Peace News*, 17 February 1961:

> The societies we inhabit today are crippling human beings. We are bludgeoned by the devices of authority into a vast paralysis, an inability to affect events, a fear that our anxieties and aspirations must remain private. We know that our values and institutions are terrible confessions of social bankruptcy, yet we feel it pointless to attempt to cope with our social problems. Men are dependent on vast and impersonal societies. These societies are highly ordered, controlled by powerful autocracies, and they are essentially totalitarian in their organization.

It is felt that society (the institutionalized aspect of society, not its communal one) has rejected certain values which are important. These values are really those that Hayek mourns, and it is illustrative of the complexity of modern life that few of the protesters would accept Hayek as an ally for the simple and absurd reason that he bears the label 'Right' and they still like to think of themselves as 'Left'. Some years ago Arthur Koestler showed how valueless these terms have become but not much notice seems to have been taken. It is this usage of the concept of alienation which is implied in references to the 'alienation of the intelligentsia', since it is not estrangement from society which disturbs them so much as estrangement from certain of its normative components.

Alienation from societal values is by no means necessarily total. Some degree of conformity may be highly functional in sustaining deviance from values which relate to matters of principle and which have important implications for the social structure. Thus the common use of the term 'alienated man' is misleading, for it is not usually man in his totality of social roles and attitudes who is at variance with society, but more commonly man in a limited number of spheres only.

Modern capitalism claimed that it could deliver the goods. By and large, it has done so. It has also managed to accompany this achievement with considerable political freedom and in its later stages, with a remarkable degree of sexual freedom. Yet the world in the middle of the twentieth century seems to be mentally sicker than it was a century earlier. As Adlai Stevenson said, the danger is not of becoming slaves again but of becoming robots. Beyond the alienation implicit in modern government and industrial organization, beyond the special-ized alienation of the intellectual, there is another degree of special-ization which applies to every individual and which seems to derive from the total impact of man and his world—a situation where man finds himself at variance with his ethos. Erich Fromm calls this mode of experience one in which 'the person experiences himself as an alien' *(The Sane Society)*. He goes on:

> He has become, one might say, estranged from himself. He does not experience himself as the centre of his world, as the creator of his own acts—but his acts and their consequences have become his masters, whom he obeys, or whom he may even worship. The alienated person is out of touch with himself as he is out of touch with any other person. He, like the others, is experienced as things are experienced; with the senses and with common sense, but at the same time without being related to oneself and to the world outside productively.

This condition is almost total in modern society. It pervades the relationship of man to his work, the things he consumes, the state, his fellow men, himself. Man has created a world of man-made things as it never existed before. He has constructed a complicated social machine to administer the technical machine he built. Yet this whole creation of his stands over and above him. The more powerful and gigantic the forces he unleashes, the more helpless he feels as a human being. He is owned by his own creation, he has lost ownership of himself. This is how J.J. Gillespie sees the modern worker: 'In industry the person becomes an economic atom that dances to the tune of atomistic management. Your place is just here, you will sit in this fashion, your arms will move x inches in a course of y radius and the time of movement will be .000 minutes' *(Free Expression in Industry,* 1948). The manager, on his side, sees the process as a whole and not as a part, yet he is also alienated from his product as something concrete and useful. His aim is to employ profitably the capital invested by others. He also deals with impersonal giants—competitive enterprise, national and world markets, giant consumers who have to be coaxed and manipulated, giant unions, giant government.

Bureaucracy, which used to be seen as a demon, has become a monster. Not a corner of a modern state is free of it. Big business and government administration are conducted by bureaucracy. Bureau-crats are specialists in administration and things and men. Owing to the bigness of the apparatus to be administered, and the resulting abstractification, the bureaucrats' relationship to people is one of complete alienation. The bureaucrats consider the people they administer with neither love nor hate, but completely impersonally. The manager-bureaucrat must not consider feelings if he is to carry out his professional work efficiently; he must manipulate people as though they were figures or things. Because of the vastness of enterprise and division of labour, these bureaucrats are necessary, and they receive almost godlike respect because of it. No-one is in a position to see the situation whole. The bureaucrat ties the parts together, but experiences no involvement. 'The giant state and economic system', writes Fromm, 'are not any more controlled by man. They run wild and their leaders are like a person on a runaway horse, who is proud of managing to keep in the saddle, even though he is powerless to direct the horse.' And so we speak, complacently, of economic laws, 'the future' and determinism. The worker has become dehumanized and exists as an appendage of the machine. Ahead of us lies automated industry, in which the worker will lose even what contact he still has with the product either by touch or sight. He will observe what is happening to the product as shown on dials and panels, and he will make adjustments through buttons and controls. But this situation is beyond the concern of my novelists.

Richard Hoggart makes an effort to arrive at a correct balance between the old and new forces that mould society, especially in its cultural aspect, in *The Uses of Literacy,* 1957. The outer world becomes more and more streamlined, the family comes to be regarded, even more than formerly, as something real and recognizable. 'It would be difficult to overrate the centralization of modern life: it is easy to overrate the sense of anonymity which so far visits most individuals.' The streamlined world tries to fill the vacuum created by the sense of alienation. Togetherness, the gang sense, all-pals-together, are the aim of the entertainment industries—holiday camps have cheer-leaders for the 'lads' and 'lasses', football pool promoters issue invitations to join the 'gang', 'circle' or 'group', radio producers, disc-jockeys and advertisement broadcasters all specialize in fake intimacy. 'What a phoney sense of belonging all this is, which is offered by the public pals of this publicly gregarious age; it would be better to feel anonymous: one might then be moved to some useful action to improve matters'. The modern 'aliens' joined the Communist Party or the Peace Pledge Union or the Left Book Club or the Social Credit Party in the thirties and the Common Wealth movement in the forties. They wanted to do something about their situation but they felt frustrated, particularly by the variety and magnitude of the problems they encountered—'by a sense that, though they appear to be expected to be knowledgeable about so much, to have views on so many things like good democratic citizens, there is really nothing they can effectively do to solve any of the problems.'

There are some who claim that a state of classlessness is emerging in our society, in so far as the special cultural features noted by Hoggart apply equally to all the existing income groups. 'The great majority of us are being merged into one class', Hoggart writes. 'We are becoming culturally classless'. The clearest example of this trend is to be seen in the new-style women's magazines, compared with the old.

In an article entitled 'The Present Human Condition' in a magazine called *Perspectives,* No. 16, Erich Fromm, who has made this area of human experience his special study, asks what kind of man our society needs to function smoothly. He replies that it needs men who co-operate smoothly in large groups, who want to consume more and more, and whose tastes are standardized and can be easily influenced and anticipated. Men who feel free and independent, who do not feel subject to any authority or principle or conscience, and yet are willing to be commanded, to do what is expected, to fit into the social machine without friction. Men who can be guided without force, led without leaders and prompted without any aim except the one of being on the move, functioning, getting ahead. Modern capitalism has succeeded in producing this kind of man. His life forces have flowed into things and institutions and these things, having become idols, are not experienced as the result of his own efforts but as something apart from which he worships and to which he submits. His idols represent his own life forces in an alienated form. The worker has become an economic atom that dances to the tune of automatized management. 'The meaninglessness and alienation of work result in a longing for complete laziness. Man hates his working life because it makes him feel a prisoner and a fraud. His ideal becomes absolute laziness, in which he will not have to make a move, where everything goes according to the Kodak slogan: "You press the button; we do the rest." '

When a man never postpones the satisfaction of his wishes (and he is conditioned to wish for only what he can get), he has no conflicts and no doubts. No decision has to be made. He is never alone with himself because he is always busy, either working or having fun. He has no need to be aware of himself as a person because he is constantly absorbed with consuming. He is a system of desires and satisfactions. He has to work in order to fulfil his desires, and these very desires are constantly stimulated and directed by the economic machine.

The Role of the Intellectuals

British intellectuals have always fought shy of being labelled a minority group—which would, in the terms of the preceding section, be an alienated minority. They show considerable points of difference from their continental counterparts, however, identifying with their society in a way not normally found elsewhere. It is a measure of the unbroken traditional strain that runs through British society that a large section of the British intelligentsia are, by and large, supporters of the *status quo*. Through their links with the public schools, the ancient universities, clubs and similar élitist institutions, as well as often through ties of kinship, they have ready access to spheres of influence and prestige often denied to intellectuals elsewhere. The critical, Left-wing British intellectual is often the product of these circles and his attitudes are based on fashions rather than convictions. After a period he is liable to revert to the ideals of the class from which he came, sometimes in his way of life rather than his expressed views, which he may retain in contradiction to his actions. This gives him a certain agreeable notoriety. Noel Annan has commented on 'the paradox of an intelligentsia which appears to conform rather than rebel against the rest of society . . .' Even in the highly politicized atmosphere of the thirties those who aligned themselves with the Left-wing cause included only a small minority of the intellectuals, a fact which their public 'visibility', prestige and dogged publicity obscured. Edward Shils wrote of them: 'Never has an intellectual class found its society and its culture so much to its satisfaction . . . Fundamental criticism of the trend of British society has become rare . . . The British intellectual has come to feel proud of the moral stature of a country with so much solidarity and so little acrimony between classes' ('The Intellectuals: Great Britain', *Encounter,* April 1955).

There may be a link between this characteristic of the British intelligentsia and another contrast they exhibit with their counterparts in Europe—their greater concern with cultural rather than economic or political values. French, German and Italian intellectuals have tended to align themselves with economic or political groups to a much greater extent than British intellectuals. Some continental writers have commented, not very favourably, on the normal divorce between artistic and scientific interests to be found among English writers. An Aldous Huxley or an H.G. Wells, interesting rarities in this country, would have seemed fairly normal on the continent. Because of the unbroken development of English society and the character of the educational institutions that moulded the ruling classes and well-to-do, from whom most English writiers derive, a training in the arts and humanities has remained the dominant background for the educated Englishman. Taking University Vice-Chancellors and College Heads as being reasonably representative of such people, we see how strongly entrenched such training still is. In 1935, 68% had been trained in the Arts, 19% in Science, 13% in Social Science and none at all in Technology. Thirty years later (1967, to be exact) the proportions had changed but Arts still held the ascendancy, the figures being 48%, 41% 9% and 3% respectively. The extraordinary thing about this situation is that it refers to the country where the industrial society first took root.

The majority of English writers come from the middle class, and their interests and preferences have a bias towards the humanities. T.H. Pear wrote that English social psychology is, on the whole, an account by middle class writers of middle class behaviour, and the same can be said of English fiction. The result is a general failure on the part of English fiction to give anything like a reasonably proportioned picture of English life. Most people in England live and work in large industrial towns. No such impression would be gained from reading English fiction, even if an attempt were made to study a scientifically determined sample. The six novelists I have chosen, on no would-be scientific basis at all but simply on the grounds that they have established reputations and, at some time or other, have enjoyed a large readership, range in origin from the aristocracy to the lowest level of the middle class, the area where it merges with the working class. But they are writers, they have been subjected to the educational pressures characteristic of this country, and the milieu they describe is largely (one feels it might be accurate to say inevitably) a minority one.

One last point. In the thirties a majority of the European intellectuals, many in the United States, and a vocal group in Britain were supporters of the political Left. This has changed since the war, when there has been a pronounced movement towards the Right, which may be accounted for by changes in social conditions, under the influence of welfare legislation or by changes in the character of the intellectual élite itself (See T.B. Bottomore, *Elites and Society*, 1964). Some sociologists have discerned three élites which have attained prominence in modern society: intellectuals, industrial managers and bureaucrats. The two latter are exceptionally united in their attitude towards society. It is only among the intellectuals that one finds sharp divisions.

This has been a very rapid and necessarily uneven survey of an extremely complex subject but it has been essential to describe the pattern against which these novelists have produced their work. In the following chapters, as I review their writings (and always with the emphasis on their fictional writings), I shall be enquiring to what extent and in what manner they reflect the following aspects of our society: its considerable inequalities; its division into recognizable classes, despite merging at the frontiers; the characteristics of these classes; the almost universal impulse towards social climbing notable in British life; the ease with which certain individuals assimilate and are assimilated; the decline in the genuine spirit of democracy; and, seeping through the whole fabric like a dense fog, the alienation of modern men and women, whatever their status, and their growing helplessness before the huge structure of bureaucracy.

II

Elizabeth Bowen—Connoisseur of the Individual
(First Fiction: *Encounters*, 1923)

Homes of the Rich

Elizabeth Bowen was an only child who became the owner of Bowen's Court in Ireland on the death of her father. Her ancestors had been Cromwellian settlers. Her grandfather had owned large estates in both Tipperary and Cork, he was known as the Master and everyone went in dread of him, just as if he had been invented by Nancy Mitford. He was a just man, but hard. The Protestant Irish landlord exercised more or less absolute power in the nineteenth century, and if he misused it he was hated. The house was lavishly kept up. The household contained nine children and eight indoor servants, and there were frequent visitors. When Elizabeth's father succeeded to the estates it was found that severe retrenchment was necessary. Labourers were turned away from the farm and most of the indoor servants were dismissed. It was difficult to keep things going. By the 1940's Bowen's Court was not immediately attractive. 'A great cold grey stone house, with rows upon rows of windows, ringed round with silence, approached by grass-grown avenues ... It is miles from anywhere you have ever heard of; it is backed by woods with mountains behind them; in front, it stares over empty fields. Generations have lived out their lives and died here. But now—everybody has gone away.'[1]

Although Miss Bowen covers a fairly wide social range in her writings, the characteristic background is the wealthy home. This is often lovingly described. In a story called 'Foothold' (*Joining Charles*, 1929) Janet and Gerard live in a late Georgian house, which is admired by Thomas, a visitor. The marble squares of the floor were

1. Bowen's Court was sold in 1961, and has since been pulled down.

good, sufficient reason alone to buy the house. There were 'square-panelled doors, leaf-green in their moulded white frames in the smooth white wall.' Bowen's themes are never wealth, always style, but in a bourgeois culture they usually go together. The forms are observed. After dinner Janet leaves the men (her husband and one other) and the port 'circles'! There is a butler in the house who makes one appearance only in the story. 'The butler appeared in the doorway. "Dinner . . ." said Gerard'. They recognize that six or eight people are working full time to keep them in luxury. The title story of this volume ('Joining Charles') is set in the house of a banker. In 'The Jungle' social habits among schoolgirls are contrasted. Rachel speaks of the excellent meals her cook prepares and asks Elise if she stays up late for dinner. Elise replies scornfully that her family don't have late dinner, but supper, and she has stayed up for that ever since she was eight. Rachel's only thought was that Elise's people must be very eccentric—it never occurs to her that they might not be quite the thing. Mrs Moysey (in the story of that name) lives on her own and has at least three servants.

Society (with the capital letter) is stamped with style[1]. This was the impression gained by the poor landowner's son when he visited South-stone, (perhaps Bournemouth) before the first War. ('Ivy Gripped the Steps', *The Demon Lover*, 1945).

> Everything was effortless; and to him, consequently, seemed stamped with style . . . People here, the company that she kept, commanded everything that they desired, were charged with nothing they did not. The expenditure of their incomes—expenditure calculated so long ago and so nicely that it could now seem artless—occupied them. What there was to show for it showed at every turn; though at no turn too much, for it was not too much. Such light, lofty, smooth-running houses were to be found, quite likely, in no capital city. A word to the livery stables brought an imposing carriage to any door: in the afternoons one drove, in a little party, to reflect on a Roman ruin or to admire a village church.

This not only hits off Southstone but is a beautiful example of Miss Bowen's middle style, intelligent and economic. Mrs Nicholson, who lived in this town, was the widow of a businessman for whom South-stone was 'the high dream of his particular world'. If he had lived it is

1. In *Pictures and Conversations* she admitted she regretted the decline of duelling.

doubtful if he would have made the grade. The golf course had been his real object.

If style was the aim money was the means. Rosanna Detter ('The Inherited Clock', *Demon*) lived in very comfortable circumstances. She made bequests to charities, legacies to old servants, gave £5000 to her sister Addie and was at the time of writing dividing the rest between two young relations. When Paul (one of them) married she gave him a £500 cheque for the honeymoon. She lived at Sandyhill, which stood among pleasant grounds with ilex and a high flint wall. She had inherited it with 'substantial wealth'. There was a good view of the Channel above the ilex groves. The rooms were well heated, papered with brocade, and constituted a museum of 'discredited *objets d'art*' which had always been kept spotless. A long way from Priestley's journey.

Some of the families were going downhill, as families will. Wealth will not maintain itself forever. Stella Rodney, a widow, has given up the 'last of her houses and stored her furniture' and taken a furnished flat when the war begins (*The Heat of the Day*, 1949). This novel is about loss of identity and loss of social function, for she lives in surroundings that are alien to her. Money is difficult. We have the case of a rich class that does not replace the losses incurred by the passage of time, taxation, wear and tear, etc. Between the wars she had travelled, as all Bowen characters do, but that has naturally ceased. Yet inheritance can still come to her assistance. Her son Roderick is left a mansion in Ireland which he has never seen. It sits in three hundred acres. Stella's lover, Robert, belongs to a family which has a large house ('size of a considerable manor, rose with gables to the height of three ample storeys'), built about 1900. But the sense of intimacy, of life still going on, that is so essential to home, is missing, just as it disappeared from Bowen's Court. Robert's father is dead, the house is up for sale, but no one ever comes near it. In the early work of Elizabeth Bowen house and owner form a kind of centaur. War breaks this. In *The Heat of the Day* the process is complete, the divorce is spiritual as well as physical.

Then there is the pastoral element, the house that is not only rural but is part of a village. The well-to-do middle class inhabit such Arcadias, but a little spoiled—drowsy and rural instead of urban and chic. Two sisters live in West Wallows, in a large cottage with half an acre of garden 'already gladey and glittering with the first greens of spring' when 'The Easter Egg Party' starts (*Look At All Those Roses*, 1941). 'Their lives had been one long vigorous country walk . . . they cut ice in the village of West Wallows', writes Miss Bowen, with her inimitable way of characterising people. But here we have not only a house, we have a community.

> West Wallows was more than a village: it was a neighbourhood. From the wide street branched roads that led past the white gates of many homes. The rector was tactful and energetic, the squire unusually cultivated; there were a number of moderate-sized dwellings—some antique, some quite recently built. Inexpensive sociability, liberal politics, shapely antique family furniture, 'interests', enlightened charity set the note of the place. No one was very rich; nobody was eccentric and, though few people hunted, nobody wrote letters against blood sports. The local families harmonized with the pleasant retired people who had settled here. Probably few neighbourhoods in England have such a nice atmosphere as West Wallows.

In addition the village pond had white ducks, there was a saddleback church tower, and a beacon on top of 'the steep, green, nursery rhyme hill. The quaint old sign of the Spotted Cow made the children laugh.' There are those going downhill, though not many of them. The atmosphere of departed glory is not uncommon in Elizabeth Bowen, but it is rarely stressed. One feels it is better to keep up appearances and not to labour the obvious. Such bald reporting as this comes seldom and then as a shock:

> Nothing new appeared in the squire's home; and what was old acquired a sort of fog from being ignored. An austere, religious idea of their own standing not so much inspired as preyed upon Gavin's parents. Caps touched to them in the village could not console them for the letters they got from their bank. Money for them was like a spring in a marsh, feebly thrusting its way up to be absorbed again: any profit forced from the home farm, any rents received for outlying lands went back again into upkeep, rates, gates, hedging, draining, repairs to cottages and renewal of stock. ('Ivy Gripped the Steps', *The Demon Lover*)

The life of the rich depends on servants. They abound here. They are part of the accepted furniture. This is true even of the suburban stories, for between the wars most middle-class families with any pretensions tried to keep a maid (whom they referred to self-deprecatingly as the 'slavey') and the better-off ones ran, or tried to run, to a cook. In Bowen's work they are always there—not noisily but noticeably. In 'The New House', *Encounters*, 1923, we read: ' *"Janet!"* she called down a dark archway. "Janet, *tea!* The master's in" '. Such a cry echoes down the corridors of these stories like the ghostly cries of a Gothic novel.[1]

Servants act as a buffer against the outer world. They are also a useful classifying tool for they know (perhaps better than the mistress) to what group a caller belongs and how he should be treated. For example, Braithwaite, the Michaelis servant in *The House in Paris*, 1935, knew the difference between showing someone in and asking him to wait. In Naomi's case, it was obvious that she wanted something and therefore was no lady. The servant might be occasional, even in quite a superior family, especially if she was some kind of specialist. Miss Fox came to stay for a week to sew, to prepare the family for the summer season. 'She was of that difficult class that has to have trays all the time. Too grand for the servants, she had to be fed in her room . . .'' ('The Needlecase', *The Cat Jumps*, 1934) Another category that did not fit in easily was, of course, the governess. 'Reduced' in *Look at All Those Roses*, 1941, starts with two little girls going upstairs with their governess. She has been acquired at cut rates because she gained notoriety in a murder trial where, though acquitted, she had been under suspicion. Her kind edge their way through the stories without much impact. Frederick, in 'Tears, Idle Tears', is seven and in the charge of one.

Elizabeth Bowen comes from an ancient social tradition which was always proud of its social cohesion. The new industrial society was divisive, setting family against family and man against man in its competitive fury. The old landed families used to keep their retainers for a lifetime and regard them as one of the family, even if underprivileged. The new mill-owners and the professional men who ministered to them were intent on maintaining distinctions, if only to show the world who was really who. In narrow, steep London houses the domestics slept under the rafters. Elizabeth Bowen used, as a child, to take one of the servant's babies off for the afternoon, climbing with him to the top of hay-ricks, sailing paper boats on the stream. The children lived and played together until the time came for one lot to go away to school. That was the end. But in industrial society even this degree of intimacy disappeared. Class divisions became more rigid, and in consequence sympathy and understanding grew less.

1. But she was aware of the post-war change. The visitors in the first chapter of her unfinished work, *The Move-in*, are astonished to see the cap of a parlourmaid through the window. 'The species, so far as they knew, had been long extinct.'

Where Other People Live

The new class that was pushing upwards lived in the most appalling places. Markie (*To the North*, 1932) told how he had once spent a weekend in the country, 'impure country where London's genteelest finger-tip touches the beechwoods'. He had not enjoyed it: 'doors opened with arty latches, the house stank of cold steam from imperfect heating'. He went for a walk.

> Down there, between the dreary trunks of the beeches, houses lay like a sediment in the cup of the misty valley: great gabled car-cases, villas aping the manor, belfried garages where you could feel the cars get cold. There were no lights, not a thread of smoke from a chimney. Afternoon stupor reigned; there was nothing more that they wanted; down there they all sat in the dark. Gardens extensive and cultured, with paved paths and pergolas, ran up the sides of the valley, some had lakes where a punt could measure its length, not turn, some bird-baths for sparrows to drown in. To Markie the foreshortened villas appeared enormous, bloated as though by corruption . . .Then someone's wife opened a cold piano: she tinkled, she tippetted, she struck false chords and she tried again. God knew what she thought she was doing.

It is rare to find a passage where the symbolism is so true and effective: so accurate in its own right and so suggestive in its symbolic function. Markie has a contempt for 'placid pools in the life-stream', anyway. Bowen's allusive method is perfect for indicating decay in the midst of plenty.

In 'Attractive Modern Homes' (*Look at All Those Roses*, 1941)—the very title an ironic declaration—we have something less pre-tentious but nearly as horrid. Estates are purgatories to Bowen, no matter who lives in them.

> This new town they had come to had a mellow, ancient core, but was rapidly spreading and filling up with workers. The Watsons had been edged out to this new estate, the only place where they could find a house. And how un-ideal it was. An estate is not like a village, it has no heart; even the shops are new and still finding their own feet. It has not had time to take on the prim geniality of a suburb. The dwellers are pioneers unenobled by danger. Every-body feels strange and has no time for curiosity. Nothing has had time to flower in this new place.

The horror of suburbia was still one of the dominant facts of the

English environment four years later in some of the stories collected together in *The Demon Lover,* 1945.[1] The girl in 'Songs My Father Sang Me' recounts her family experiences after the first War. The words describe a place to live in; the impression left is a sad dreariness of the spirit.

> The first thing *I* remember, upon becoming conscious,[2] was living in one of those bungalows on the flats near Staines. The river must have been somewhere, but I don't think I saw it. The only point about that region is that it has no point and that it goes on and on. I think there are floods there sometimes, there would be nothing to stop them; a forest fire would be what is really needed, but that would not be possible as there are no trees. It would have looked better, really, just left as primeval marsh, but someone had once said, 'Let there be bungalows'. If you ever motored anywhere near it you probably asked yourself who lived there, and why. Well, my father and mother and I did, and why?— because it was cheap, and there was no-one to criticise how you were getting on. Our bungalow was tucked well away in the middle, got at by a sort of maze of in those days unmade roads. I'm glad to say I've forgotten which one it was. Most of our neighbours kept themselves to themselves for, probably, like ours, the best reasons; but most of them kept hens also; we didn't even do that. All round us, nature ran riot between corrugated iron, clothes-lines and creosoted lean-to sheds.

Then there is the seaside resort, brilliantly portrayed in *Death of the Heart,* 1938, or *Eva Trout,* 1969. Miss Bowen gets the feel of it, the rawness and the windiness. Eva (in the latter novel) takes a house in Broadstairs and is met by Mr Denge, the agent. His description of the town shouts boredom at us between its stilted lines. 'Broadstairs is also animated in the evenings, more rather than less so out of season, when, less overrun by visitors, we are more exclusive. You will find in the better part of the town hotels with an international *cuisine,* not to speak of restaurants. Those, Mrs Denge and I and our little circle frequent, on occasions, that is, from time to time.'

But *Eva Trout* is remarkable for its adjustment by an author, who has left her youth far behind, to modes of living of a new younger

1. Villas became the 'dominants of the stories I started to write' *(Pictures and Conversations).* She was infatuated with them, 'unhistorical gimcrack little bubbles of illusion.'

2. i.e., after birth.

generation. Having the ability to hit off a scene in a brief phrase (a girls' school, much of it consisting of huts in the garden: 'enlightened huts, consisting so largely of glass that in them you still felt outdoors'), Bowen can also capture an alien way of life unerringly. Eva takes a house at Broadstairs and decides to equip it in the modern manner. She is mentally backward, slightly unbalanced, but knows what a modern girl needs. (She is also the first, incidentally, of Bowen's heroines to go to America—at least, functionally.) And here is her drawing room.

> Outstanding examples of everything auro-visual on the market this year, 1959, were ranged round the surprised walls: large-screen television set, sonorous-looking radio, radio-gramophone in a teak coffin, other gramophone with attendant stereo cabinets, sixteen-millimetre projector with screen ready, a recording instrument of B.B.C. proportions, not to be written off as a tape-recorder. Other importations: a superb typewriter shared a metal-legged table with a cash register worthy to be its mate; and an intercom, whose purposes seemed uncertain, had been installed. What looked like miles of flex matted the parquet. Electronics had driven the old guard, the Circe armchairs, into a huddle in the middle of the floor . . .

There is no indication that Eva needed this equipment, or even used it, but she had to have it. She was a modern girl, and Miss Bowen knows what goes to make a modern girl, whether in 1930 or in 1960.

The Classes

'Into the novel goes such taste as I have for rational behaviour and social portraiture', she wrote in the introduction to a selection of stories published in America in 1959. The short story, she said, 'allows for what is crazy about humanity'. Realism is neither her forte nor her interest, yet she has an intuitive grasp of what is characteristic and essential that puts the reader in a much closer relationship to the life she portrays than any methodical description could do. There is an aspect of life which Virginia Woolf called 'the social farce', and she said it was overplayed. It is 'the consuming futile', what does not matter. It used to infuriate Woolf because it threatened her with its demands. It is time-consuming and exhausting, and it is also intellectually puerile. Yet most social novelists devote the greater part of their time describing it. Bowen avoids it more rigorously than most, far more than, say, Rosamund Lehmann, for whom it appears at times to be the very stuff of life.

Nevertheless, there is an aspect of middle class behaviour which can only be called farcical. Bowen sees it clearly and knows it would be false to ignore its existence. It is a disagreeable actuality. It is an important part of *The Heat of the Day*, 1949, where English middle class society is shown *in extremis*. Robert's sister, Ernestine, represents all that is crass and insensitive in English middle-class life: the philistinism, the absence of fine feeling, the self confidence based on a charade view of existence, the extreme extroversion, the reduction of everything to a simple equation in morals. Talking of her dog, she said he had wonderful faith in human nature. 'Of course, he came to us as a pup and I am glad to think none of us ever let him down. I often think that if Hitler could have looked into that dog's eyes, the story might have been very different.' One can hear her saying it. Plummily.

In *The Death of the Heart* we are given a picture of those whom the pretentious imagine are not quite-quite. Portia goes to a kind of finishing school in Cavendish Square. She is discovered reading a letter, which she holds under the table. Miss Paullie, the headmistress, suspects that Portia is not really quite the class of girl she likes to have. She has already told her that she should not carry her handbag about with her indoors. It's a hotel habit. '*Sins* cut boldly up through every class in society, but here misdemeanours show a certain level in life', Miss Bowen writes with her tongue in her cheek. In the same novel there is Mrs Heccomb, Anna's governess, who had married a doctor whose first wife had died, leaving a boy and a girl. They had grown up rough: 'the fact was, though one did not refer to this, that her husband's first wife had not been quite-quite.' As for the second Mrs Heccomb, she also found her level. She lived on the sea-front, which was rather commercial. Most of her friends lived in balconied villas or gabled houses up on the hill.

Morality, the abiding interest of the middle classes, had a geographical disposition that Mrs Heccomb's neighbours were quick to grasp. Pauline, a schoolgirl in *To the North*, 1932, was made aware of it. She went for a ride on a No. 11 bus at the recommendation of the housekeeper.

> The No. 11 is an entirely moral bus. Springing from Shepherd's Bush, against which one has seldom heard anything, it enjoys some innocent bohemianism in Chelsea, picks up the shoppers at Peter Jones, swerves down the Pimlico Road—too busy to be lascivious—passes not too far from the royal stables, nods to Victoria Station, Westminster Abbey, the Houses of Parliament,

whirrs reverently up Whitehall, and from its only brush with vice, in the Strand, plunges to Liverpool Street through the noble and serious architecture of the City. Except for the Strand, the No. 11 route, Mrs Patrick considered, had the quality of Sunday afternoon literature; from it Pauline could derive nothing but edification.

But under no circumstances would she have recommended a No. 24, which went down Charing Cross Road. Pauline blushed at the very mention of the place.

Somehow the middle class—the real solid middle bloc of the middle class—never changed. Karen (in *The House in Paris,* 1935) 'had been born and was making her marriage inside the class that in England changes least of all. The Michaelis lived like a family in a pre-war novel in one of the tall, cream houses in Chester Terrace, Regent's Park. Their relatives and old friends, as nice as they were themselves, were rooted in the same soil.' They were serene—they still appear in books but they make tame reading. 'They were not rococo, as the aristocracy are supposed to be, or, like the middle classes, tangles of mean motives . . .' Here we come up against the familiar difficulty of terminology, whereby the middle class is in fact an amalgam of classes, ranging from the small shopkeeper and poor professional man to the company director and fashionable doctor. Karen belonged to the well-to-do, what is often called the upper middle, and was thoroughly aware of it. 'She saw this inherited world enough from the outside to see that it might not last, but, perhaps for this reason, obstinately stood by it.' Her brother had come through the war safely and married a woman with property in the North, which he managed. He hunted two days a week, sometimes published clever satirical verses and experimented in artificial manures. It was a world she sometimes wanted to escape from but intended to stay in, through her own marriage. With her mother she went to private views and the Opera. Certain things were established—for instance, if you wanted a bed, you went to Heal's. It was necessary to keep the classes separate, it was better to inbreed than to marry outside your class. The man she was going to marry was her cousin's cousin.

Now contrast this existence with that of a lower level in the middle class. Living in small houses, there is a great sense of intimacy. The 'plunging manner' in which Dickie Heccomb (*The Death of the Heart,* 1938) bathed and dressed was heard all over the house. By contrast, 'at Windsor Terrace, with its many floors and extended plumbing, the intimate life of Thomas was not noticeable.' Rich women live at a

distance from life and very often they do not see their money. Miss
Bowen comments that it is said that the Queen (who is the standard)
never carries a purse. The middle class envies and despises, or perhaps
pretends to despise, the upper class. 'Contented wry decent girls like
Daphne (Heccomb) are the bad old order's principal stay.' She never
failed to attack Anna but was the kind of girl you would be likely to
see watching a fashionable wedding or socialites arriving for a first
night. (She and Dickie were the children of a doctor's widow, who had
been governess to Anna.) Life was a combination of pretence and
realism. You were told that the Corona Café at Seale (seaside) was
run by ladies; if you went to a party at the Heccombs you might be
called upon to roll up the carpet or stick flags in sandwiches.

The bourgeoisie have a weapon, though it is a feeble one. They feel
at a disadvantage with the rich and the well-to-do, with the upper
classes and those they imagine to be upper class (for they are easy to
deceive, as one side of them wishes to be associated with such people).
For instance, Daphne is furious with Portia because Portia saw her
holding Eddie's hand at the pictures. There is only one thing to do,
accuse her of being common and vulgar. Scorn is the only answer. 'I
had no idea at all you were so *common,* and nor had Mumsie the least
idea, I'm sure, or she wouldn't have ever obliged your sister-in-law
by having you to stop here, convenient or not. This all simply goes to
show the way you're brought up at home, and I am really surprised at
them, I must say.' Such people are psychologically insecure, and have
to strengthen their position by some kind of aggression. One can see
it in Daphne's admirer, Mr Bursley, who is in the Army and comes up
the path 'with the rather knock-kneed walk of extreme social consciousness.'

The two wars were tremendous blows to the middle classes, both in
their material circumstances and their self-confidence. Bowen
illustrates the effects of both wars. In the story 'Songs My Father
Sang Me' a girl talks about her father and his failure to find work
after the first war. 'To think of all we expected after the war', her
mother kept saying to him, day after day. She got him the offer of a
job, through friends, selling vacuum cleaners. He said nothing, simply
stared. 'Then I suppose you want us to starve?' she said. 'In the
Square' (*The Demon Lover,* 1945) shows us what happened during the
second war. This time they lost their servants, whom they had
managed to cling on to during the interim. You answered the door
yourself. 'These days, there is no-one to . . .' you mumbled apolo-
getically. There were fewer lamps, some had been put away with the
bric-à-brac that used to be on the tables and in alcoves. You notice a

film of dust on the bulb. The sixteen-year old nephew is very independent—'But these days I suppose everyone is?' The house, a smart one in a London square, is now shared by her husband's secretary and a couple of caretakers in the basement (they are also very independent) with a son who is a policeman, who sometimes sleeps at the top of the house, and a schoolgirl daughter who comes in when she thinks they're not about. It is true, this situation was formed by the impact of war itself, but there was to be no complete return to normal.

The lower classes rarely impinge on the others. When they do, they are seen from the other side of the fence. They are usually represented by servants. An early novel, *The Hotel*, 1927, is interesting in this respect. The Pinkertons have their own maid, who is suitably coarse in her diction. A porter smiles (we are in Italy). There is a little fun at the expense of the boots who was called Antonio because of the song. The only guest who appears to consider the feelings of the staff is Tessa Bellamy and ironically her life consists of lying on a sofa, getting fat. She does not like to give the staff unnecessary trouble but is rebuked by Sydney, who says they are paid to take trouble. Tessa even thinks it unfair to keep the waiters hanging about once dinner is ready.

The outer world is barely recognized. (Their dependence on the world, in Marxian terms, is not acknowledged, it is as firmly pushed out of view as the comparable society in Henry James). It is once deplored that there is nothing in the papers except politics, which always go on and on and so lose interest. One doubts whether they have any effect at all. One lady mentions a pit disaster which draws forth the disdainful reply: 'Miners always seem to be getting into trouble. One is so sorry, but it is difficult to go on and on sympathizing, especially out here where one gets on just as well without them—they burn wood, you know, and do everything else by electricity.' But some White Russians had inhabited a villa in the neighbourhood. They were admired as a race apart—they had been too perfect to survive, not too imperfect or stupid. Milton, the clergyman, suggests they had had no value. Miss Pym, who can never control her thoughts or her tongue sufficiently, blurts out: 'If you come to think of it, what is the good of *us*?' When pressed to be more explicit, she blunders on and explains that she means their class. Someone suggests she is a Socialist. She asks, 'Must one be a Socialist to wonder sometimes what is the good of us? Because one can't help it (without wishing to attach oneself to any party) these days, when so much is in the melting-pot.' Miss Hillier feels such talk is bad form and falls back on the necessity of their all setting an example. 'People do notice—even the Italians notice.' Miss Pym wonders if the local population might not think them all lazy, and even thinks that the waiters might —— but she is told she is getting acutely self-conscious because the 'creatures are positive parasites'.

Parasites! And sometimes worse—they get too independent. Miss Bowen, who is very good-mannered, does not say unpleasant things about working people. Some of her social climbers tend to sniff about them. But it takes a thief to catch a thief. In 'Oh, Madam . . .' (a story in *Roses*), the house has been bombed, the windows broken. The old servant is reporting on the situation to her mistress, her greatly respected mistress, who has been away. 'If I can just get these glaziers —they expect you to whistle. It's not good for a trade to be too much in demand, is it? It makes the working people ever so slow.'

I have a feeling that Miss Bowen's most remarkable achievement is her last novel, *Eva Trout*. It was a greatly changed world from that of the 1920's, when she had started. But she had noticed the changes (by no means all novelists are able to do that) and, what is so impressive, she had incorporated them in her work. Her description of Eric Arble cannot be dismissed in the usual way, i.e., superb in the delineation of her own class, Miss Bowen is less sure of touch when she goes outside it . . . Eric had tried fruit-farming, and when it failed he became foreman in a garage belonging to a cousin. 'He nowadays caught the seven-thirty a.m. bus into town, intercepting it at the crossroads, and usually made it home on the six-thirty p.m.' There was an old Anglia at home, but this was for his wife. And here is Eric coming home, the day's work done.

> He seldom came in saying anything. He saw no need to. On the contrary, he came back into a room as though not conscious of having gone from it. Once he was there, he was there. He gave but one sign of having been far afield: invariably he brought back the evening paper. Quite often he quite simply sat down and read it. Who would have thought this man had been gone a day?—but that by what had happened, might have arisen, been done or not done during the day away, he was still to a certain extent preoccupied.

Snobs and New Rich

Miss Bowen traces very carefully the effects of families going up and families going down. She most delights in observing those who think or hope they are going up and try to adjust their behaviour accordingly. There were some in her first book, *Encounters*. 'The New

House' and 'The Return' show people trying to use their money to buy improved status, and in the case of the Tottenhams failing completely. In her Preface to the 1949 reissue Miss Bowen showed her distaste for this story ('The Return'), calling it showy but hollow. It was a situation she had thought up rather than felt. Where the character is more sympathetic (as is Herbert in 'The New House') the difficulties of adaptation nevertheless persist. One may rise with a certain amount of grace, but the past cannot be blotted out.

> Every step of Herbert's through the disordered house was a step in a triumphal progress. Every echo from the tiles and naked boards derided and denied the memory of that small brick villa where he and Cicely had been born, where their mother's wedded life had begun and ended; that villa now empty and denuded, whose furniture looked so meagre in this spaciousness and height.

Houses are very important to Elizabeth Bowen. They soak up personalities from their occupants, and become practically living beings. This accounts, of course, for one of the theories of hauntings.

In 'The Working Party' (*Joining Charles,* 1929) we have Mrs Fisk, a young farmer's wife, who had a room 'in which she never felt comfortable but always entirely ladylike'. The most difficult adaptation was attempted (if that is the word) by Eddie in *The Death of the Heart,* 1938. Eddie is one of Bowen's most interesting characters, being a sort of pre-view of the youth of a later generation. He is a proletarian who has been to Oxford, is always on the verge of protest, and has a barely-concealed contempt for those who consider themselves his betters. 'The brilliant child of an obscure home', she calls him, the Lorenzo type, who 'was taken up, played up, played about with, taken down, let down, finally sent down for one idiotic act.' His rich, cultured friends made a monkey of him, so that he was ashamed to go back home. Matchett, the old retainer, naturally doesn't like him, she 'sees through him'. She sums him up with: 'Manners? He's no class'. It was the last thing he pretended to have, but others of his origin either expected him to have it or to submerge. Bowen never makes fun of him. She feels uncomfortably keenly his situation. To his credit he was no snob. He just realized he didn't belong and never would belong again.

Jocelyn Brooke, in his British Council and National Book League monograph, refers to the vulgarity of the Heccombs in *The Death of the Heart.* They are sharply contrasted with Eddie. They, unlike him, are always 'aping the wrong kind of smartness'. They are perpetually betraying what Brooke calls 'their crass spiritual muddledom, their inability to see the simplest matter in its proper perspective'. The Heccombs were in a desperate situation. They had no money, and you can only successfully acquire class if you have it. Not only does wealth excuse a certain amount of gaucherie, but it will pave the way perfectly for the next generation. A good plan is to take your wealth and your pretensions abroad, as Lady Latterley did in *A World of Love,* (1955). A wealthy Englishwoman, with a past, she takes a castle in Ireland. The people she invites tend to be very much of her own type, except for young Jane and an old man named Terence, who is represented as being rather more real than the others. Jane looks round Lady Latterley's bedroom and supposes that it must be 'a replica, priceless these days, of a Mayfair décor back in the 1930s.' There was a great deal of gossip about Lady Latterley—the number of baths she had installed, the lovers and servants who had left her, the failure of her guests to arrive or, once arrived, to leave, the delays, the non-deliveries, the breakages, leakages and general exploitation she had endured. It was her fault for being so rich. 'She was *nouveau riche;* but, as Anthonia said, better late than never.'

Such people are immensely concerned with status symbols. Lady Latterley's status symbol was her whole way of life. For the miserable Heccombs it had to be something very carefully chosen, such as an up-to-date dance record or a second-hand car of the right make. Eva Trout is the daughter of a millionaire and she has inherited his wealth. She is astonishingly lonely and unattached for one so rich. She is a little queer which possibly puts people off. She is friendly with Henry, the bright son of an impoverished parson, now an undergraduate. He won't let her bring her Jaguar to Cambridge. A Jag is a status symbol to a business man. It shows he's a bit better than you might think from looking at him. By the same token, it is a differentiation symbol to the artist or the academic—it tells you that its owner is not quite sure of himself. 'Ostentatious' is the word Henry uses. Eva has the wealth; Henry has the nous.

Although many of Bowen's characters are in reduced circumstances they have rarely fallen in the social scale. The fact is that in England, if a man's family has stood high for some generations, it is almost impossible for him to fall very far, if he stays in this country, for his relatives will rally round him. Bowen does not show the fall but she illustrates and explains the hanging on. The keen interest in family ramifications underlies the desire to maintain family position. Every individual, however undeserving, is a little piece of the family.

Abroad

Bowen's characters are Irish or English or both, but their area of activity extends beyond the boundaries of the two countries, particularly into France and Italy. Western Europe is part of their natural habitat.

It is partly a matter of class and partly a personal reaction. In the Preface to the reissue of *Ann Lee's* (1926) she said that her principal stimulus originally was travel. At the time she had been living in the English Midlands, outside Northampton. Some of the stories came from there but 'otherwise I drew on the distant, rather than the nearer, scene. Some days I caught a train and went to London; I visited Ireland to see my father; every spring brought me two weeks in Italy; in late summer my husband and I travelled in France . . .' During childhood it was London that drew her myth-making and romantic nature.

> It loomed darkly somewhere at the other side of the water; I thought of it (when at all) as an entity, at once magnetic and dangerous. It was, from all I heard, a city into which no-one ventured alone, and which was to be entered only after preparation and wary forethought. It stood for the adult, and so much so that there should be children in London seemed unimaginable —in fact that there should be people of any kind was only a secondary idea: I pictured the thing as a mass of building, a somehow impious extreme of bulk and height in whose interstices was fog.
>
> ('Coming to London', *The London Magazine,* Mar. 1958)

She added that she endowed London with extremes of fashion and wealth, alongside which lay sinister squalour. It was the fantasy of a protected child, from a comfortable Anglo-Irish home, then at an English boarding school, who wintered in Italy in 1921. It shows the lure of distance, superimposed on the natural custom of the rich to travel.

The early stories and novels simply show the rich travelling, living and wintering abroad, in rather more pleasant climates, as a matter of course. The war brought this to a temporary halt and was naturally resented. After the war everyone began to travel and it lost its cachet. There are several examples in the first book, *Encounters* (1923). 'Requiescat' takes place in Italy and 'Mrs Windermere' has a background of Italy. We meet the lady from whom the latter story is named in Fuller's Restaurant, Regent's St. It is hard to imagine her outside the expatriate circles of Italy. She is in full bloom, over mature, the hothouse product of a *rentier* civilization.

> Her lustrous eyes looked out mournfully, contentedly, from under pouchy lids, through the long fringes of her hat; her *retroussé* nose was powdered delicately mauve, the very moist lips had a way of contracting quickly in the middle of a sentence in an unpuglike effort to retain the saliva. Curly bunches of grey hair lay against her cheeks, a string of Roman pearls was twisted several times round her plump throat; her furs were slung across her bosom and one shoulder; her every movement diffused an odour of Violet de Parme. She had not removed her gloves, and opulent rolls of white kid encircled wrist and forearm; her sleeves fell back from the elbow. She was an orthodox London edition of her Italian self.

There are three Italian stories in *Ann Lee's*. At times Italy appeared to be little more than an English holiday province. 'It seemed so odd to everybody else to meet Italians staying on Lake Como', we read in 'The Contessina'. *The Hotel*, 1927, is set in Italy. It is Miss Bowen's most sustained account of well-to-do idleness. A lady in a needlework group says she would go mad if she didn't go abroad. Abroad means company, the communal life which is so despised when adopted by other countries as State policy. (No social group is so well prepared for communal living as the English upper class, with its background of public school and foreign hotel. Only a misunderstanding, fostered by such irrelevancies as nationalization and expropriation, keeps the truth from them.) This lady describes the unbearable strain of life in a drawing room, where books and the telephone are such poor substitutes for company.

All these people have enough money to live without working or, at least, to take long expensive holidays. Few could be called rich. They all regard themselves as a cut above the generality, but only the Honourable Mrs and Miss Pinkerton can claim aristocratic membership. They keep aloof, in a self-imposed privacy. Sydney Warren, the most intelligent of the guests, sums them up. 'They were stupid but not, she felt, vulgar; all this lace and leather, monograms everywhere and massive encrustations of silver meant less to them, probably, than to herself, to whom wealth and position would have been conveniences to be made use of.'

The conversation of the Pinkertons is a good example of that mixture of inconsequence and private information that characterizes their class (and is so strongly marked in a Nancy Mitford novel).

Mrs Pinkerton sat turning over the pages of *The Tatler* and talking to Rosina while she embroidered.

'I see', she said, 'the Wyntons' girl is to be married.'

'Ah?' remarked Rosina, snipping with her gilt scissors. 'Who is he?'

'A Barre, apparently.'

'Are there Barres? I never heard of any. Where does it say he comes from?'

'It says here', replied her sister-in-law, looking at the paper closely, 'Hampshire'.

'There are no Barres in Hampshire', said Rosina definitely'.

'Then it is another of these marriages'. They both sighed.

These two ladies cannot understand how anyone can go to Nice, which they have been told is a kind of French Brighton. One of them begins to suggest that it might be too expensive, but is angrily checked by the other.

Such people are the most pathetic of all the hotel dwellers: they have the pretensions without the money to support them. They did the best they could in a hotel that was not, to be frank, one of the best. They had rooms on the sunny side and could patronize the view from a balcony. (Elizabeth Bowen has hard words for the view: 'The spiritual, crude and half-repellent beauty of that changing curtain, so featureless but for the occasional passing of a ship.') They barricaded themselves behind jalousies. They just managed to understand that a hotel of this description did not have a private suite with a bathroom, so they had reserved for their exclusive use the bathroom opposite. Unlike the other, more bourgeois occupants, they demanded privacy and would pay what they could for it. Naturally, you had to dispel loneliness before you could get a taste for privacy.

It was important to advertise remoteness from the bourgeoisie, from which all came, except the Pinkertons. There were certain rules to be followed. Some of these I shall list later when I consider L.P. Hartley, especially his *The Go-Between*. Punctuality was a suburban virtue. It wasn't done to arrive for dinner at the earliest advertised time—if one did, then one retreated quickly. Certain words were middle-class, e.g., Mrs Kerr was puzzled when Sydney said she hadn't wanted to 'intrude'. It seems probable that Sydney's use of the word was a minor blow for independence, breaking away from the claims of a lady whose background was mysterious and whose style indeterminate.

Whenever the English intelligentsia consider the French they are immediately assailed by strong feelings of inferiority. (The lower classes never suffer from such a *malaise*.) Bowen is quiet about the French, apparently admires their culture but is never silly about them. The typical English middle class approach is beautifully illustrated in 'Shoes: an International Episode' (*Joining Charles,* 1929). The Ahernes are staying at a French hotel. Mrs Aherne wanders round in her dressing gown smoking a cigarette, 'feeling French and sophisticated'. She tried to express joy when café waiters brought her *La Vie Parisienne.* 'They wouldn't bring *that* to most Englishwomen!' she thought. Then her shoes disappear. Edward tries to calm her by saying that the best type of French were becoming increasingly Anglophil, and someone would soon return the shoes, which must have been taken in error. He suggests that someone is trying to copy them, and Dillie immediately changes her tone. Now, she felt, it was they who were setting the fashion. 'You know, I'm quite sure if brogue shoes came to be worn over here generally, there'd be quite a change in the Latin attitude towards women'—an attitude she didn't care for, especially the ogling.

When she feels that Edward is paying a little too much attention to a French woman (in fact, it is entirely formal), she declares viciously that French women are 'hard'. The story depends for its effect on certain misunderstandings over two pairs of shoes. What hurts more than anything is that the waiter thought her brogues belonged to her husband, while the Frenchwoman's shoes 'radiated sex-consciousness'. The uncertainty and lack of confidence of Dillie are portrayed with the greatest subtlety. The story ends with the English couple walking away, talking loudly about the Latin mentality. They are made to appear like a couple of extrovert, self-righteous barbarians.

The continental background is present, though rather tenuously, in the excellent novel published in the same year (*The Last September*). This is in a setting of Irish country houses during the Troubles. They are all burning away like mad in the last paragraph. The life described is that of the provincial aristocracy, snobbish and unaware: large façades, mounting lawns, surrounding plantations and a chauffeur. The inmates and their guests have usually travelled in Europe, or intend to, though it has done little to fracture their Irish impermeability. The Naylors owned Danielstown. Myra was 'interesting', cultivated, sketched beautifully, knew about books and music. She had been to Germany and Italy, 'everywhere that one visits acquisitively'. (Once more Miss Bowen finds the right word.) Francie Montmorency, who was visiting with her husband (he had foolishly sold his family estate and now had no permanent home), was ordered abroad for successive winters. To complete the picture, Myra and Francie had been presented the same year.

To the North, 1932, starts with two of the main characters returning from Italy. Later there is a weekend in Paris. *The House in Paris*, 1935, centres on one house in Paris. Leopold has lived in Rome and Spezia. The Michaelis family were once at Florence. The unseen Mrs Arbuthnot, who is going to receive Henrietta, lives at Mentone. Karen spends some time in Germany. The nine-year old Leopold speaks knowingly of France and Italy: 'Nobody goes to France when they can go to Italy'. Abroad is a good way of getting rid of inconvenient acquaintances. When the Monkshoods get tired of Eddie and want to get him off their hands, they simply give up their flat and go to live in a foreign country (*The Death of the Heart*, 1938). This novel is a good example of one of Bowen's virtues, her ability to establish character without fuss. It starts with a man and a woman standing on a foot-bridge in Regents Park. They are warmly dressed (against the winter cold) and are obviously well-to-do. The woman, Anna, is married and employs three servants and a charwoman. Thomas, the husband, is in business with capital transferred to him by his mother. They are familiar with the continent. Thomas's father had divorced his first wife and with his second, Irene, trailed up and down the Riviera. Irene died in Switzerland. Portia, their daughter (a magnificent piece of character creation), was born in Mentone. During the course of the story Anna and Thomas go for a continental holiday.

There is the same picture of wealth and ease on the move in the volume of stories entitled *The Cat Jumps*, 1934. In 'The Good Girl' an Englishman and two women gently bounce across Italy in a Rolls Royce with a valet. Mrs Letherton-Channing ('The Little Girl's Room') lives in an Italianate house in Berkshire. The guests felt like expatriates and coal fires roared under mantels crusted and swagged with glazed Della Robbia lemons and bluish pears. One of the guests called it Little Italy. In 'The Apple Tree' we have one of those lonely little Bowen girls who have no parents (rich parents disappear rather more quickly than poor ones) and occasionally visit relatives on the continent—in this case, an aunt and uncle at Cannes.

But the war breaks it up. People have to come home. Once home, they can't get out. *The Demon Lover*, 1945, has an air of frustration, people cannot go abroad, there are no servants, life itself is decaying. In 'The Cheery Soul' an aunt has been turned out of Italy because of the war. There is one sad reference to a happier time, in the ivy-like story called 'Ivy Gripped the Steps'. Mrs Nicholson goes abroad and sends Gavin a picture postcard from Mentone. But this was before Sarajevo, let alone Hitler's invasion of Poland.

Hotel Life

It is perfectly natural that, with people who are so often on the move, hotel life should figure prominently. The hotel is the natural habitat of a considerable number of Bowen characters. It represents a never-never land of people who are semi-intimate, semi-friendly and semi-acquainted. In the first book of stories there are two named 'Breakfast' and 'Lunch', which is significant, for they are hotel meals, and meals rule hotel life to a much greater extent than home life. In *Look at All Those Roses* 'A Love Story' is a hotel story. The love is unsatisfactory, the war makes everything doubtful and impermanent: a hotel is the obvious symbolic setting (not that Miss Bowen uses hammer-symbolism of the type apparently admired by some academics).

The Hotel, of course, is central to our interest. It is devoted to the life in a hotel on the Italian Riviera, where nearly all the guests are English—in fact, we never meet any who are not. One guest thinks of 'the whole band of white hotels like palaces along the line of coast into which their own seemed now to be knitted.' The guests are 'weighed down by their leisure'. A child's insight sums them up: 'people in hotels, hardly *alive* . . .!' They were a species of their own and must appear to the local Commune as such: English visitors. The conception of this life or imitation of life as something endless and unbroken oppresses Mrs Lee-Mittison. She is looking, with barely realized envy, at a villa: 'she felt sick at the thought of their hotel bedrooms that stretched, only interspersed with the spare-rooms of friends, in unbroken succession before and behind her.' The crushing truth about this existence was its dullness, its constant struggle with boredom, so that one snatched at the most insignificant detail as a diversion. Tessa Bellamy had nothing to do but lie on her sofa. She was waiting for the menu to arrive (she paid an extra five per cent to have it brought in advance); it 'gave one something to think about during the morning'. Such a life gathered rules to itself as a kind of protection, though they were not always helpful. For instance, reading was an obvious outlet, but then an unwritten rule decreed that it was not really done to read before lunch.

In *To the North* the lovers stay in a Paris hotel, not a particularly smart one, but it was by choice, not for economy. *The House in Paris* shows us children at a seaside hotel and again, lovers. Lois in *The Last September* confesses some of her dreams to the sophisticated Miss Norton, who is staying with the family; she has never been abroad, and more than anything she would like to stay in a hotel by herself. Perhaps for the young of the Irish gentry a hotel was a symbol of escape, a richer world, the exotic. *Death of the Heart* is more hotel-ridden than any other novel except *The Hotel,* but in a different way. Portia and her mother had lived all their lives together in continental hotels. They are in the past at the time of the telling of the story, but they brood like ghosts. Meanwhile Major Brett actually lives in cheap hotels in London, a life of well-to-do poverty. There is a great deal of the philosophy of hotel-living in this novel. Portia's character has been formed by their demands and requirements. It would be possible to make a collection of shrewd observations on hotel-life. Anna noted that nothing that was Portia's ever seemed really to belong to her, and it was difficult giving her a present unless it was something to eat. 'It may be because they always lived in hotels'. And Portia notes how you keep hearing other people in hotels; in a flat you keep quiet so that others shouldn't hear you; but a house is itself quiet rather than the inmates. Thomas said it was 'pretty awful' but it was the pretty awful of the rich.

'The Shoes', which has already been mentioned, is set in a French hotel *(Joining Charles).* 'Good Girl' *(The Cat Jumps)* is another hotel story. 'Love' (in *Look At All Those Roses*) suggests the end for it is about a derelict hotel. In 'A Queer Heart' the husband dies, most conveniently, in a hotel. Many of the stories in this volume appear to mark the end of an epoch, a pleasant epoch on the whole, with the hotel as a pleasant convenience. Eva Trout is a Portia of a later generation. She had lived in a series of hotels like Portia, she was now an orphan, largely unwanted, with nowhere in particular to go. The only difference was that Eva had money. Whenever her father arrived at a new hotel he used to telephone down for a governess, and then a stenographer. 'They could also always obtain a horse for me, a masseur for my father's friend, a hypnotist to allow my father to sleep', said Eva.

It is not surprising that Elizabeth Bowen wrote the story of the famous Dublin hotel, the Shelbourne, in a book bearing its name and sub-titled 'A Centre in Dublin Life for more than a Century'. But the Shelbourne contrasted with most of the hotels in her fiction. They were resorts for exiles and lovers, the homeless and the unwanted. The Shelbourne was seen and described enthusiastically as a home and a friend.

Speech

Bowen is fascinated by the speech of the lower middle and superior working classes. Throughout her novels and stories there are brilliant reproductions of the mode. By its use she is able to establish the social standing of a character without further description. There is a good example in the story, 'Dead Mabelle', in *Joining Charles*, 1929. Two bank clerks converse.

> Jim removed his pipe thoughtfully. 'Upon my word', he began, 'upon my *word!* You really *are* you know. I mean really, old man—!'

And later Jim says, 'Oo-hooo, we don't think. No, we *don't* think—.' When William is angry and sends Jim packing, and then apologizes, Jim is very nice about it. 'Say nothing more about it, old man. I quite understand. Beg yours, I'm sure'.

The main characteristics of this type of speech are pretence (because it is felt that these rather arcane phrases are those used by their social superiors) and poverty of content—in fact, conversation moves through a series of exclamations, which disguise the fact that nothing is said. Elsewhere people of this class talk stiltedly, making a tremendous effort to be correct, hoping not to give themselves away. There are examples of this in *A World of Love*, 1955. Here we have an Irish background, which makes the novel largely irrelevant to my purpose, but the household is half English. The setting is a country house owned by Antonia, although her illegitimate half-brother Fred Danby farms it. She has married him off to the fiancée of her brother Guy, who was killed in the first war and dominates the book (or is meant to—it is entirely unsuccessful). Lilia is a typical Bowen portrait of an English lower middle class woman—she is sentimental, quick to misunderstand and spiritually heavy. This is how she speaks: 'How many other offers do you imagine I might not have always had, if I had chosen to lift a finger, instead of staying faithful to Guy's memory? That, of course, you would never understand'. One is made to feel she tries out each word carefully before using it. She also has gentility: 'Antonia had given her espadrilles but she would never sink so low.' We are told that Lilia had been 'whirled by the courtship out of her natural sphere (suburbia merging into the Thames Valley).' At times there might be just a touch of caricature. If so, it is not evidence of cruelty but of the exuberance of the author's imagination with all its delights.

The conversation of the bank clerks is echoed by that of the girls (perhaps typists) in 'Love' (*Roses*, 1941). They are having a quiet holiday. Bowen reproduces their clichés with telling effect. 'It gave us quite a shock'; 'you're always on about tea'; 'I must say it was a bit slow'; 'What are you up to, then?' said Edna, ever so sharp; 'I could have slapped Edna, being stubborn like that'; 'Oh, give over, Edna, do'; 'oh my goodness, I could have dropped!'; 'so then I piped up'; etc., etc., But despite this Bowen retains her keenness of observation and sharpness of feeling. 'Her wrists were as thin as wire, with gold bracelets slipping into her cuff.' In a darkened room one of the girls sees a row of mackintoshes hanging up, and first thinks they are corpses.

Miss Bowen herself gives a clue to the distinctive element in this kind of talk. It is when Joanna is lunching in a restaurant with Mary Dash during the war ('Careless Talk', *The Demon Lover*). 'Every tongue struck its own note, with exclamatory English on top of all.' Exclamation, sometimes to the exclusion of everything else, as with the bank clerks. Conversation punctuated with 'Darling!' 'My dear!', 'How frightful!' and so on.

In *The Heat of the Day* Louie and Connie take over from the two girls in 'Love'. They are also counterparts of a couple higher in the social range: Louie equates with Stella (whom she admires extravagantly the only time their paths cross) and Connie is a less privileged Ernestine. It is rare for a writer to cover the minor distinctions of class so effectively as Miss Bowen does. The effort of identifying with her characters enables her not only to get speech patterns exactly but also causes her occasionally to drop into them herself when describing the girls. Sometimes this can be done with satiric intent (One of Rosamund Lehmann's characteristics) but with Miss Bowen one feels that she is influenced by her own progeny. 'She was on duty at 23.00, which would be only too shortly' sounds like one of the girls, but is in fact a comment by the author. And, it is implied, it is necessary at times to become slightly vulgar, to let the hair down, to forget one's noble pretensions and admirable background. Sanity requires relaxation. In the same novel poor Cousin Nettie feels the world is insupportable and diplomatically goes mad and is shut away in a home, where she is perfectly happy. And why? Because 'she carried with her the lasting dignity of a world in which it was impossible to say, "Oh, come off it!"'

Each novel becomes slightly more mannered in its handling of speech rhythms and structures, but she never forsakes reality. Miss Bowen becomes bolder and more exact—a writer has to be bold if he is to put down what is rather than what his readers want or believe to be. *Death of the Heart* was remarkable for its precision of speech. *Eva Trout* takes us into a new world, a generation apart. Eva asks Catrina (a little girl) why she stays so still. Catrina replies, 'Anywhere to go is too far'. Democratization of behaviour is one of the more

notable trends of post-war life. It has been accompanied by democratization of speech. Miss Bowen has been aware of these changes and
has incorporated them into her work. Few writers can keep pace with
society after the age of forty.

Keeping in Touch

The greatest compliment I can pay to Elizabeth Bowen is to say that
she has advanced the novel a notch higher than when she found it in a
quality that is difficult to pin down: is it comprehension? understanding? awareness? consciousness? There have been few to
acknowledge her achievement, perhaps because she has consistently
stood on her own. The normally well educated person cannot always
follow her (including myself for some of the time). Is this a confidence
trick? Her transparent integrity refutes the idea. She attempts to move
into regions where words are not quite sufficient to impart her feeling.
It is the kind of thing poetry sets out to do. Her prose is often poetic in
spirit though never pseudo-poetic in form.

There is a conflict between those who are aware of complexity at
the heart of things and the *simplists,* those who are irritated by
subtlety, the Maoists, the Red Guards, the Che-men, all of whom want
immediate answers with no grading, who want to establish a peasant-
mental society, with no challenge, no aims beyond stomach and
bourgeois idealism—for that is what it is, though masks are always
worn. It is a new outburst of romanticism and it finds a strong echo in
the TV parlour. On the other side are those who are aware of personal
ignorance, who believe truth is a citadel that can only be reduced in a
long campaign. Bowen is as aware as anyone else of the decadence of
modern society. She would like man to raise himself to a new,
virtually unexperienced level. Her closest allies cannot go so far so
they take the only other line which possesses a dynamic, which is
descent.

She believes that intelligent people are increasing. There is no
hedging about this, no casual use of words like 'relatively': 'education,
I suppose', she writes in a letter to V.S. Pritchett (*Why Do I Write?* an
Exchange of Views between Elizabeth Bowen, Graham Greene and
V.S. Pritchett, 1948). But she feels these intelligent people are closing
in on the artist, who uses more than intelligence, and she has a rat-
nightmare, as of Bishop Hatto being devoured by the rats. 'The worst
it boils down to, really, is that people these days have a mania for
being shown round factories'. This is shrewd. 'Showing people round'
is one of the constant stand-by's of even the most enlightened

educationist. There seems to be a belief in automatic assimilation. Quality is ignored.

It is obviously a restless age—but Lady Waters in *To the North* has enough commonsense to see that all ages are restless—and in this she shows more wisdom than many journalists and bishops. She goes on, prodding into the heart of the matter: 'but *this* age is far more than restless: it is decentralized. From week to week, there is no knowing where anyone is.' It is in 1934, with the publication of the volume of stories called *The Cat Jumps,* that the changing times are brought into focus.

The longest story in the collection is called 'The Disinherited'. It is also the most socially 'aware' with an awareness that Bowen doesn't usually exhibit explicitly. There is frequently a rebelliousness implicit in her writing, though usually it is barely discernible. But here it is given its head. It is not a simple movement of revolt that is being codified but rather an aristocratic discontent with the modern world which could parallel the thrust from below, rather like what happened in the French Revolution in certain quarters. The story starts with a new housing estate which faces the old village at the foot of the hill. Two ways of life confront each other. Mrs Archworth belongs to the older way and doesn't like to see the hill cut up for building plots. But she admits that times are changing and she calls on the newcomers in her Daimler.

It is the prosperous new middle class that the aristocrats can't abide. In a satisfactory world the mass of the population would be happy with their tasks and their masters would be living elegantly and without strain. In 'The Good Girl', for example, an English party motor through Italy and come to Varese whose inhabitants were occupied in the manufacture of stockings: 'it seemed delightful that they should be so busy'. It was different in England. The Harveys (he had retired from the Civil Service and was now honorary secretary to a society) lived on the estate. It was characterized by a subtopian niceness which maddened Davina Archworth, who had made friends with Marianne Harvey. The estate was exclusive. Lots could only be purchased on condition that houses of a fixed value should be put up. 'You undertook not to keep chickens, put up a frame garage or hang out clothes.' The estate, with its rawness, 'its air at once hygienic and intellectual, revolted Davina. The Harvey living room looked to her 'nullish with, here and there, the stigmata of intellectual good taste'.

We are told that Davina, being naturally aristocratic, loathed refinement—and the estate thrived on refinement. She meets some old friends in an empty country house. They were all enemies of society, having been led to expect what they did not get. In her need of money, Davina demeans herself socially and borrows off the chauffeur. (We are never told if she gave anything in return—it probably wasn't necessary.) He hints that she's after something else and warns her to keep away. 'I know your sort. Well, I'm through with all that. I'm buying not selling, these days. You keep your place, Miss Archworth, and I'll keep mine. You can't have it both ways.' The irony is that Davina is unable to keep her place. Society is in flux. It is the age of Lady Chatterley.

In another of these stories, 'The Little Girl's Room', a rich, uncared-for little girl indulges in fantasies about the people she knows. They are all the products of hatred and contempt. Her Greek tutor says, 'There has been the Revolution', and her mathematics tutor adds, 'Reading is running with blood.' But not even the new middle class in their hygienic villas are happy. Life is messy, unsatisfying ('Firelight in the Flat'). The sudden solution, born out of despair, seems to be to get out of subtopia and start a chicken farm. Would it work? The pity of it is that many of these people hate the world they have brought into existence by their own effort, even through their own dreams. It had once seemed natural to get what they could from the rich because if the rich lost their wealth, they, less well endowed, would get some of it. But the way it had happened didn't please them. In 'A Walk in the Woods' (Look at All Those Roses) it is Sunday and Londoners are walking in (probably) Epping Forest. 'They looked about them, dissatisfied, acquisitive, despising the woods because they belonged to everyone. Had they not profoundly dreaded to trespass, they would have preferred the property of some duke.'

Miss Bowen was keeping up, and not much escaped her sharp eye. In 1964 and again in 1969 she produced works which, despite all the evidence, still surprised by their contemporaneity. The first of these, The Little Girls, is completely and unquestionably post-war in spirit. There are no signs of an aging writer trying to appear up-to-date by superficial tricks. The ladies (who are the three little girls grown up) are well-to-do middle class, products of St Agatha's, Southstone, which is within view of the French coast on a clear day. They are calculating, modern, not easily abashed. In addition to the TV aerials and Mini-cars, it is assumed that everyone can cook now, unless they eat out. If they do, it is for business reasons. One of the ladies obviously hasn't read Macbeth and is on one occasion placed at a disadvantage because of it. This would not have been likely before the war.

Two of the families lived with a degree of bourgeois style. The third was Army and therefore always on the move and living among other people's belongings. Mrs Piggott (before the war) had been a widow, employed a cook, a maid and a jobbing gardener. After the war her daughter, Diana, also contrived to live in style, though the reality was not so impressive. The façade is maintained by Francis, a Maltese who had been acquired and would not leave, and could be referred to as the butler, and alternate widows who cleaned. Sheilah had to make do with her husband's devoted nurse, who did a bit of everything. Social consciousness is rarely more than a flicker in Bowen's work but there are occasions when her characters have to make ritual acknowledgment. Hermione, a schoolgirl 'colouring with social consciousness' said that her goldfish came from Harrod's.

These ladies have to face up to such bitter things as a shortage of money. In the past her characters had often been rich and usually comfortable, though they avoided the subject with natural good taste. One of the girls, Clare, has become a successful business woman and runs a chain of gift shops. She cannot afford to waste time: 'Time's money'. One of the others does allow herself the pleasure of twitting Clare on this matter on one occasion, but it is half-hearted. Clare's gift shop resembles the travel agency in To the North but she is much more business-like and money-minded than those girls ever were. But such places are last resorts, not quite so contaminated by the commercial spirit as pots and boots. They were reserved areas. Two of the women actually sit in a car listening to the Light Programme on a transistor, which is part of the car's furniture. Before the war art meant concerts and new exhibitions. Sheilah had been a very promising little dancer. She used to dance at charity performances. Her parents, especially mother, would never have allowed her to dance for money, professionally. But now she has an audition in London. She was turned down because she had picked up vulgar dancing habits (at polite charity performances) she would never be able to lose.

In Eva Trout again one notes the open-minded acceptance of a new world and new people. There are none of the stupid prejudices which mar the work of Rosamund Lehmann. The year is 1959. Eva is a rich heiress but her mind is under-developed. This can be partly attributed to her upbringing as a modern nomad. Her father hadn't worried much about her education—it simply meant phoning for a governess.

> He took her to Mexico, where they were joined by Constantine; then, business calling him to the Far East, dropped her off with a Baptist missionary family in Hongkong, reclaimed her, left her in

San Francisco with some relations of her chiropodist's, caused her to be flown to him in New York, flew her from thence to Hamburg, where he picked her up later and asked her if she would like to become a kennel-maid, decided it might be better for her to go to Paris and was about to arrange things on those lines when she said she would like to go to an English boarding-school: one for girls. Two years having elapsed, his daughter was on the eve of being sixteen.

The tone of this is quite different from anything that has gone before. It is maintained throughout the novel, and through a wide social range of characters. Eva's young friend, Henry, a parson's son who will not become a parson himself but has no obvious niche in society, is at Cambridge and is appalled by the idea of the competitive society that lies in wait for him. How Eva will chart her way through its complexities is anyone's guess. But with her earnest innocence we can contrast the flippant social adjustment made by Willy Trout's old friend and assistant, Constantine. This is a barque that will never sink. He has a London office, 'the whole set-up reeked of expense accounts'. Lunch seems his most important function. Can you wonder the country is in the state it's in, asks Eric Arble, who has a garage, does real work, and is very conscientious and a bit dim.

III

L.P. Hartley—Tarnished Glamour
(First Fiction: *Night Fears*, 1924)

The Modern World

Hartley doesn't like it. There is no equivocation, no attempt to be 'fair', to look at things from other angles, as with Elizabeth Bowen. The world is going from bad to worse. The distaste is increasingly implicit in his work, and when things become unbearable there is the occasional explicit statement. Hartley begins his story, 'Mrs Carteret Receives', in the collection of that name, 1971, with a brief essay, almost in the manner of Arnold Bennett, on the social change that has taken place in England since the turn of the century. The motor-car, he says, has corroded the 'democracy of place and local habitations.'

To begin with, ours is an ugly world. The English part of it is worse than many other parts. In 'Three, or Four, for Dinner' (in the collection, *The Travelling Grave,* 1948) two Englishmen see a couple of tramp-steamers moored in a Venetian canal. One says, 'This reminds me of Hull. Good old Hull! Civilization at last! Nothing picturesque and old-world. Two ugly, useful old ships, nice oily water, and lots of foreign bodies floating about in it.'

The distaste increases with Hartley's maturity. He finds life sufficiently enjoyable during the early years to ignore its worst manifestations. But the war inevitably drags things down. By the time he wrote *The Boat,* 1949, he was quite disgruntled. The epigraph from Emily Brontë prepares us:

> Gaze on the wretch, recall to mind
> His golden days left long behind.

It will be useful to consider this novel in some detail.

It could be viewed as a subtle Right Wing apologia if one felt that Hartley were at all interested in making such a thing—which he never was, or not in such crude terms. If the Conservative Party had been more aware they would have adopted it as a cultural mascot, just as other political groups have adopted *Animal Farm* and *Lord of the Flies*. It is a protest against the idiotic class attitudes which became so prominent during the war. The dominant symbol (Hartley being very partial to such devices) is a flood. The flood overwhelms and brings everyone to their senses and destroys evil. Timothy Casson, like the more famous Eustace, has it easy and lives on a legacy. This is the ideal situation, and its social implications are never considered. Also like Eustace he cannot resist fantasies of grandeur, tremendous self-dramatizations, accompanied by a wretched sense of personal inadequacy. That such a character should be presented in such detail in four consecutive books suggests that Hartley feels these qualities in himself.

We are in the Age of the Common Man but, if we take sides with our author, we don't feel at home in it. The period is the early stages of the war, but is set in an English village (West Country, with a view of the Welsh hills), among retired and evacuated populations. Timothy is always trying to adjust himself to new circumstances, although he has no understanding of social structures. The village of Upton is divided into two nations, but they are not Disraeli's: they are the old stagers and the newcomers. It is war within the middle class. The working class form a comic chorus in traditional English literary style, and they are also beyond communication. No sooner does Timothy feel that he is beginning to understand them than something begins to baffle him anew. His gardener tells him that there is a similar cleavage among the working people. Some of the lower classes realize that things have changed and that their labour is in short supply. When Beattie, his cook, phones a friend, she says: 'The tables are turned now, they can't talk to us like they used to, they know they can't get anyone in our place.'

The class war, however, is within the traditional middle class (between Orwellian sub-groups) rather than between the major social divisions. Miss Vera Cross, who turns out to be a Communist Party agent, dedicated to causing social unrest (this is a bit hard to take, because her field of operations seems so petty and remote from the real struggle, and one wonders what Stalin's agents are doing there), wants to enlist Timothy with the newcomers (mostly business wives from the towns) against the retired colonels: 'We're tired of being high-hatted by all these stuffed shirts'. Edgell Purbright, the rector's son, says the retired gentry are finished. Symbolically, he and Vera fall in love. The rector himself disapproves of the new trend because the local landowner (Mrs Lampard) has done up dilapidated cottages for weekend businessmen, leaving several labouring families homeless. She has unwittingly hastened the process. She goes mad, which is symbolically unobjectionable.

Much of this is satire on Left Wing romanticism. Timothy's socialite friend, Magda, writes of a Russian girl's deep-chested laughter 'which no European corrupted by centuries of bourgeois culture, can hope to understand.' This is typical of the idiotic kind of statement one heard during the war when thousands of people, including many rich and even of aristocratic background, were emotionally stampeded into acceptance of communism as the complete answer to everything. One of the paradoxes of our time has been that the first scientific approach to politics, Marxism, gave rise to one of the most irresponsibly romantic political movements in history. Timothy is infected. He is a sitting target because his intelligence is undeveloped, his motivations are luxurious and aesthetic, he has nothing to do and the devil finds work for idle hands. When we left Eustace at the end of the famous trilogy, he was already going that way. Timothy becomes impressed by the uselessness of the fishermen (that is to say, the retired gentry) who, he imagines, will not let him use the river for boating. 'Almost for the first time Timothy felt himself warmly proletarian, a champion of the have-nots against the high-ups.'

Urged to take action by Vera, lectured in letters from Magda, Timothy came to appreciate the virtues inherent in the proletariat. 'It might not be such a bad thing after all, he said, if we were governed by them, for their feelings were still direct and natural, not vitiated by theories of behaviour.' In another letter he writes: 'I don't approve of people being allowed to hand on their money, of course . . .', but while the law is what it is he must (fortunately) act within its framework. Timothy owes everything to a legacy, and he is here telling his friend Tyro that he is leaving his estate to him and two other friends. In a letter to Esther he asks if she can find him servants, for he has given his own servant notice. He doesn't mind what sins they may have committed—'in any case, it's society's fault, not theirs.' Timothy is an excellent example of the willy-nilly and absolutely superficial embracement of socialist belief encountered during the war. It wasn't socialism and it wasn't sincere. A puff of wind could have blown it away.

In a way this book comes closer to social commentary than most books of the period, even those which adopted a socialist philosophy and were intended as criticism. It is about social fantasy which, in its results, is as real as social reality. (What people think is as important as what people do.) Vera was no fool, though. After the River Revolution (in itself an absurd, though tragic affair) 'the labourers would be less willing to touch their caps and the bosses would not get out their fishing tackle with the same confidence as before. The two nations would be conscious of their apartness, their irreconcilability; and the rift would widen in preparation for the final struggle.' Water will wear away a stone. And Vera was right, for the change has come. But Timothy was a mere fool. Miss Chadwick, his landlord, advises him not to make friends with his servants. 'Their outlook is so very different from ours. Kindness is so often constructed as weakness or worse, and familiarity is always a mistake.' This is a basic tenet of the English social creed. The policeman says the same thing about the evacuees, for the police are a bridge between classes, in the pay of the upper and middle. Hartley gives this philosophy a cruel twist when Timothy makes his blow for equality by rowing his boat on the river and giving two little boys a ride. All the mothers want him to take their own children. When he is compelled to refuse, one says: 'I didn't think you'd descend to favouritism. What's the good of gassing about the freedom of the river, when you've packed your boat with your friends?' Timothy's friend Esther does not sympathize with his betrayal of the group, though she does not put it so crudely. It is necessary for them to stick together, for people need an example to look up to. This, in its halting way, is the crux of the matter: there must be an élite.

The war is definitely seen as a watershed: on one side lay the Land of Cockayne, on the other it sloped away to the Bad Lands. 'The White Wand', a story which gave its name to a collection in 1954, pressed the point home. C.F. is telling his story:

> All through the war, in England, stopping in strange hotels up and down the country, and not only at hotels, I had been the victim of innumerable acts of pilfering—don't tell me, Arthur, please don't tell me, that the war has done our morals any good. All the little trinkets I possessed—yes, and necessities, too— were pinched from me—watches, watchchains, cuff-links, travelling clocks—even the shirt off my back, when it was new enough. The war turned us into a nation of thieves . . .

It will be recalled that economists and sociologists often claimed that the war had had an excellent effect on morality—it had reduced privilege and introduced a remarkable degree of solidarity. But C.F.

didn't agree. Originally he had tried to cultivate his responses to the variety of life but since the war he had stopped. What was the point of trying to maintain civilized behaviour when those who were loudest in defending it were the first to abandon it? He flatly contradicted the solidarity theory, asking 'for how many people the steady warmth of personal relationships perished in the burning heat of September 1939? Certainly with me it did; I felt I had nothing to give out or to take in . . . The blight of political hatred was on everything.' And when the war was over he felt that people were always waiting for some specific event to take place (for example, the hydrogen bomb to be perfected or the Korean war to come to an end) before they would attempt to return to a post-war habit of life. Such references to current political events are extremely rare in Hartley's work.

But his feelings about society led him to write the kind of novel that it is certain he is least fitted to write, and that one of his admirers would never have foreseen. This was *Facial Justice,* 1960, an essay in science fiction. In it he presents the Uniform State, which is the characteristic Dystopia of the English liberal. In this society it was unwise to show a marked Personal Preference, for it led to inflammation of the ego. Citizens were graded into Alphas, Betas and Gammas. 'Alphas are anti-social.' In fact, like other egalitarian states, it was governed by an élite, who were the Alphas. But these were 'pure' Alphas, the Inspectors, specially chosen by the Dictator. Those who did not quite come up to standard were called Failed Alphas, and were encouraged to merge with the Betas. The women were even Betafied, which involved a facial operation which reduced them to the mediocrity of the middle rank. Gammas, who were unattractive, gained by the operation. For women were graded according to beauty, and it was anti-social to be more beautiful than your neighbour.

The social poles were Equality and Envy, Good E and Bad E, Good Egg and Bad Egg, as the jargon had it. Mention of either involved the speaker in a ritual dance: 'a few jerky, gymnastic capers for Envy, a long intricate, ecstatic exercise for Equality.' There were time-saving concessions: a curtsey for Equality and a token spit for Envy. It followed that one must not mention 'bad luck' for luck is a leveller, therefore good. You should always look your own height for there is nothing higher. The Horizontal View of Life (On the Level) was generally accepted. At eleven o'clock the population ate pastilles, coloured violet, with an E engraved on them. Laughter was discouraged, but was permitted for five minutes a day to get it out of your system. Cinemas showed films of the horrors of war twice a week and attendance was compulsory unless a doctor's certificate could be produced. Everyone had the same income and money could only be transferred in return for an official receipt. There were no such things as tastes, only taste—the *reductio absurdum* of Good Taste. By the time Jael, the heroine, was Betafied (against her will) four-fifths of all women had the same Government-approved face. The remainder were Gammas, ugly by comparison. When Jael attacked the regime she used ridicule based on the regime's own principles. She suggested it was unfair and an abuse of privilege for some to enjoy better health than others, and suggested the injection of the healthy with some form of not necessarily serious illness, 'so that the level of physical and mental well-being in the New State should be roughly regularized—no one too ill, no one too well.'

This state was a juvenilocracy. Citizens were treated as if they were children. Slogans regulated every aspect of life (as in *Brave New World*) and were usually alliterative. The method was even applied to foreign countries, all foreign relations being excellent. The adjectives varied but were always favourable—Belgium was beautiful one day, brave the next, bountiful the next, and so on. If anyone called Belgium beastly he was fined, as he was if he didn't know the adjective of the day, if challenged. This seems so pointless the childishness of the regime rubs off on the book. At times it irritates through its perverse lack of perceptiveness, its uncritical criticality. Paradoxically, few children were seen on the streets. Radioactivity had caused a high degree of male impotence and the children were carefully segregated. A stranger might have thought it an exclusively adult community. This is one of Hartley's keener insights, for in fact the adults were mentally immature.

The Dictator was never seen but was occasionally heard when he addressed the nation in a broadcast, which could be heard throughout the country. The automatic reaction to any mention of him was the exclamation, 'Dear Dictator'. This is clearly a variant on Big Brother. A daily dose of bromide maintained obedience. The Dictator called his subjects Patients and Delinquents to remind them of their fallen state. This is after the Third World War when the people have emerged from their underground shelters. Each person was obliged to take the name of a murderer or a murderess. (This theme is from *Ape and Essence*.) They wore sackcloth and had ashes in their hair. A confirmed Delinquent wore PS (Permanent Sackcloth). As always, the organization of this totalitarian state involved opposition to home and family. 'Families were still permitted but they were very much frowned on, and the majority of children were brought up in crèches . . .' Homes were still on trial but were considered a hotbed of bad

influences, especially Bad E (like personal beauty). They were as
uniform as possible but each had something particular to itself—an
ornament, or the arrangement of the furniture—which made it
individual and therefore a standard of comparison. Individualism was
naturally abhorred. Private Motoring was not allowed, being considered dangerous, decivilizing, egotistical and ideologically unsound.
The Motor Expeditions (Country) Service was for the benefit of a few
backsliders. And here is a hospital sister praising organization:

'. . . making them do all the right things at the right time! If I
listened to every moan and groan and squawk and squeak, do
you think I should get *anywhere?* Discipline, discipline is what
matters . . . There isn't a single one (i.e., of her patients) that
hasn't wanted something special doing for her—more food or
less food or different food, more light or less light or no light,
more wireless or less wireless or louder wireless or softer wireless
or no wireless, they simply have no idea of collective action,
they think that being ill (and it's their own fault they are, in most
cases) entitles them to special consideration.'

Life was planned, everything was made as pleasant and easy as
possible, to inhibit the need for personal effort. The result was a
suggestion of liberty that was entirely specious. It is here that Hartley
does put his finger on one of the crucial aspects of our time. In one of
his addresses the Dictator managed to oppose the Voluntary Principle
to Free Will. 'Has not the motto of our régime always been Free Will?
Would any of you, standing, sitting or lying (alas, you are all of you
fond of lying), who hear these words, dare to say that since the time
our envoy led you from the Shades, into this unpromising land, you
have ever acted under compulsion? That we have ever forced you, our
dear subjects, to do anything you did not want to do?' Of course not;
before any of them acted, they were always first persuaded that they
wished to do what they would be compelled to do. Jael's revolt
eventually takes the form of demanding the right not to be equal. She
puts this to her committee, formed to discover and destroy the
Dictator. In the Bad Old Days people accepted variations in liberty
and a lack of equality because they considered them to be the consequences of luck: 'it hadn't been earned, it hadn't even been stolen.'
Jael wrote of the Dictator, sarcastically: 'Long may he live to make
the New State safe for mediocrity!' There was no conflict between
the generations, but sex conflict flourished. It was one of the foundations of the state. Beautiful women were Betafied to reduce the
tensions of Envy. Men were not touched. Jael revolted against this

and became a man-hater. She wanted men's looks to be Betafied but they were horrified at the suggestion. But this aspect is poorly integrated with the main theme.

What a surprise! That Hartley, the least political of my six novelists, should write such a book! The reason is that he was the unhappiest of my six. Unlike Waugh (who admired his work), he could not enjoy his blustering. There is a certain amount of band-wagon in Hartley's choice of theme but it enabled him to express his abhorrence of modern trends of uniformity, standardization, statistical administration and communalization. His talent is not suited to this kind of theme—most of his ideas seem to come from Huxley, Orwell and Heard, he has nothing to say about the modern state that has not been said before, and what he does say is clumsily expressed. The rebel, from the liberal-individual standpoint, is Jael, but all her plans go astray and usually lead to bloodshed and chaos. In the end she even replaces the dead Dictator, who had also been a woman. What does Hartley mean? That a Dictator is inevitable? That his rule will be better for us in the last resort than one of freedom and personal choice? No clear message comes through, and much of the detail remains obscure. I think the most likely interpretation is that dictators and leaders of revolt belong to the same category of political man. Revolutionary Djugashvili is Dictator Stalin.

Hartley is much more successful when he is dealing with the minor aspects of life. In *Poor Clare,* 1968, he makes a comment on freedom, but domesticates it. He says that Italy is a freer country, in some ways, than England. This point is repeated in the story, 'Mrs Carteret Receives', in the collection of that name, 1971: 'it must be said that most Latin countries, if not so democratically governed, are socially more democratically-minded, than we are, and this is true of all ranks of society.' This has nothing to do with the polls or leading articles. It sounds like heresy to an English patriot, who regards freedom as his personal property, but the remark contains a whole philosophy, that of the Edwardian man of leisure. In England attempts have been made to safeguard freedom by legislation. The rich safeguard their freedom by bribes, but the rich are disappearing. The poor need the paraphernalia of Bureaucracy, which appears to some to be the major enemy of personal freedom. Again in *Poor Clare* Hartley refers to the fascination that ugliness has for modern man. Is this part of the same complex? Possibly—Hartley is not an analytical writer. The inspiration of Gilbert's ugly music was conflict. He used his friends as sparring partners as well as sounding boards. As a result he composed *Sinfonia Disorientate*. His music was modern and dissonant—in

Edwards's opinion (which is Hartley's) ugly. 'It didn't appeal to me but it did, no doubt, appeal to people who were at odds with them- selves and with the world.' He refers to Gilbert's music as 'all that chaotic, life-destroying stuff, which is about as much like art as a town hit by an atom-bomb!' How can you expect people who demand conflict and thrive on it to understand and appreciate nineteenth century freedoms?

In *The Love-Adept* 1969 we are given another picture of The World We Live In which is more successful because it is contained in Hartley's familiar manner: the personal and the domestic. It is about a novelist who is writing a novel, and corresponding with four ladies all named Elizabeth. He asks one how he should finish his novel and adds, it could be murder, as 'they could all, with the approval of the permissive society, plead that they were suffering from "diminished responsibility" '. Hartley's distaste for the permissive society is so pronounced I am leaving it to another section, along with his most bitter denunciation in *The Betrayal*.

Hartley likes to present himself (often as a first person narrator) as an elderly man of rather pliable character who is never quite at ease in his environment. One of the ladies in *The Love-Adept* (his strongest critic) accuses him of bending over backwards to be a man of his day! She tells him what people are like and it is probably a list of the things Hartley dislikes most about the contemporary world.

> You don't realize that people of today don't want to step out of the ruck; they want to be in it and *with* it, in all senses of the term. They want to keep up with the Joneses, they don't want to outstrip them, they just want to be with them, they are ruled by *fashion,* a factor you never seem to take into account, but fashion is the ruling passion, and of course it doesn't encourage individualism, or eccentricity, how could it? . . (Teenagers) only want the emotions that are within their range and by which they can be communicably excited, such as train-wrecking, telephone- kiosk breaking, throwing bottles at football matches, fighting with each other at the seaside, here or abroad, or battling with the police and then accusing them of brutality. Apart from these stimulants, this release for their egos, their ideal, which they will never realize, is to bask semi-nude on a deck-chair or some ocean-going cruise, or to bask, still semi-nude, on the beach of some West Indian island, ready for a bathe or just returned from a bathe, with a sub-tropical sun beating down on their nicely tanned or badly blistered bodies, and a white-coated black-faced waiter hovering by, handing out dry martinis.

She goes on to say that the only kind of humour that will draw people together is sick humour, perhaps a joke about the atom bomb, because they feel a common calamity is threatening them. There is no happiness or reasonableness today, so you must not try to get your effect from pretending there is a background of it, and making a contrast. We are all aware that the future is going to be very unpleasant, and our humour consists in making brief comments on that unpleasantness. Being *with* it is the key, people today don't want contrasts, they are only interested in intensifications of the horrid fact.

She also finds fault with his treatment of children, especially the way they talk to each other ('they talk like little grown-ups, each aware of the other's identity . . .'). Children today probably regard their elders as enemies or potential enemies, who frown on their proper pastimes of bottle-throwing, etc. She explains that she uses 'proper' in the original sense—pastimes that are natural, inevitable, even desirable. 'I don't use the word as you would, ironically or sarcastically, to denigrate our youngsters aged between twelve and twenty. They are only acting according to their natures, relieved from, or rebelling against, parental control.' How should they feel or act differently? If there is to be blame, it should be of their elders whose nationalism and submissiveness to *their* elders have made two world wars possible. That we are already on the road to the society of *Facial Justice* is illustrated by the little boy who talks to Granny Kirkwood. He said that all did well at school but none did best and when asked how this was possible, he replied, 'Because it would make the others jealous.' This negativism seems to be the natural end of democracy to Hartley.

His dislike of the age, which makes itself felt in his post-war fiction, receives emphasis in his best-known essay, 'The Novelist's Responsibility', which is not only printed in his own book of essays, bearing the same title, but also in *Essays by Divers Hands,* Vol. XXXIV, 1966. These are the Transactions of the Royal Society of Literature, and are edited by himself. In his Introduction to this volume he calls our period a 'drab age'. The essay, which he read on 17 March 1963, stresses this impression. Three writers, he says, have helped to undermine the individual's sense of responsibility: Dostoevsky, Marx and Freud. Behind their dogmas lay another, more insidious idea, that of the Little Man: 'a poor, puzzled creature, pushed around by everyone', who has become almost a symbol of man in the modern world. He is nondescript, essentially *little,* from whom nothing much, either good or bad, could be expected. He became the hero of the modern novel, but he had no heroic qualities, so the heroic qualities became unfashionable and to have them was to be anti-social.

In fiction the individual has been devalued and his stature has shrunk. One cause was the enormous amount of suffering and inconvenience endured during the war, so that people ceased to expect a happy, easy or even physically safe life. 'What was one broken heart when so many millions of hearts had been broken?' People today suffer from a state of 'diminished responsibility'—the excuse for breaking your word or your appointment is now 'enshrined in the Statute Book'—and you can literally get away with murder. Compassion is now fashionable but it is for the criminal, not the victim. 'If the question "Whither Fiction?" is raised, the novelist will have to make up his mind which side he is on. Is he to write: "She was a beautiful woman, witty, clever, cultivated, sympathetic, charming, *but,* alas, she was a murderess?" Or is he to write: "She was a beautiful woman, witty, clever, etc., *and* to crown it all, she was a murderess"?'

In a letter to Peter Bien he wrote:

> My great enemy was the State. . . . When I was at Oxford for a short time in 1915 and 1916, and again in 1919 . . . Herbert Spencer, Mill, all the individualist and *laissez-faire* writers, were utterly out of fashion—I suppose they still are. Not only had socialism triumphed over them, but 'political science' was against them. The political philosophers we were told to admire were Hobbes, Locke, Rousseau, Bosanquet (even possibly Macchiavelli), because they all exalted some form of human *association* (usually the State) at the expense of the individual. As I thought that all our troubles came from the State, I was infuriated by this—and the idea of the State having a sort of entity of its own, to which we must sacrifice ourselves, drove me nearly frantic . . .
>
> (Printed as a footnote in *L.P. Hartley,* by Peter Bien, 1963)

Bien says that in *Facial Justice* Hartley took Vera, the immoral communist of *The Boat,* 1949, and magnified her into an impersonal government system. But he does not attribute this to implacable economic or historic forces. A people gets the government it deserves and a tyranny comes when individuals show themselves incapable of the moral alertness necessary to a free society.

When a novelist writes out of conviction, as Hartley does, his meaning will often be revealed in oblique ways. Bolshevism is not a subject that crops up often in his work, but when it does in *The Sixth Heaven* Hilda said that at least it stood for something. Hilda could not bear sloppiness or pretentiousness, she loathed the idea of living beyond your income, or trying to adopt a style you were not accustomed to. She is also very domineering. W.W. Robson, discussing William Golding in *Modern English Literature,* 1970, said that a more profound study of 'the impulse to dominate' might be found in Hartley's trilogy. If Vera is a preview of an impersonal system, Hilda prepares us for the earnest commissar, longing out of love to compel us to do what is right.

The Wonderful World of the Aristocrats

Hartley was not an aristocrat, nor are his heroes, but they all love the aristocrats. Like his heroes, he has always lived in close proximity to the most privileged section of our population and he has shared some of their privileges. He was educated at Harrow and went to Oxford, where he got to know the Oxford and Asquith family. Many of his stories and novels take us into homes of the nobility. In the stories in particular, castles are in vogue, e.g. 'The Killing Bottle' and 'Conrad and the Dragon', which is a fairy tale and reflects the childlike obsession that is so strong in Hartley's work. Substitute castles (country houses) are even more in evidence—in 'Feet Foremost', 'The Travelling Grave', 'Cotillon' and 'Monkshood Manor' and several of the novels. Valentine in 'Home, Sweet Home' has a nightmare in which he discovers his old home has become a home for disturbed children (*Mrs Carteret Receives,* 1971). The U/Non-U polarity has always interested Hartley, long before Professor Ross and Nancy Mitford turned it into a game, and scattered through Hartley's work are many examples which did not appear in their *Noblesse Oblige.* For example, in 'The Corner Cupboard' (*Two For the River,* 1961) Philip Holroyd engages a cook and is saddened when she calls the sitting-room the lounge. In the same collection ('The Pampas Clump') two men, aged forty-one and thirty-eight, entertain two women to dinner. The women leave the men to their port and later the men 'join the ladies', a desperate attempt to maintain a tradition in miniature. Hartley seems to be fascinated by the ephemera of upper-class behaviour. Long before he bewailed modern manners he celebrated the fancies of the rich. One could have forecast his post-war reactions.

His first book, a collection of stories called *Night Fears,* appeared in 1924 and is undergraduate in tone. It is largely concerned with a world of privilege. The leading story, and one of the best, 'The Island', is a spine-chiller and is set in a fantastic Usher-like house, with a maze of corridors, jutting into a furious sea. 'The New Prime

Minister' is marked by allusive conversation between the new man of the hour and an old school friend, and reflects the kind of society where all important men (and most of their women) come from a tiny social group, all known to each other. 'A Portrait' begins with a house party but moves to a tedious discussion betwen a lady and an artist, who is painting her (for the Academy) for the second time in ten years. Here is a sample of the conversation, from the lady, replying to the artist who said he slept like a log. 'The simile is unworthy of you. Why use it in preference to the better and truer one? We sleep like tops. It is only when the day comes that we begin to flag, to wobble and throw ourselves about, hither and thither, in ludicrous and ungainly movement. No wonder such a pitiable spectacle induces Providence to chastise us into uprightness.' One thanks God for Hemingway, Bennett having apparently failed. This is aristocratic literature with a vengeance.

The only exception is to be found in the title story, 'Night Fears'. An untypical class angle is introduced by a stranger who reminds a night-watchman of his sorry lot. One has a suspicion that he is the Stranger from the Third-Floor Back out for a walk.

'Do you like this job?'
'Oh, not so bad', said the man carelessly; 'good money, you know.'
'Good money', repeated the stranger scornfully. 'How much do you get?'
The night-watchman named the sum.
'Are you married and have you got any children?' the stranger persisted.
The night-watchman said 'Yes' without any enthusiasm.
'Well, that won't go very far when the children are a bit older', declared the stranger. 'Have you any prospect of a rise?' The man said no, he had just had one.
'Prices going up, too', the stranger commented.

An unusual tone for Hartley. But the motive of the stranger is neither economic nor social reform; it is part of a dramatic plot, a fiendish one in the event.

It is in the Eustace trilogy, particularly the two latter volumes, that the enthusiasm for the aristocracy reaches its peak. *The Shrimp and the Anemone,* 1944 is an extremely sensitive and beautifully controlled study of childhood. The urge to know the aristocracy has its seeds here but is barely recognized. But there is an entirely different atmosphere in *The Sixth Heaven,* 1946. The period of events is fixed.

The Cherringtons left Anchorstone, first for Wolverhampton and then for Willesden, in 1907 when Eustace was eleven. The action of the novel takes place in 1919. Eustace is now at Oxford. He has a private income and aristocratic, wealthy friends. All his friends 'tended to be rather well off', like Stephen Hilliard, whose rooms had been redecorated in black, scarlet and lilac, with valuable pieces of furniture and *objets d'art*. Eustace used to look down on to Carfax, black with people, none of whom seemed to realize that a few feet above them was a summit of social eminence to which they could never attain. It is only fair to add that Hartley's treatment of Eustace's social climbing is pleasantly ironical.

Eustace is terribly excited when he realizes his boyhood dream and is invited to spend the weekend at Anchorstone Hall. He imagines himself showing Stephen the window of his bedroom. Stephen was even slightly jealous of Eustace because he numbered among his friends a very minor foreign royalty. Then there was Antony Lachish, 'a freshman of ancient family and winning manners who went through Oxford like a ball of quicksilver.' When Eustace went to church during the Anchorstone weekend the church was filled with fishermen and farm labourers, or more often their wives. 'They looked so conscious of their collars that you could tell that they wore them but once a week. Eustace felt like a first-class passenger whom circumstances had obliged to travel third.' It was here that Eustace met Lady Eleanor (Nelly), who was to have such a great influence on his life. She took a great interest in local events, used to get up plays and entertainments for the village people, and helped with charities. 'She was adored there', said Lady Staveley. Eustace, a sucker for the feudal virtues, believed it.

But Eustace was by no means sure of himself. He had mastered the intricacies of upper-class speech, and when a workman, asking the time, called him 'mate', he feared his own accent would militate against matehood. This was, of course, really a matter for congratulation. But he wasn't nearly so sure of 'correct behaviour'. When staying at a country house he wanted to go into his sister Hilda's room to see how she was getting on, but was afraid it might not be done. He had given her a wristwatch and now worried about whether she ought to wear it at dinner or take it off. The responsibility for this momentous decision was all his, for she wouldn't know. Did one leave one's shoes outside the bedroom door in a private house? (The answer, given many years later in 'The Shadow on the Wall', *Mrs Carteret Receives*, is that you do not.) In one of his self-accusing dramatic fantasies, a servant wonders where he was brought up—obviously not in a gentleman's house. (It is the judgment of the servant that is the cruellest of all—remember poor Eddie in Elizabeth Bowen's *Death of the Heart*.)

Then there is what one says, as against how one says it. Here, perhaps fortunately, the upper class is not completely united. Stephen would indulge in arty talk of the kind that would appal Dick Staveley of Anchorstone Hall. But then Stephen was not really class, coming from a family of solicitors. He talks about music in a way that, according to Simon Raven, causes the hackles of the lower classes to bristle. Beethoven: 'gigantic gestures against a hostile sky'. Brahms: 'those steamy wallowings—let him stew in his own undergrowth'. Boccherini: 'that sugared eighteenth century chit-chat of "Haydn's wife", as they called him', etc., etc.[1]

Eustace, a delightful but anxious little boy, develops into a young man who deliberately destroys his own personality in favour of an aristocratic similitude. In *Eustace and Hilda,* 1952, the third book of the trilogy, we see him in Venice, the guest of a female member of the English aristocracy; he is almost a gigolo, 'dancing attendance'. It would appear that he has reached his haven, but we learn from a letter from Lady Staveley at Anchorstone Hall that Venice is not what it used to be. Rather queer people go there now. There used to be some really nice English people who had houses there, and one or two Americans ('half English, of course'). One old lady used to make enquiries about the people she 'received'. Hilda, too, is getting on. She is seen at the Ritz with Dick Staveley—what's more, seen and reported by Lord Morecambe. Eustace is photographed with Lady Nelly in *Gossip* and Barbara (his younger sister) writes to say how *thrilled* they all are (even Aunt Sarah, though she won't admit it) to think of him in such *exalted* circles.

The wonderful thing about the aristocrats is that they needed no excuse to exist, unlike other people. Eustace, for example, had to be explained as a writer, another guest as an Olympic hurdler. Count Andrea di Monfalcone might not be important but he fitted in and 'no doubt there were countless fine shades of understanding that she had with him that she could not have with Eustace.' He became positively abject in his admiration of the aristocracy. They wore their clothes so

---

1. We are given a different picture of university life in *My Sister's Keeper,* 1970. Here the tone is more earthy, less pretentious. Instead of art, literature and music, the young men discuss society and morality. A later period is intended ('those days', when long hair was becoming fashionable) so a clear-cut comparison is not possible.

gracefully, something he could never do. He used to stuff so much in
his pockets Lady Nelly said he looked like the Michelin man. 'All
situations could be met and on their own terms, if only one knew how.
But he would never master the gradations between a bathing-suit and
an overcoat.' The aristocracy was like a hermetic society. At the most
one could enjoy reflected prestige, as when the bank clerks were
deferential to him. This was only partly because he had money, even
more because he moved in the right circles.

Some of the mysteries of Establishment behaviour were revealed to
him. Eustace always felt that other people's principles were better
founded than his own. Lady Staveley was conventional, which meant
doing things in a certain way, a known way. 'It's the technique of
living, as practised by the experts', said Lady Nelly. 'It may not take
you very far, but you'll always feel you are on the right road, and in
good company.' You can still get into trouble but people will be on
your side so long as they know that in spirit you still toe the line. (This
was the mistake made by Timothy Casson in *The Boat*.) You can do
an immense number of things so long as you do them in a certain
way. Here is an example of aristocratic ruling, from Contessa
Loredan, about ladies: *On peut coucher avec un gondolier, si on le
désire; mais on ne danse pas avec lui.* This shocked Eustace greatly.
But the rules of sex did not apply to marriage. Aristocrats didn't like
mixed marriages, i.e., cross-class. For instance, Hilda had not been
brought up in the same world as Dick. They would never find the right
things to say to each other. At a party Miss Cherrington wore a red
dress. Lady Staveley wrote in a letter to Lady Nelly: 'my dear, there
was nothing really *against* it, it would have looked all right on the
stage, I dare say, but it wasn't right for Anchorstone.' Aunt Sarah
shared this view of social climbing, but from the other end: 'no good
ever comes of trying to climb out of the class of society into which
you are born.'

Hartley's fascination with the aristocracy gets a new twist in *The
Brickfield*, 1964 and its sequel, *The Betrayal*, 1965 because here the
tables are turned and Denys Aspin, a young aristocrat, works for the
first-person narrator as his secretary and companion. Denys's fore-
bears would not have deigned to speak to Richard's! Richard sometimes wonders if he would have found Denys attractive without the
background of Aspin Castle. In fact, Denys is not aristocratic at all—
he was adopted by an impoverished branch of the family and he
turned out to be rather wild. As soon as Richard learns this he not
only begins to have a lower opinion of Denys but Denys actually
begins to behave badly. Richard has to fight against what he feels is

disloyalty in himself: 'the fact that Denys was or might not be a true Aspin, made no difference, indeed, it only served to show up Richard's snobbishness, as if he had valued his friend for his name, not for himself. My secretary, Mr Denys Aspin of Aspin Castle! I pay him, it is true, but he lends me the lustre of his ancient lineage, so we are quits.' Richard's lack of reality where aristocracy is concerned becomes apparent when he discovers how Denys has been cheating him. 'The dishonesty, the calculated cheating, landing him in for hundreds—it was rather much. No Aspin would have done it. But Denys wasn't a real Aspin, he was only a nominal one . . .' Richard had previously gloated over the romantic probability that the original Aspins had been border cattle thieves and gangsters. Now the likelihood was revealed that Denys's biological origin had been proletarian, and Richard understood that the proletariat had quite different moral standards from the middle and upper middle classes.

The pronounced social changes that have occurred since the war have brought home to Hartley the possibility that a new kind of aristocracy may be forming. *My Fellow Devils,* 1951, treats the tensions between this new group and the conventional old English squirearchy. Margaret Pennefather comes of a well-heeled family that lives in considerable style (they employ a chauffeur) in a small town not far from London. She becomes associated in an unexpected way with Colum MacInnes, a leading film star, and eventually marries him. Although Colum went to a minor public school he is not considered a 'gentleman' by acquaintances such as Margaret's father or Stuart, her best friend's husband. In fact, his vocation would proscribe this. Margaret is a magistrate and is known for her good works. She has a strong desire to do good and is convinced that Colum suffers from a poor background. She hopes she can save him from himself and his friends. Her desire to serve others is linked with a fascination with the opposite, the romantic and the glamorous. This is her fantasy of Colum MacInnes:

> . . . a rough little boy with ragged clothes and pleading eyes, a juvenile delinquent with a bad home background, who had never had a chance, but who had been brought up before her and to whom she was now going to lend a helping hand. No, he should not go to an Approved School if she could help it; she was going to try what kindness could do. She would, in a sense, adopt him; take him into her comfortable, pretty house; and there, with Nick and her father helping, she would reform him, teach him to be clean, orderly, affectionate and honest; and after years, many

years, of good food, good example and good treatment and good education, he would emerge into the world, a good citizen.

This was before she married him—while she was still engaged to another man, in fact. It represents a decent, upper class view of the less fortunate (in traditional terms, that is, not financial) and exhibits great social optimism.

The new aristocracy (in this case, the film world) lived in much greater style than the decaying remnants of the old. Party-going was the favourite activity. Colum had a staff of three: Richards (the butler), the cook and the resident house-parlour-maid. 'Colum never had the smallest difficulty in getting servants, indeed he had difficulty in keeping them away, for nearly every day some beglamoured girl wrote offering him her services—sometimes free. Thus the servant problem, the modern housekeeper's supreme concern, did not exist for Margaret.' But this sort of relationship was disturbing to her. 'To Margaret service was a blessed word.' She came from that solid, rural, squirearchy-J.P. belt that accepted the existence of social duties in return for privilege. Nothing could be further removed from the world of the film star-pop-trendy executive.

Limbo

If Hartley's work aspires towards aristocratic harmonies it is rooted in the class that used to be called 'the backbone of England': a class that is no longer sure of itself, is often intensely miserable, filled with envy, engrossed in self-pity. We see all these states in Hartley's work, but we also see aspects of an earlier phase, when the middle class was content with its lot and convinced of its usefulness. *The Brickfield* is largely about a period that has passed away. It is the kind of novel that makes a small impact on reading it but stays to ruffle the mind. It is heavy (at times, turgid) with nostalgia. It evokes the late Victorian and Edwardian provincial life lovingly. Changes in social feeling are stressed, for example, the attitude towards money. Mr Soames was a gentleman farmer, and not a very efficient one—but why should he be, when it wasn't necessary? His possession of independent means set him apart from the other farmers. 'It would now, but in a different way. There was no socialistic feeling that they had no right to their wealth, but it put them in another category.' They were 'living upright', which meant they had private means.

The chief character, Richard Mardick, comes as usual from a respectable but not wealthy middle class family. His father was a bank manager and he had an interest in a brick works, more as a hobby than a source of income. It brought in about £500 a year, which in fact doubled his salary (at the beginning of the century). Richard went to the grammar school, along with the farmers' sons. His grandfather, himself a farmer, had many servants (groom, shepherd, carpenter, gardener, two house servants and a charwoman, a foreman at each farm, farm labourers, grooms and horses) but he didn't have an easy time. The servant question was not acute then, as it is now. 'With my grandfather it wasn't a status symbol, still less a sign of wealth, to have a certain number of dependants. For a man in his position they were necessities, not luxuries. The farm and the farmhouse couldn't do without them. It was an inelastic, semi-feudal system; he *had* to live in that way, it didn't mean that he was well off.' In those days farmers could only just make both ends meet, even in South Lincolnshire, where things were easier.

The aristocracy in this novel is represented by Denys Aspin (already referred to), who was Richard's secretary. Denys pretends to be apologetic about his ancestors, saying they were probably 'a shady lot'. They were Border chieftains, the Aspins of Aspin Castle, and the ruin was still in the family's keeping. There are still a few advantages accruing to the aristocrat—he is addressed as Honourable which is useful in shops and for getting things on tick.

The Perfect Woman, 1955, is set in another sector of the middle class. It is rooted deep in suburbia and for once there is no bourgeois-aristocratic tension.[1] There is a marked sense of restlessness and ephemerality compared with the world of the Lincolnshire farmers. Isabel's husband, Harold, is an accountant for whom assessing a person's income is a routine enquiry. He mistrusted Alex Goodrich, a novelist, especially his tendency to joke about money. In the end, he felt, everything went back to income. We are not really so far away from Eustace, who was ruled by monetary considerations. And like Eustace he was impressed by those in a higher social position but in his case the gulfs to cross are minute. They are between grades within a class, not between distinct classes. Poor Isabel was much more aware of her class situation because she was secretly ashamed of it. When she knew that Goodrich was coming to stay she felt she would have to apologize for 'our suburban home'. She was sufficiently

---

1. The same can be said about the Hancock family in *My Sister's Keeper*, 1970. At the back of the house is a gravel path with a herbaceous border on one side and a lawn on the other, both separated from next door by black split-wood palings.

realistic to know that, however superior she felt towards Harold (as a clergyman's daughter), times had changed and in fact it was Harold who was conferring the favour when they married. There had been a reversal of fortune within the social grouping. She is a romantic, longing to belong to a cultured society, aching to express her sensitivity, scorning the brute cash that kept her comfortable. She despised her own milieu and believed herself superior to it. One of the most prolific sources of modern romantic sentiment derives from the revulsion from suburbia. She goes for a walk outside her home town, on the cliffs, and identifies her lover, Alec, with the ocean.[1] But what a difference on the other side! 'Low hills rose behind the town, green hills already fledged with autumn yellow, and pimpled over by a rash of villas. One of those red roofs, nestling so snugly and smugly in the foliage, was hers . . .', and she turned her eyes back to the sea.

Three middle-class approaches to life are contrasted, and Isabel is their battle-ground. Harold's plans for the children's future are unflinchingly bourgeois and solid. 'I'm all for them getting on in the world, as you know, but I haven't got extravagant ideas for them. I want them to develop on the lines that we have—and be safe, reliable sort of people with a stake in the place and in the country. People you can look up to, but no frills, no sob-stuff—solid, you know, and just above the average.' In comparison Alec was pretentious. He said he had a feudal relationship with the country people, although he didn't

1. Hartley's work is full of symbolism, usually well handled. One of the weaknesses of modern criticism is its compulsive search for the symbol and its uncritical admiration of it, just for existing, no matter whether it is well or badly integrated. Hartley's use is often subtle, though occasionally heavy-handed (as in the prominence given to the shrimp-anemone tension) and one feels that he has perhaps been pushed into this by undue attention to the academic critics. On the other hand, the misuse of symbolism is one of Eustace's worst mental disorders, and Hartley admits this after Eustace has returned to his old haunts and is compelled to face the wreckage of all his high hopes. When Isabel identifies the sea with her lover she is avoiding reality in typical Eustace fashion. 'He turned from the lighthouse and looked over the cliff. The sea was far out, and straight in front of him, beyond old Anchorstone, the mussel-bed, the great black sandbank, extended its giant strength like a stranded whale. No, not like a whale—Hamlet had laid that trap for Polonius: it was a sandbank, and like a sandbank, and no good would come of seeing it as something else'. (*Eustace and Hilda,* 1952) In an interview with Francis King held at Glebe House, the P.E.N. H.Q., on 12th November 1970, Hartley denied that the shrimp-anemone symbolism was conscious. 'I had written half the book before I saw that the eating of the shrimp by the anemone was a symbol of the relationship . . .'

really 'belong'. 'Anyone they look on as gentry they treat as such. Before the war they did, at any rate. Everyone seemed in their right place and not spilling into someone else's . . .' Alec benefited from his discovery that most people are prepared to take you at your own valuation. And then finally, a minor strand, the progressives Isabel had mingled with during the war when she had roomed with another girl in London. They had been left behind but occasionally she remembered them, occasionally she felt guilty because she had not always measured up to their ideals. Their ideals were of classlessness (on the whole, a middle class emotion, as they are the people who get squeezed, but even so, they form a small minority of their class), a society where all should be equal, where no-one should be 'just above the average'. They preached the end of the individual. 'We don't want tragedy or catastrophe or any high-powered emotion, because the individual doesn't count any more.' Modern fiction (they might be discussing the work of Alexander Goodrich) 'mustn't be about people wanting to get on, in any sense, because (a) there's no where to get to, and (b) we don't *want* to get ahead of other people now, we don't *want* to jump the queue!'

But there weren't many who thought like that. Most of them, in this minutely graded hierarchy, were intent on social climbing. The situation was rather like the one provided by football pools—a small win will bring a better car or even a small yacht, while a large one opens the way to the public schools and (who knows?) a peerage if the money is used discreetly. Talking about Lady Ditchworth and her dead husband, Eileen Faulkner says tartly: 'When he made his pile out of whatever it was—something slightly shady—which he did in an incredibly short space of time, they were wafted into spheres far, far above ours, and mixed with people in the same income bracket with themselves. I don't know whether they ever quite made the grade, socially, I mean' (*Poor Clare,* 1968). Lady Ditchworth was well aware of her situation. She was said to have replied to a titled woman who had been rude to her: 'My name may not be as good as yours, but it's better at the bottom of a cheque.' In a sense, this is Hartley's version of the class war. The other war he recognizes (referred to in an earlier section) is psychological and grounded in generational differences.

Now we can see Eustace, Hartley's most famous creation, in his true setting. He is lovable in his innocence, his concern for truth and his determination not to hurt others. He is also a disgusting little crawler whenever wealth or rank are concerned. His own accession to wealth enables him to become the intimate of aristocrats and to squander his personal gifts of character. Money is revealed as an evil—it permits the worst characteristics (which need it) to triumph over the better (which don't).

Eustace is only too willing to use his elder sister Hilda to further his social ambitions, that is, to become a guest at Anchorstone Hall. Stephen Hilliard sees it as a sacrifice, leading to tragedy, and writes to Eustace: 'I see now that you meant her to marry Staveley. But perhaps I'm wrong, perhaps you only wanted to use her as a rung in the social ladder. How cleverly you contrived that visit to Anchorstone . . .' When his younger sister Barbara and her husband Jimmy discuss what to do with Hilda after she is paralysed, various alternatives are mentioned—and now Eustace is going to stay with them. This is all a burden but Barbara points out to Jimmy that he likes Eustace, 'in spite of his being rather a toady'. She adds, 'I wish he wouldn't speak about his friends in that low, respectful voice.' Eustace tries to persuade himself that his mistakes were not due to wickedness (or the modern equivalent, a flaw in the character) but to his habit of turning all experience into fantasy. 'The temptation to see things larger than life, to invest them with grandeur and glamour and glory—that had been his downfall. Everything, he told himself, could be traced to that; above all, his wish to aggrandise Hilda and make her the Lady of Anchorstone Hall.'

The Lady of Anchorstone Hall! Hilda was in fact intended to be a governess and the misery of this state, as illustrated by a score of Victorian novels, seemed to have eaten its way into her soul already. Her attitude to the future is one of acquiescent helplessness. In the end, Eustace is compelled to face reality. In the third book of the trilogy he returns to Anchorstone, where he had spent his childhood and nourished the dreams which so nearly destroyed himself and his sister, and now he has to acquire a new conception of reality. In Venice he had bought his way out of trouble and into people's regard. He had treasured a piece of masonry from Anchorstone Hall which Dick Staveley had given him. It was a worthless talisman and eventually he knows he must get rid of it. He needed a substitute (but Anchorstone had no antique shop) and anyway, such objects were useless and dust-collecting and static, and he could no longer afford such indulgences. So he bought a bicycle—it had high practical utility, it was a vital part of industry, essential to the proletariat. He began to feel the joy of intimate association. Eustace was really unregenerate, passing from the influence of one symbol to that of another. This is the first instance of the attraction of proletarian associations, later developed so crazily in Timothy Casson in *The*

Boat. The world was changing, Eustace realized that his dreams were not the stuff of life. While Eustace dutifully pedalled his bicycle, exulting in his developing social conscience, Bert Craddock, the old cab-driver's grandson, got a scholarship to St Joseph's. To revert to sporting allusions (and none are more apt for our time) Bert was winning promotion, Eustace suffering relegation.

Eustace and his type, living through their symbols, felt that machinery created a kind of social watershed. The aristocracy, even when its position was grounded on industrial wealth, centred their interests on land, horses and foreign travel. Their fortunes came from the use of machinery, but their pose was to reject it. When Eustace uses the phrase, 'throw a spanner in the works', Stephen protests, 'What unpleasant metaphors you use. I don't think machinery's a fit subject for ordinary conversation . . .' He then lists a series of mechanical objects which suggest he knows far more about their existence, if not their use, than he would have us believe. Ignorance of machinery is a pose much appreciated in certain quarters. Barbara, who had no time for poses, married Jimmy, 'a representative of the Better Sort rather than of the Finer Grain'. Jimmy treated life like a machine that would go if set up properly and given plenty of oil and power. 'These both existed in his own nature; the power was steam rather than electricity, the oil was crude, but not sticky or glutinous. Messy Jimmy might be, but it was the messiness of the engine-room or the garage, a creative messiness inseparable from energy and movement . . .' Eustace felt left out of it. He was aspiring to the horse culture, Barbara was content to accept the internal combustion machine.

Barbara and Jimmy Crankshaw represent the traditionless but vital class that is setting the pace in contemporary society, challenging and replacing the exhausted older stock. Peter Bien, in his book on L.P. Hartley, writes: 'In the Eustace series, the union of Barbara and Jimmy, though not central to the plot, is the only positive, creative, happy outcome of the events therein . . .' They are the kind of people we like to call 'Americanized'. (In fact, the only book of Hartley's where both the ambience and the characters, and hence the social comment, are American is the early *Simonetta Perkins,* 1925). Hartley devotes most of his literary energies, within the middle class framework, to marginal characters such as writers, film stars, well-to-do expatriates, or dilettantes such as Alexey, one of the leading characters in the novel-within-a-novel of *The Love-Adept,* 1969. He wasn't an artist but he had done well enough in business to retire in his late forties. Such men are becoming increasingly rare because few have the leisure to pursue joint vocations. Too often Hartley's work is marred by triviality; insignificant people are given as much attention as more noteworthy ones; all are treated with equal respect. *The Boat* in particular fails through this lack of discrimination. A story like 'Mr Blandfoot's Picture' (*The White Wand,* 1954) is much too kind to the society of Settlemarsh. The vein of satire, which is all it deserves, is, if existent, extremely thin. This is odd because elsewhere Hartley claims that one of the requirements of good fiction is that the leading characters should be interesting. In itself, such a dictum begs a lot of questions. One wonders to whom and from what standpoint, and at times one feels it is position in the class hierarchy that determines the quality of the treatment.

Servants and Others

'Foreigners refer to distinctions of class more openly than we do', comments L.P. Hartley in 'Three, or Four, for Dinner' (*The Travelling Grave,* 1948). Lurking behind the paraphernalia of what is called Society are the workers. In writers like Hartley these are as untypical as many of his middle class characters: servants, chauffeurs, yeomen farmers barely distinguishable from labourers. Trouble with retainers is a perennial subject in the post-war novels—it crops up in *The Boat, The Betrayal* and stories in *The White Wand.* Servants are so touchy. You have to be so careful. 'Unless he kept watch on his tongue he might lose both his retainers' ('The Corner Cupboard', *Two For the River,* 1961). The trouble is 'they're all so class-conscious nowadays', says Mrs Marriner in 'The Waits' (same collection). She is talking not specifically about servants but of the class they come from.

There are certain types of behaviour that belong to the working class only, and one is puzzled to find them cropping up elsewhere. For example, Richard in *The Brickfield* knew that his aunt had got into some sort of trouble connected with love. 'I knew, by hearsay, that servant-girls and suchlike did, but never imagined that love could lead anyone of our sort into "trouble" '. Actually, she was not in that sort of trouble. 'Trouble connected with love' is the theme of this novel, the tragedy of ignorance, no matter what the class. Nevertheless, Hartley does seem to regard the middle class (the solid, traditional middle class of farmers and professional men) as beleaguered, and slowly yielding to influences from below. The 'proletarianization' of English life is a favourite theme of his. One finds it in his description of 'Restbourne', an unidentifiable coastal resort, with its 'appalling vulgarity'. Having used the term 'proletarianization', he continues: 'It is the apotheosis of the synthetic. I dreaded it, and when I got there it was worse than I remembered—an exhibition of what was, to my middle class mind, a substitute for every form of pleasure.' ('The Face', *Two for the River*). Hartley believes in class and fears the destruction of the class structure. According to Paul Bloomfield, author of the British Council and National Book League pamphlet on Hartley, *Facial Justice*, 1960 is about the abolition of class. The motive is envy.

Working class characters play an important part in two of Hartley's novels, a strong auxiliary part in a third, and in a fourth one of the leading characters is a yeoman farmer whose way of life is much closer to that of one of his labourers than it is to that of, say, a novelist or a retired business man. This is *The Go-Between*, 1953, one of the finest novels of our time. It describes the events of a very hot summer at the turn of the century, with the Boer War in the background. Leo Colston celebrates his thirteenth birthday during the course of the period. The story is told by him looking back from his sixties, an old and empty man. Leo is from a small village near Salisbury, grandly called Court Place. He stays with his schoolfriend Marcus at their Norfolk mansion, Brandham Hall. Of the two, Marcus (who is a snob) is the more impressed, but entirely on a comparison of names. Court Place was very old and the bishops of Salisbury once held court there, but it was an ordinary house, set back in the village street behind looped chains. The child-hero is immune from the more pressing cares of life because his father had been a book-collector, although the proceeds of the business supported him in later life, not now. His father was dead, and he lived with his mother on her money and a pension.

As with Eustace, it is the story of a boy who is fascinated by his social superiors, and who apes them whenever he can. When he is invited to stay with Marcus, the latter's mother writes grandly that although it is the Season neither she nor her husband have been well . . . The house belongs to the ancient Trimingham family, but the tenants are the Maudsleys, in business. The ninth Viscount Trimingham is a guest in his own house—he hopes to marry Marian Maudsley. Half a century later his grandson is living in a small wing of the house and the rest is let to a girls' school. The story centres on the ill-starred attempt to break through the very pronounced class barriers, for Marian is having an affair with a local farmer. How this extraordinary though possible relationship began we are never told. It ends in disaster. Leo was 'acutely aware of social inferiority'. He himself felt out of place among rich people, a misfit. Marcus makes unflattering references to 'the plebs', and identifies his mother with the same feelings. After the cricket concert in the village hall (where Leo had had a singing triumph), Marcus said, 'Anyhow, we've said goodbye to the village for a year. Did you notice the stink in the hall?' Ted Burgess, the farmer-lover, is a solidly attractive character. When he catches Leo sliding down his rick he bawls at him first, but his tone changes when he discovers that Leo is from the hall. Leo is delighted. He had felt a similar change of attitude in himself when he discovered Trimingham was a Viscount. 'I did not despise him for changing his tune when he knew where I came from: it seemed to me right, natural and proper that he should, just as it had seemed right and proper for me to change my tune with Trimingham when I realized he was a Viscount.'

Marcus is a constant fund of information about class behaviour. Leo asks him how long engagements last. 'In the case of grooms, gardeners, skivvies and such-like scum, it may go on for ever. With people like ourselves it generally doesn't go on very long.' (The violence of his language can be partly discounted because it was part of a game he played with Leo, but the content was sincere enough.) Leo was puzzled when Marcus said his mother was a hysterical type because he thought hysteria was something only servants had. When Leo started to cry in front of Ted he didn't feel ashamed: 'I had an instinct that, unlike the people of my own class, he wouldn't think the worse of me for crying.' Then there were the things that were done and not done. Very frequently these marked the border line between middle and upper classes rather than between upper and lower. Only cads wore school clothes in the holidays. It was wrong to go to breakfast in slippers, that's what bank clerks do. You can put them on after tea. (This was hard for Leo, though he didn't let on; his father had worked in a bank and always came to breakfast in slippers.) You shouldn't fold your clothes when you undressed and put them on a chair. 'You must leave them lying where they happen to fall—the servants will pick them up—that's what they're there for.' When hot, you shouldn't mop your face with a handkerchief, but dab it. At breakfast, men ate their porridge walking about but not the women—who were, incidentally, never called ladies. As for a made-up tie, it was the mark of a cad. In his more recent work Hartley has reacted to another type of inhibition, originating at a different social level. 'You mustn't use the word "servants" in these days', says Ralph in *My Sister's Keeper,* 1970. In 'The Prayer' (*Mrs Carteret Receives,* 1971) we are told that the word 'staff' has replaced it.

The Hireling, 1957, actually has a working man (a car-hire driver) for its hero. Leadbitter is not a pure proletarian, out of the industrial melting pot. His family background is 'shortage of money' but no details are given. His status is a marginal one, virtually a servant of the rich, and eventually he sets up for himself. He becomes his own man and is no longer a working chap. Even when he was an employee he was always striving to rise socially. His customers had something he was hoping to acquire. In telling his story Hartley has picked up the We/They jargon. 'No wonder that his customers were "they" to him, beings of an alien, if not hostile race, idle, capricious . . .' He was just as unreal to those who employed him. 'To "them" Leadbitter was just part of the car's furniture, with as little personal feeling as the car had, whereas Leadbitter had no moods, or was supposed to have none, and couldn't break down, he couldn't afford to. For at least half his customers, Leadbitter didn't exist as a man.'

This novel contains Hartley's expression of the alienation effect in modern society. Leadbitter had very little to thank his patrons for.

> In the nature of things they treated him with less consideration than he treated them. Many a time they kept him waiting till the small hours, at a night club or a dance, without the offer of a sandwich or a cup of tea; many a time they cancelled a good job at the last moment, without apology or the promise of redress; sometimes they forgot about him altogether. They took his patience under their thoughtlessness for granted; they didn't seem aware that he had feelings to hurt or interests to injure, and some of them talked together as freely in his presence as if he wasn't there.

Lady Franklin feels the difference in their positions, though not as keenly as he does. On one occasion she felt she had been talking down to him and tried to make amends. 'It's the difference in our social positions, she thought, that makes me use this artificial tone— that, and the effort to be more articulate than I am normally, or have grown to be.'

The Love-Adept, 1969, has another chauffeur-hero, Jock, who resembles Leadbitter in being physically strong, unimaginative and humourless. The author of the novel-within-a-novel imagines Jock's first meeting with the actress, Pauline, who becomes his mistress, as embarrassing, 'with Jock oily and greasy and dirty in his working-clothes, and perhaps unshaven.' She liked him better that way than when he had smartened himself up. James Golightly's chief critic reminds him that he has used the Lady Chatterley situation in a previous novel, which implies he must be fond of it. As the same can be said of Hartley himself, it is impossible to avoid identification. My impression is that Hartley has a slightly pathetic desire to make himself more familiar with working class conditions and attitudes. I am led to say this not only because of this recurring situation but also because of a scattering of comments and asides which appear throughout his fiction. In the post-war work they become more frequent, paralleling the greater confidence of the working class which appears to affect Hartley in two ways: he recognizes it and he hates it.

In an imaginary reply to his critic James defends his use of his trio of characters, especially in their social aspect: actress-business man-chauffeur.

> It happens . . . quite often, and more often than it used to, because the changing structure of society makes such irregular relationships more possible and more probable, and more permissible. They weren't probable, though they weren't impossible, fifty or sixty years ago, when Strindberg wrote *Mademoiselle Julie. Then* it shocked people that a well-born girl should fall in love with a footman: it wouldn't shock people now. Footmen may be a dying race, but they have their counterparts in other walks of life.

In the chapters of the novel that are quoted Jock's plebeian nature is stressed. In the restaurant with Pauline and Alexey he munches his chop (he eats much more than they do) 'with his knife and fork spread facing each way on his plate'. He had too much white shirt-cuff showing above his thick wrists, and pulled his sleeves down when no-one was looking. He had a simple way of finishing an argument. If it happened in a bar, he would take the fellow outside and thump him.[1]

The normal class relationship in Hartley's novels is between an embattled employer and his domestic servants. Leadbitter and Jock represent attempts to get outside the circle of the home, and in each case they are portrayed as individuals. In *The Betrayal* Richard is everybody's victim. We are immediately reminded of his place in the social structure when he answers the telephone and hears 'quite a

1. This novel is dedicated to Elizabeth Bowen, who must have been working on *Eva Trout* at about the same time. In her novel there is also a working man whose would-be mistress, a rich girl, helps invest in a garage. Pauline does the same for Jock. At one stage in their careers both girls drove Jags. Is it possible that Hartley and Bowen were both inspired by the same relationship which was known to each of them? In other ways, the novels are vastly different, including the major themes.

cultivated voice—the voice of someone you might know.' Lower
middle and working class harpies feed on him. All the time he is
aware of the gap between them and him but can do nothing about it.
'Oh dear', he thought, 'these people! Their ways are past finding out.'
Just as the ruling class is 'Them' to the working class, so the servants
are 'They' to Richard. He discovers you can't have domestics without
domestic troubles.[1] He wants to make people happy, but as soon as
they grasp this they take advantage of him. They would probably like
it better if he were a martinet. The two daily helps, Mrs Cuddesdon
and Mrs Stonegappe, didn't like Denys presumably because he was a
gentleman. But Mrs Stonegappe wouldn't accept this and said to the
doctor: 'he's no more a gentleman than you or I are'—a text on which
a fascinating study in social relationships might be written. The
servants tell tales about each other, but pretend all the time to be the
souls of righteousness. 'You know what those people are—they
cannot admit they are in the wrong, or they lose face, and, among
each other, never hear the last of it. They *have* to be in the right.' A
new mood had come over the working people. They were determined
to assert their equality, even their superiority. Class battles raged
incessantly.

Hartley returns to this theme in 'The Prayer' *(Mrs Carteret
Receives):* 'if Anthony wasn't easy-going with them, indeed if he
criticized them—their cooking, their driving, the friends of both sexes,
or any sex, that they brought into the flat from time to time, their
unwarrantable absences or their sometimes more disturbing presences
—at the faintest hint of criticism they departed, almost before the
offending words were out of his mouth.' The exploitation of the classes
was being stood on its head.

The Money Obsession

I have assumed all along that the reader is acquainted with Eustace,
Hartley's most famous hero. Eustace is a beautiful study in growing
up: a boy who is kind-hearted, generous, always worried, given to
fantasy—and obsessed with money. He is also determined to become
the familiar of aristocrats, and underlying the claims of tradition,
breeding and vast estates there is an unsentimental concern for wealth.

1. Hartley's approach to servants is quite different from Snow's. They
always cheat Hartley and he knows it. It seems very likely that they cheat
Snow's well-meaning characters, but the latter would not admit it. It was
necessary to maintain a fiction of trust, democracy and mutual respect.

A title brings credit, even in a democratic age, as Denys Aspin admitted. One is reminded of Lady Brett Ashley in Hemingway's *Fiesta*. When the count says a title does him no good, it only costs a lot of money, she replies, 'Oh, I don't know. It's damned useful sometimes.' She tells him he hasn't used his title properly and adds, 'I've had hell's own amount of credit on mine.' Now Eustace is not so crude as to want entry into the charmed circle of the aristocracy for mercenary reasons, but he is convinced that the possession of wealth is one of the mainsprings of social life.

The Shrimp and the Anemone appeared in 1944. One of the main themes of this very fine novel is the corruption that follows on wealth reflected in the mind of innocence. One is tempted to see it as a complex of symbolism, in the manner of the modern literary don, but that would be no more than a transcription. Most of what passes for symbolism debases: the novel should be a revelation, not a piece of spiritual algebra, which is the balm of the inferior mind. It would of course be easy to make out a heavy symbolic argument that, let us say, Eustace's legacy brought him at one and the same time wealth and a conviction that he was going to die, and therefore that money and death are qualitatively alike—but this is the kind of half-baked use of symbolic equivalences which has nothing to do with the writing of fiction. In fact, *The Shrimp and the Anemone* would be a better book if its author had not opened with the imagery from which the book gets its title. Nearly all the book is intensely living but it starts in the lecture hall.

From the first page onwards we know that Eustace is agonized by an over-active conscience, which includes the social conscience. His heart bled for the shrimp, he longed to rescue it—but how could he rob the anemone? And then, shouldn't he be helping Hilda build up the bank? And so on, right through to the time when he's planning his will and thinks that some poor boy might like his sponge, toothbrush and flannel—once they'd been well dried, of course.

We are always aware of the social hierarchy. Eustace is convinced that most of his acquaintances are higher up the ladder than he is and that he is lucky to know them. He is surprised that the Steptoes invite him to a picnic for they are the kind of people who probably have one every day, whereas for him it is an exciting rarity. Nevertheless, Eustace is proud that his father is a chartered accountant with an office in Ousemouth. There are plenty of unfortunates below them. Although he stood in considerable awe of Mr Craddock, who hired out the horse and carriage, for Aunt Sarah the old man belonged to the category of things that had not been properly washed. The

Steptoes had a very clear view of life in general. They knew that Mr Johnson's was 'a potty little school' for tradesmen's sons, that the South of England was socially superior to other parts, that there is a world of difference between Cliftonville and Margate, where trippers go, and that Anchorstone should be pronounced Anxton. (This is an important part of the upper class code: Wiveliscombe-Wilscombe, Cirencester-Sister, Cholmondeley-Chumley, Beauchamp-Beecham.)

The period is about 1906. Though relatively poor (Mr Cherrington speaks in some awe of a colleague who is in the thousand-a-year bracket) they feel obliged to have a nanny for the baby and also a daily help. Families were judged by the number of servants they employed. Minney saw three different ones while she was at Miss Fothergill's. The behaviour of the rich towards their servants and the poor in general was baffling but had to be learnt. Eustace was alarmed to think that the coachman would have to wait for Dick when the latter called to see him. (Eustace would have dashed off immediately.) On the other hand, Minney was surprised to find Dick pouring tea for himself, yet in some way it was understood that this confirmed his rank. Dick spoke easily of 'family retainers' and had to translate the term for Eustace.

The Cherringtons had their full share of bourgeois narrowness, particularly Aunt Sarah, Mr Cherrington's sister, who looked after his family after the death of his wife when Barbara, the third child, was born. She had a fierce dislike of all gambling and games of chance, which even extended to making a decision by tossing a coin. She was irritated when her brother relaxed after the day's work—it was something she felt he had to stop and so she used to bring up awkward family matters. (Hilda adopted her aunt's view without resistance— cards, for instance, were a waste of time.) Aunt Sarah didn't want to accept Miss Fothergill's legacy, and certainly was against telling Eustace about it. It would spoil him. Hilda told Eustace it wouldn't be *good* for children to be rich. In the sequel, *The Sixth Heaven,* Aunt Sarah shows a poor opinion of Eustace. He has always had it too easy.

Mr Cherrington was not rich enough to send Eustace to a fee-paying school, therefore he did not go to school. A state school was out of the question. One day, if Mr Cherrington could afford it, he might go to the Rev Johnson's prep school, but we all know what Nancy Steptoe (greatly admired by Eustace) thought of that: not much. Miss Fothergill commented that he ought to be at school. As she says it he is conscious of the darn in his blue jersey and tells her he has lessons at home. Eustace puts the position beautifully: 'Daddy can't afford to send me to a good school and Aunt Sarah won't let me go to a bad one.' As for Hilda, it is generally accepted that she will become a governess. It is not a fate to look forward to, but their poverty seems to make it inevitable. An aura of hopelessness hangs around Hilda, and we find it repeated in *My Sister's Keeper*, 1970, which again has childhood lack of means (one can hardly call it poverty) as a background. 'Daddy isn't rich enough to give any of us a pony', wails Gwendolen. She never expects to eat asparagus again as there are so many of them to bring up and educate.

In absolute terms the Cherringtons are not poor. In the framework of the English social system they scarcely count. Money is the key. Money and its power and the corruption that can emanate from it are never absent long, as a pervading threat. Eustace naively says to the driver on the way to the picnic, 'It's very hard to make money, isn't it?' At times Hilda makes a virtue of the family poverty—just as there is a hole in Eustace's jersey, so there is a ladder in her stocking when Dick calls, and she hopes he sees it. She refused to learn to ride a horse because she knew she would never be able to afford one of her own.

Mr Cherrington is not above using the family poverty as a threat. Because of Eustace's irresponsible behaviour he fell ill and there were heavy doctor's bills and a nurse, which meant that Hilda had to have a room outside. It was suggested that they might have to leave Cambo because they had no money left. Eustace feels that his father will never be able to spend much time with him again because he will be so busy earning money to make up what it cost him to pay for the illness.

Then Miss Fothergill's legacy changes the situation completely. Mr Cherrington immediately begins to live in a more expansive way, and we learn from *The Sixth Heaven*, 1946 that he was drinking too much in his later years. 'Who would have thought the old lady had all that money!' he mused, echoing Lady Macbeth, and thus equating money in the mind with blood, life itself. His sister Sarah can see nothing but danger coming from the new wealth: how could he control Eustace, who would be getting £700 a year, much more than himself? And what would be the position of Hilda and Barbara, penniless sisters of a well-to-do young man? (In fact, these dread forecasts were not realized.) When Eustace becomes rich, everyone's attitude towards him changes. He notices this (they are kinder, more considerate), but he doesn't know the cause. Mr Craddock now finds it possible to bring the carriage down the rutted track to Cambo—in the past he had waited at the end of the lane. Nancy tells Eustace he won't ever have to work, he'll be like Dick, live at home, play golf, shoot, hunt and go to Homburg or Carlsbad. But probably most important of all, from Eustace's point of view, he will able to enjoy himself more in the bath. He had a game (flooding cities) but he used to suffer from fears such as having his leg sucked down the plughole by escaping water or, a more rational one, that the water might overflow, sink into the floor and dissolve it, and let him down into the drawing room, costing his father several pounds. Now he would be able to cover any such disaster.

We see what Miss Fothergill's legacy really did to Eustace in the second book of the trilogy, *The Sixth Heaven*. It took away his initiative. He is aware of this, tries to wish he hadn't had it, but cannot quite manage it. Aunt Sarah is convinced that he has received no benefit at all from the legacy; it has removed the circumstances that might have strengthened an already weak character. Stephen, a more positive man than Eustace, despite his precious way of speaking, tells Hilda (who has Aunt Sarah's distrust of money) that it is not 'just an extension of one's emotions: it has a reality of its own which one ought to respect'. He says that Eustace is not to be trusted with money: 'he thinks it is just a natural adjunct of benevolence.' In fact, Eustace hovers on the edge of a different world but never quite belongs to it. Lady Nelly tells him that when she married Freddie 'he hadn't a penny—I mean, about a thousand a year.' Eustace's father had once spoken in some awe of a colleague who earned that amount. Now he betrays his background and says, 'It doesn't seem very much.' Mr Cherrington was a nine-to-five man, who regarded one evening drink as a luxury. The Staveleys got their money from a coal-mine in Derbyshire, which is mentioned as frequently as the unnamed product that supported the wealth of the Newsomes in James's *The Ambassadors*.

In the third volume, *Eustace and Hilda*, 1952, Eustace discovers that money can buy anything—except, of course, happiness. Temporary depression can easily be put right by a visit to the bank. Hilda is in trouble with the governors of the clinic she works at—he will send her a thousand pounds to carry out repairs. He wires the money. 'He left the post office lighter in step, lighter in heart, lighter by a thousand pounds.' In fact his sister is passing through a grave psychological crisis but he makes no effort to understand it because it would disturb his personal idyll. Without the money he might have been forced to help Hilda in the way she needed. But Eustace was getting accustomed to buying his way out of difficulties or into personal favour. By overpaying the boatman on the ferry he won special smiles, even a return to fetch him after the ferry had left, and

considerable pains to see that he was safely disembarked. 'Such
attentions pleased Eustace very much.' And yet his money is not
inexhaustible and even Eustace is finally compelled to adopt a higher
degree of realism towards money, exactly what it can do and what it
cannot. When he returns to Cambo he has an altercation with the
cab driver and is heard to say, 'I'm sorry, but I think sixpence is quite
enough.' In a later edition this was changed to, 'Sixpence over the fare
is quite enough.' Hartley explained to Peter Bien that he wanted to
convey that Eustace has become more realistic about money matters.
Previously he would have given two or three shillings and thought
nothing of it. He is being reborn.

It is natural that money should never be far from the consciousness
of Leadbitter, the working class hero of *The Hireling,* 1957. He is
always striving to improve his position and this requires money. His
greatest step forward is made when Lady Franklin gives him a cheque
that enables him to pay off the instalments on his car. His concern
with money is contrasted with her indifference, as a wealthy widow.
He did not envy her indifference but took it as a fact of life. She warns
him that money is not everything and says that when he gets rich he
may find that money will lock the door on his prison—or at least,
fail to unlock it. ('It would take a good deal of money to lock the door
on me', thought Leadbitter). When he buys a powerful new car he
feels he will now impel recognition, and it will be through the power
of money. Sometimes he takes a young couple in his car. The girl,
Constance, says rich people never seem quite real: 'Their problems are
not the same as ours, and all that freedom of action—it's like a fairy
tale. They float around, they don't belong—there are not enough of
them, now, to make a social unit. They are an anachronism, a vestigial
survival . . .' This is rather over Leadbitter's head. What he notices
when he has some money to his name (in his case, a flourishing
business) is exactly what Eustace noticed in Venice—the banks
behave differently. Before, if the clerks even raised their heads, it was
only to show blank faces. But now he was welcomed by smiles and
even the manager put on a friendly air: 'Of course, old chap, of
course', and practically bowed him out.

Money still provides the ground-bass for *The Betrayal,* 1966.
Superficially Richard should have no money worries, but he is constantly cheated by his employees and he becomes worried about his
security, as Eustace used to be. Richard could recall times when his
parents were anxious but when he asked his mother what was the
matter, she used to say, 'It's about something you wouldn't understand, my darling—something to do with money.' When they passed

the Abbey his mother always told him to look away so that he would
not see the ugly buttresses in the form of an M. The ugly M, she called
it. On one occasion he thought of ugly words starting with M, and one
was Money. Richard owed his material prosperity to the Brickworks,
left him by his father. His novels had brought in only marginal wealth.
'His first novel had come out in the twenties, when it was still possible
for an author, or anyone else, to keep the bulk of his earnings from the
clutches of the Inland Revenue. It was only his first novel that had
brought in money—it had been filmed and dramatized. But when his
earnings from authorship fell off he still had the Brickworks and it was
not necessary for him to ask: 'How can I please the public better?'

I doubt if there is a contemporary writer who has illustrated more
emphatically the fundamental role played by money in our society
than L.P. Hartley, nor the subtle changes in its value relative to human
service or the consequent erosion in the morality of its use. In 'The
White Wand' we read that CF had come to stay in Venice for a
month. He lost the services of his gondolier after a quarrel, and did
not replace him. By saving this money he was able to stay a little
longer—and yet it must have been so little! It is always embarrassing to see someone trying to play the role of the cosmopolitan and at
the same time having to count the pennies. As Richard's financial
situation became more and more difficult *(The Betrayal),* his solicitor
advised him to sell his shares in the Fosdyke Fundamental Brick
Company, and to buy shares in Juvenile and General Hair Stylists. It
was the traditional remedy, realising capital on stock. But there is a
new tone in this transaction, a symbolic change from solid values to
something more frivolous. Immediately the Fosdyke shares soar and
the J. & G.H.S. fall to a quarter. So much for values. As for morality,
it was his solicitor who bought his Fosdykes. It is the end of an era for
Richard. Money still counts, but you have to have it. Hartley's
characters are usually without it, or enough of it, or if they have it
they are likely to lose it. But the marginal men, like Alexey in *The
Love-Adept,* 1969, are all right. This is the story of a trio, two men
and a woman, who are emotionally and sexually implicated. They
break up and go their own ways with their own desires. 'Alexey was
the luckiest, because besides having money . . .'

IV

Rosamund Lehmann—Twilight of the Rich
(First Fiction: *Dusty Answer,* 1927)

Rich Men, Right People

Rosamund Lehmann's name is associated, largely through her brother John, with sympathies for the poor and unprivileged. Sympathy was perhaps the least she could give. She was the daughter of a well-to-do M.P., with a nurse and nursemaid, domestic servants and gardeners. The staff is listed in *The Swan in the Evening,* 1967. There were Goodman, Gooden, Bob Field, Stacey, Seymour, Edith, Ethel, Rhoda Annie, Sarah, Mabel, Nellie, Cloudie, Mrs Almond—though I am sure they did not all serve simultaneously. There was James in the pantry, Mrs Slezina, and William Moody in the stables. There was a Victoria and certainly two horses. Down by the river was a boathouse, with two tiers of racing craft, a catamaran, a canoe, a light skiff and a big punt. Oliver was the boatman.

All her novels are concerned with the well-heeled and prosperous, although to varying extents. Judith of *Dusty Answer,* 1927 lives in a comfortable middle class home with plenty of unseen money to support it. 'Gardeners mowed and mowed, and rolled and rolled the tennis court; and planted tulips and forget-me-nots in the stone urns that bordered the lawn at the river's edge . . .' A butler and a nurse are casually mentioned, and she shared a governess with the girl next door. The children next door sometimes came to tea with her: 'exquisite China tea in the precious Nankin cups which always appeared for visitors. Everything in the house was precious and exquisite. . . .'

Years later she stays with Martin at his mother's Hampshire estate. Martin's father had been a colonial Governor: Sir John Fyfe, K.C.B. Martin (like his cousin Julian) had been educated at Eton. In the drawing room was a portrait of the Governor. 'There were some books in glass-fronted bookcases, some goodish furniture and china; one or two good water-colours and some indifferent ones; abundant plump cushions in broad soft chairs and couches. It was a house that showed in every detail the honourable, conventional, deeply-rooted English traditions of Martin's people.'

Judith's parents seemed to spend much of their time in Paris. Later, as Miss Earle, she travelled with her 'elegant and charming mother, staying at the smartest hotel and prominent in the ephemeral summer society of the health-resort.' Judith did not go to school because, like Nancy Mitford's Uncle Matthew, her father didn't approve of girls' schools. She was coached by a vicar, had music lessons from a man who came from London, and her father taught her Greek and Latin. In fact, she was about as unrepresentative of the average contemporary woman as could be imagined. Her worldly mamma says to her: 'If you were a little more stupid you might make a success of a London season even at this late date . . .' This was the protest of the young, to point out that stupidity was a social asset if allied with a solid financial cushion. It was pleasant to have enough money to accuse the assured and comfortable smart world of hating ideas and unconventionality with impunity. Normally there were no job fears. Martin, for instance, acted as estate agent for his mother when his father died.

In *A Note in Music,* 1930, we are in the presence of hunting people. Tough to a degree they are. An old aunt breaks a leg, but is not unduly put out: 'will anything kill her?'

> Norah had relations all over the country: a couple of hard riding, close-fisted maiden aunts in a stone barracks on the moor; a family of cousins, who, living on a large estate, sent sons into the services, kept daughters at home uneducated, moulded to their sagging tweeds, organizing girl guides, breeding Sealyhams, riding to hounds inelegantly, astride on comic ponies, or following the hunt in a derelict Ford; finally, a bearded elderly cousin who lived in a charming house in a green valley, collected first editions, prints, tapestries, and early English water-colours, and dwelt together in a certain haze of culture and mystery and tobacco-smoke: dwelt, moreover, in almost unbroken silence, for his wife was stone-deaf, and spent her days in the rose-chintz drawing room, the world forgotten, reading the French and German classics; or in the garden, tending her rockery, looking at her roses and delphiniums.

This is below the Etonian level, but still well above the normal spheres of English life, especially in the North of England, where they live. Annie, the maid at Mrs Fairfax's little house in a dull town street, is excited when her mistress brings home a young man in hunting pink, and asks him if he would like a boiled egg. 'She had been with a hunting family once, and she knew what pink coats meant at tea-time. Mrs Fairfax, poor soul, would never have thought of it.' Distinctions had to be drawn between ladies and would-be ladies. For example, everyone thought of Mrs MacKay as a 'well-bred woman; one distinguished her indubitable County blood; her detachment was intangible and unspoken: unlike that of Mrs Fairfax, that disagreeable woman, snobbish and exclusive without any justification whatever . . .' And out at the house of Norah MacKay's rich relation you could see men 'pacing shoulder to shoulder, talking as men talk once they have recognized in each other the mutual background of country gentlemanhood.' Inside the house the country gentlemen could be sure of feeling at home.

> Tall groups of unshaded candles in five-branched silver candlesticks of elaborate Georgian design lit the long polished table. An ancestor by Raeburn hung above the mantelpiece; and there were other portraits all round the room—portraits military, political, fox-hunting; beribboned, satin-clad, waxen-fleshed, rounded of arm and breast, maternal or maidenly. Upon the far wall a vast Salvator Rosa storm and wreck made more tenebrous the shadows.

Invitation to the Waltz, 1932, is concerned with yet another sector of the British rich. The Curtis family belong to the new industrial aristocracy created during the nineteenth century. They are not as prosperous as they were. They live in a stone square house built at the same time as the Tulverton paper-mills in the middle of the century. The interior is imagined by an observer who looks at the house from outside. A catalogue similar to those already quoted springs to mind.

> You see rooms crowded with ponderous cupboards, sideboards, tables; photographs in silver frames, profusely strewn; wallpapers decorated with flowers, wreaths, birds, knots and bows of ribbon; dark olive, dark brown paint in the hall and passages; marble mantelpieces vapid, chill, swelling as blancmange; the watercolour performances of aunts and great-aunts thick upon the walls; worn leather armchairs pulled up to hot coal fires: you smell potpourri and lavender in china bowls; you taste roast beef and apple tart on Sundays; hot scones for tea—dining room tea

on the enormous white cloth, beneath the uncompromising glare of the enormous central light . . .

Obviously poverty is not yet a problem. But the family line is growing thin. You never knew what the boys would get up to these days. Victorian grandees tended to have such unsatisfactory descendants. A horrid vision of a final James who doesn't have a car and doesn't make the regular journey to and from the mills spreads gloom. But all the same, there is a pattern. Somehow, there will be sufficient continuity to see the family through. There is something alarming, even wicked, but tough and energetic.

Apart from the two parents, there are two girls and a boy. The family are looked after by a nannie, a cook and a domestic named Violet. The boy is taken for a nature walk once a week by a woman from the village. The sisters had been to the day school in Tulverton and Katie is to be 'finished' in Paris—not at a school but with the family of a professor. These girls hardly ever go anywhere. Friends of the right type and class are not readily available. It is, therefore, all the more necessary to maintain a front. They tend to become hypercritical to show their superiority to the world outside. A letter from a young man is criticized adversely. 'A bit finicky, to my mind. Bank clerkish. Spotty, with glasses. "Most kind"—that's distinctly shady. It's what Miss Mivart would say. Why couldn't he say how ripping of you. . . .'

The great day is when they are invited to a dance at Meldon Towers. They feel distinctly like 'country mouse cousins'. In fact, an actual cousin is there, but she is one of the house party, one of the establishment. Two brothers are said to have a special gramophone for the bathroom: 'what a delirious standard'. The young men talk mainly of hunting and shooting. Olivia makes a tremendous bloomer when asked if she goes out, and says she goes out every day: it turns out that *out* means hunting. Nevertheless, even these golden youths have to work. Nine-thirty till six, every day in the City. They agree it's slavery. Olivia meets one upper-class rebel, an unsavoury undergraduate who calls himself a poet and despises everybody. He speaks disrespectfully of their hostess, Lady Spencer, whom he calls 'a tin-plated dowager'. This is terribly subversive, and also exciting. More conformist behaviour comes from some of the hunting types who begin to gallop up and down the ballroom, kicking their legs up and uttering wild cries. 'Nothing like an Englishman for a rag, is there?' says the poet. 'Damn good sportsmen! With any luck they'll break up some chairs and things soon. Just for the joke of it.' They are the insensitive heroes of a dying culture. The weedy poet is to be its salvation.

The Weather in the Streets, 1936, is a continuation. Miss Lehmann's treatment of this class is never wholehearted. Her obvious admiration for a declining way of life is diluted by pricks of social conscience, and the resulting gloom pervades everything. The gaiety of her heroes and heroines is woefully depressing. Olivia goes to a dinner party at the Spencers'. Dinner is ready. 'Ha! A good meal coming, another good dinner: one of hundreds before, hundreds to come—anywhere, any time they liked. Not one grain of doubt, ever, about the quality, quantity, time and place of their food and drink . . . In prime condition they all looked: no boils or blackheads here, no corns, calluses, chilblains or bunions. No struggle about underclothes and stockings. Birthright of leisure and privilege, of deputed washing, mending . . .' Portraits of the ancestors in the hall, of course: 'here a legal wig, red robes; there the dulled splendour of ancient regimentals; here a pink satin gown, a smirk, a rose, a long neck, a white hand and breast, there a towering Victorian group, exaggeratedly fertile-domestic-blissful.' Benson, the family chauffeur, had taken her there: 'a lifetime of service, said his patient figure, standing on the steps, waiting: the last, no doubt, to wish to change his station; deploring each successive stage in the breakdown of the social scale; yet a man of intelligence, of dignity.' Sir Ronald Clark-Mathew, a fellow guest, foresaw the end of a chapter. (These old codgers did it as regularly as critics foresee the end of the novel). What will happen to all the art treasures when the present guardians have gone? Some houses are already closed for three-quarters of the year. It is not only the end of a social chapter, it will be the end of all aesthetic standards. The complacent Jeremiad drones on. 'I ask myself: who'll care a hundred years from now for art and letters?' Olivia suggests other people. He replies, 'Potted! Re-hashed! Distributed cheap to all consumers . . . Museums plentiful as blackberries. Ve long gallery at Holkhurst railed off wiv greasy ropes, guides in attendance, ve cheap excursions disgorging at ve gates and shuffling frough. . . .' They have already had to sell a Rembrandt. What will go next? What will happen in Rollo's time, unless he can make some money? An advantageous marriage would help—the traditional way out for a beleaguered class.

The variations on an aristocratic theme continue in *The Ballad and the Source*, 1944. The story is told by one of the three children of an M.P. (again). The period is just before 1914, when foreign travel and residence were a commonplace, and continuing into the war. There is mention of a butler, and a French governess intrudes from time to time. Grandmother suffered from a weak chest and used to get a dreadful cough, which compelled her to leave England and follow the sun. A friend, Malcolm, is being prepared for Winchester: 'a gentleman resident in Winchester, an ex-tutor of the college, had been found to receive and coach him.' Once again, a few words will suggest the background of culture and prosperity:

> Portraits, letters, albums in the library, family legends, all conspired to float these grandparents, dead before our birth, glamorously before us. Figures larger than life size surrounded them, mingled with them in a rich element of culture and prosperity. In that lost land it was always mid-summer; and the handsome, the talented, the bearded great moved with Olympian words and gestures against a background of marble-columned studios, hallowed giant writing desks, du Maurier-like musical drawing rooms, dinner tables prodigious with good fare, branched candle-sticks and wit.
>
> Without conscious awareness that our circumstances were a decline from all this, we did receive early intimations that our budding time was somehow both graced and weakened by echoes and reflections from the prestige of that heyday.

Miss Lehmann's novel, *The Echoing Grove,* 1953, shows, among many other things, how wealth and position and social contacts can provide a cushion against disaster which is as valuable as any other aspect of privilege. When Madeleine's son Anthony was killed in the war, Rickie 'gave her a stiff brandy and helped her to pack a bag and put her into the car, and they went first to Eton to pick up Colin and then straight down to Clarissa. Then they went on, all four of them . . . she was never quite sure where. Seven days in a little house on the banks of the Wye, lent to them, staff and all, by a friend of Rickie's in the Admiralty. . . .' In the background lurk the usual cook and nanny. Both generations of boys go to Eton—it seems the only school for Lehmann characters, Winchester surely being an aberration almost equivalent to laughing at Lady Spencer.

The novel traces the amorous careers of two sisters, in love with the same man. Originally Dinah Burkett, the wild one, was engaged to a young barrister, 'established with a sensible, a prosperous if not dazzling future, conforming to the right social pattern.' Madeleine, the elder, conventional sister, who is married to the man in question, was the Londoner, 'in the swim, never unaccompanied, never without new clothes, shored up with layer after layer of prosperous social life'. Dinah once remarks to her mother that 'I couldn't be more thankful for the good sound upper-middle stock I come of. It's meant a sort of solid ground floor of family security and class confidence that's been a great stand-by.' It seems likely that Rosamund Lehmann finds herself in the position of Dinah. Critical of the circles she moves in, yet always aware that she is maintained by them, she feels something like a court jester. It is impossible to feel impressed by a licence to shoot with blank cartridges.

Anthony Burgess, in his *The Novel Now*, comments on the increasing gap that occurs between the publication of Miss Lehmann's novels, and suggests that she is unsure of her audience or finds difficulty in making contact with the post-war world. A letter I wrote to her publishers, asking for sales figures of her novels, was not even answered. If her public is small today, it is scarcely surprising. Her novels are intensely personal; the persons concerned are not the kind to arouse much interest among post-war readers; and they are so frightfully upper class. The irritation one occasionally feels while reading Henry James is always threatening to break surface. We are confronted by people in love who talk endlessly about their problems, refining and paring down their situations, one hopes eventually to the bone—but the bone is never reached. It is a weightless nebulosity, a matter of splendid literary metaphors, a general tone of self-pity, and no revelation whatsoever. If you doubt this, turn to the long long account in *The Echoing Grove* of Rickie and Georgie trying desperately to become lovers until at last one feels, with relief, that this is at least something we won't have to follow to the bitter end, and then they become lovers after all—but consider the rhetoric! Most of the situation is skirted in a blaze of self-congratulatory candle-light. The time for this has gone. It is hard to believe that the time for it ever existed, but this genre did once have its followers. What is extraordinary is that an attempt should have been made to combine it with social consciousness. Today people have less time for self-indulgence in psychological messes, they haven't the income to support it, the schools teach sociology and the universities try to act it.

The In-Betweens

As I have already remarked, it is not easy to see exactly where one class ends and another begins. We can see the extremes of poverty and wealth but the boundaries between not-so-poor and not-so-rich are by no means clear. A middle class boy may scrape into Eton and rub shoulders with an earl's son or a corporation manager's nephew; he may work alongside a grammar school product and even be on the best of terms with him at a yacht club; you can remain aloof in a hotel but contemporary society demands a certain degree of business fraternization. In Lehmann the working class are always the working class, to be pitied and (undoubtedly) despised. But not all Lady Spencer's horses nor all her servants can keep the *parvenus* sons out of the demesne.

This is the area where changing fortunes are felt most acutely. Rickie (*The Echoing Grove*, 1953) had been heir to large estates in Norfolk, which he had sold off, except for a small Jacobean dower house that he had furnished and given to his mother. He dreaded going back; it was 'the soil and landscape and architecture of his ancestors'. He had been brought up to be a country gentleman but he had gone into business. Dinah wondered what this had done to him psychologically, but her mother was tougher.

> Rickie, I take it, inherited a certain property and like what most of you call the landed gentry—indeed so do I but without feeling called upon like you to impose a particular inflection upon my vocal chords—found himself crippled by taxation, whether justly or unjustly is a matter of opinion though I am sometimes tempted to consider it more a matter of taste. . . .

It is that 'particular inflection' that one finds most trying in Miss Lehmann's work as a whole. Mrs Burkett, who appears to have a very sound headpiece, draws attention to the curious duality one finds among the well-to-do left-wingers of the 'thirties, with their combination of Marxian economics and admiration for the aristocratic values.

The time is pre-war and there is a levelling process at work. Dinah lives with a young proletarian she called Rob. Madeleine calls and asks where he is, but can scarcely bear to pronounce his name: 'she hesitated over the semi-anonymous truncated name, feeling it stick suddenly in her throat, become a symbol for all she feared and hated —the levelling de-individualizing new order to whose massed ranks something in Dinah was committed.' Dinah's mother remembers some dreadful young man who had been brought to the house, who had explained for her benefit what was happening. 'You see, Mrs Burkett, the fact is Western civilization is in *decline* and those of us like *myself* who are *aware* of it must reflect it in our *lives* before crystallizing it in our *work*. We cannot be expected to *behave*.' But this reflection, in Mrs Burkett's view, consisted largely of trivial chatter, effeteness, bottle parties and cynical sexy novels. Rickie said (speaking of his wife's lover) that such people in fact don't behave. 'Behaviour has ceased to be a concept. I've got a hunch they simply don't know what it feels like to feel *disgraced*—personal, moral disgrace—dishonour if you like.' It is even possible that a new attitude to sex (which was later to become clearer) was becoming discernible. Dinah felt that the difference between her generation and her grandparents was much more than the obvious social economic one. 'Sometimes I think it's more than the development of a new attitude towards sex: that a new gender may be evolving—psychically new—a sort of hybrid. Or else it's just beginning to be uncovered how much woman there is in man and *vice versa.*' Now although Miss Lehmann's work is peppered with sensibility, so that it finally has the effect of acting upon the reader like a bludgeon, this is in fact about the most perceptive comment she makes on her society. It is difficult to entangle the rest from personal and class self-pity.

Let us move in the social spectrum and examine another type of changing position. 'The Red-Haired Miss Daintreys', a story which first appeared in *Penguin New Writing* in 1941 and later in the collection *The Gipsy's Baby,* 1946 is set in a hotel on the Isle of Wight during a holiday just before the first war. (The Lehmanns used to go to the Isle of Wight when Rosamund was a child. In those days it was perfectly respectable. These days, she remarks in her autobiography *The Swan in the Evening,* 1968 an equivalent family would motor across Europe with Moses baskets, collapsible cots and masses of gear.) It is an untidy and rather pointless story but socially it has some significance.

It starts with a short lecture about fiction-writing in which the author declares: 'I myself have been, all my life, a privileged person with considerable leisure.' The tale is about her childhood. Her father was a literary gent, and leisure and a fair degree of wealth are implicit. The Daintreys, on the other hand, had a great West End business, 'a store whose name was a household word.' The girl's parents told her they must be very rich, although they lived simply. There is no doubt about what kind of people the lower classes are and what is their proper place. On the beach 'nurses went on sitting with their bare feet stuck out in front, letting the sea air get at their corns.' Although this is perfectly reasonable, the reader knows that this is a world where people of quality do not have corns. But the main interest lies in the Daintrey family. Rich, yes, but—are they quite-quite, to use a term employed ironically by Miss Bowen? There is something unprepossessing about Miss Mildred Daintrey, the eldest, who plays the leading role in the story. To put it bluntly, the family fortune comes from trade; she is nice and kind but she is not sophisticated.

A widower marries her. He is after her money and he gets it. She dies in childbirth, a little over forty.

The story ends with a portentous comment. Two nephews grew up and became much like other people 'but not in the least like their relations of the two former generations. Product of an expanding age, the mould is broken that shaped and turned those out. Forced up too rapidly, the power in them, so lavish and imposing as it seemed, sank down as rapidly as it faded out. There will be no more families in England like the Daintrey family.' As they used to say in the North, shirtsleeves to shirtsleeves in three generations. Miss Lehmann sees such people as being formed in a mould which may or may not break—this one broke, but the one that shaped the Curtis family in *Invitation to the Waltz* had so far managed to maintain itself, though with difficulty.

Such people found it difficult to feel secure. They longed for the stability of the old established families, they feared the challenge of the new housing estates. When Rollo Spencer, the admired aristocrat, gives Olivia a lift home in the family Sunbeam, she feels impelled to show off by criticizing the new houses (*The Weather in the Streets,* 1936). 'Every time I come along this road there's a fresh outbreak of bungalows. *Look* at that one! *"Idono"* . . . if only I had the energy to set fire to every one of them in the middle of the night . . . except that they'd go and put up something worse. There's one somewhere called *"Oodathortit"* '. Rollo has no need of this kind of protest, and is bemused. Why does she want to deprive them of their houses, although he concedes that they are 'nasty little brutes'? She starts to lecture him: he ought to mind. 'England gets squalider and squalider. So disgraced, so ignoble, so smug and pretentious . . . and nobody minds enough to stop it.' Rollo points out that nobody can stop it if that's what the people want. She supposes he must be 'what's called a realist'. She, of course, was an idealist before the term got a bit frayed. It was very disappointing when the best people didn't agree with one's noblest sentiments.

One kept the lower classes at arm's length by a variety of devices. One was speech. 'He's ripping and he's jolly clever too. Much cleverer than me. He thinks I'm an awful ass', says a character in *Dusty Answer*. It was the middle class language of the day, which no-one but the most abject crawler among the working class population would ever resort to. There are four words that would never have passed a miner's lips, let us say. Another divisive force was religion, at least in certain circumstances. Olivia's father was an atheist—the very sight of a clergyman irritated him. The working classes might not be great church-goers (although the women were more conscientious than the men) but they hadn't adopted an atheistic or even agnostic stance. That was a matter for intellectuals. Olivia became aware of these differences on her seventeenth birthday, when she called on the village dressmaker, who had a sister renowned for her Christian patience. While waiting for the dressmaker to appear, Olivia considered the declining place of religion in her life:

> It was undoubtedly a fact that faith was failing. Nowadays, at the moment of getting into bed, when a lifetime's habit still suggested prayer, one's immediate reaction was a confused mental protest, like an impatient shrug of scepticism; and straightway, a shade uneasy, into bed one got and thought about something else. Gone this many a day were those ecstasies, that crouching low upon the pillow, eyeballs pressed to palms, till stars and coloured globules appeared, and one began to be almost sure one was in the presence of God.

Along with God went the servants. They were just as surely disappearing from middle class life, although the really rich had not yet begun to feel the draught. Those families who had served abroad, on imperial business, were the ones who suffered most. The Thomsons (*The Ballad and the Source,* 1944) had been in India. When they came back circumstances were difficult and he was reduced to a teaching job. 'I don't quite understand what father did out there—I know he was quite important. . . . We seemed to be rich in India, but since then we've been poor.' It's not difficult to know why the Thomsons found it so difficult to adjust in England. Not only were they earning much less money but you could no longer hire servants for a few rupees.

Lehmann's attitude to servants can be astonishing. Although she is often associated with the between-wars movement for greater social justice (her stories used to appear in her brother's *New Writing*), nevertheless a rather satirical, snobbish attitude towards the lower classes peeps out of her writing. When her guard drops she is liable to treat servants as figures of fun, in the traditional manner of her class. Servants are rarely allowed dignity in the mainstream of English middle class writing. Perhaps, because of their status, they do not deserve dignity. Then let them have compassion. A maid named Lucy is to see Maisie on to the train *(Ballad).* 'She tweaked Lucy's ear, and then gave her a hug; and Lucy responded to the embrace with one of those eloquent compressed looks I had observed on the faces of the dear maids at home when one or other of us was in trouble. "It's a

downright shame, that's what it is, and I don't care who hears me say
so", were the unspoken words behind the look.' There is condescension in the use of the word 'dear' and in the quotation of words put
into the maid's mouth—but the condescension, the slightly veiled
amusement, is in the mind of the adult writer, not the child. And when
Tanya fell in love with Gil and wanted to marry him she is compared
with 'a housemaid . . . howling to be made an honest woman of.' This
is another familiar stereotype of life 'belowstairs'—or 'in the attics',
where they slept. I shall return to this unfortunate aspect of
Lehmann's style in a later section.

But despite all the inborn prejudices of her class, she has another
dimension which shows itself, from time to time. She is a bit (not
unduly) worried about the moral basis of her society. One of the
earliest expressions of this is to be found in the story, 'A Dream of
Winter', which first appeared in *Penguin New Writing* in 1941 and
was later collected in *A Gipsy's Baby*. A lady lies ill in bed with flu.
She is well-to-do and lives in a country house where the old Squire
used to hold evening classes to improve the minds of the local people.
She has plenty of leisure, has friends with revolutionary ideas, and
is a member of the Left Book Club. A man comes to remove a swarm
of bees from the balcony outside her bedroom. He is on terms of easy
intimacy with her—rural but not servile. He has been observed, not
reproduced from a stereotype. When he uncovers the nest and takes
the honey, she feels she is merely exploiting the bees. The man says
there is very little honey to be taken. Then her 'Enemy' whispers in her
ear.

Just as I thought. Another sentimental illusion. Schemes to
produce food by magic strokes of fortune. Life doesn't arrange
stories with happy endings any more, see? *Never again*. This
source of energy whose living voice comforted you at dawn, at
dusk, saying: We work for you. Our surplus is yours, there for
the taking—vanished! You left it to accumulate, thinking:
There's time; thinking: When I will. You left it too late. What you
took for the hum of growth and plenty is nothing, you see, but
the buzz of an outworn machine running down. The workers
have eaten up their fruits, there's nothing left for you. It's no use
this time, my girl! Supplies are getting scarce for people like you.
An end, soon, of getting more than their fair share for dwellers in
country houses. Ripe gifts unearned out of traditional walls, no
more. All the while your roof was being sealed up patiently,
cunningly, with spreading plasters and waxy shrouds.

When the honey is taken it looks disgusting and the children don't like it. The social moral is obvious, but crude. The story ends with an even cruder symbolism: a bird which has been rescued from the cold kills (or maims itself) trying to escape, by flying into the fire.

The progressive cause of the day with which so many of Rosamund Lehmann's contemporaries identified themselves was to be found in Spain. Dinah (*The Echoing Grove,* 1953) married Jo, who joined the International Brigade and was killed. Dinah then devoted her life to the cause, and wrote a justification to her mother. She felt she was carrying Jo's torch and she would always be proud to think she had married a pioneer of the future, 'one of the heroes of the New People's Democracy that is going to be born.' Franco would be defeated, despite the bombs and tanks of Hitler and Mussolini and the British Government's iniquitous non-intervention policy. Dinah's language is strident, on the verge of hysteria, perhaps expressing her own tensions as well as her political disgust. It was the kind of language that sensitive people, who loathed crudity in their personal lives, seemed to adopt with the greatest of ease once the political button had been pressed. Perhaps it was a sort of self-punishment for being so well-shod.

The Common World

Here seems to be the paradox of Lehmann's work. The masses, on whose behalf it was necessary to work and sacrifice, were individually frightfully vulgar and invited contempt. Naturally, this is a highly exaggerated expression of her overt attitudes, but it does not falsify the spirit underlining them. In *The Swan in the Evening* she states that her glimpses of the common world had been rare. 'Often at week-ends or on Bank Holidays our aquatic efforts are acclaimed by trippers thronging the decks of Salter's River Steamers. Up towards Marlow, Reading, Oxford, down towards Cookham and Maidenhead glide these romantic and majestic vessels, packed with common people.' They danced, bawled in chorus, drank beer, exchanged paper hats and threw crusts and empty bottles overboard at the swans—a 'nasty vulgar habit'. This was the plebs seen through childhood eyes, and it took a long time for the impression to be softened. All through her novels runs this vein of contempt, which is not really eradicated by abstract political convictions. *The Swan* was published in 1968, by which time Miss Lehmann had suffered and learnt a great deal of charity. But she is very reserved about what she looks back at in the past.

On the other hand, she is a good observer. When she is not committed to a particular social slant, when she can be content with telling us what she sees, we are often given descriptions of working class people that impress by their fidelity and reality. She knows English life well enough to be aware that what is often stern on the outside can be gay beneath. As Olivia motors through the country-side with Rollo, her lover *(The Weather in the Streets)*, her happiness is answered by the external beauty. 'I remember a line of washing in a cottage garden—such colours, scarlet, mustard, sky-blue shifts, petticoats—all worn under grey and black clothes, I expect—extraordinary.' Like Elizabeth Bowen, she can be adept at the thumb-nail sketch. 'She had an altogether uncared-for plebeian appearance, as of a girl scrubbed perfunctorily with inferior soap and put into cast-off charity clothes'. This is sheer vision, for the girl described is in fact a social equal. There has therefore been no temptation to spoil the description with a little addition, no matter how small, such as a spoken cliché, to pin the girl down for what she is—in other words, the classifying passion has been kept at bay.

The best descriptions of working class people are to be found, perhaps unexpectedly, in two early novels written before social consciousness could blur the effect. *A Note in Music,* 1930, by no means her best work, nevertheless introduces dignified references to the unfortunate, which are set off starkly against the appalling snobbery which provides a milieu for her middle class characters. 'Men walked in quiet groups from their work, raced their whippets, lay on their backs in the sun; or wandered singly, hands thrust in their threadbare pockets, the unmistakeable stamp of the degradation of unemployment in their faces, their shoulders, their gait.' Pansy, a spare-time street-walker, is not an entirely successful creation, but she does not suffer from condescension; she represents hardship. 'How her legs ached; what a shame it was to have to work as she did, nine-thirty till six on her feet, endlessly shampooing, cutting, waving; and the tips next to nothing; and not a good class of shop, she knew that—a nasty cheap little place, a common class of people.' She looked after a weak-minded brother, who had had only one little job in ten months, and was now out of work again, with not a hope of anything else until the summer. It was partly his own incapacity, but it was also the state of the building trade. Norah visits houses on behalf of a charity—this was no particular sign of an awakening conscience, for it had been regarded as a traditional duty of the well-to-do Englishwoman to dispense charity all through the nineteenth century—and these scenes are among the most impressive in the book.

> She thought of the last house, where a woman had shouted to her
> from an upper window that she was behindhand with her
> washing and could not see her; and the one before where the
> mistress of the house, in gaping petticoat and bodice, and a filthy
> shawl wrapped round her head, had informed her with tipsy
> tears that she was far from well and must be permitted to return
> unvisited to the sofa; and the first house of all, where, besides a
> woman and some children, several men, in rags, long workless,
> sat all together by one relic of a fire, stared at her dumbly out of
> starved eyes in animal faces . . .

In *Invitation to the Waltz,* 1932—it is her best novel, for everything
in it is felt at first-hand—she is perfectly frank about the society in
which she found herself. The Curtis family was not from the top
drawer but it was comparatively fortunate. Most of the population lay
beneath them in layers, and one grew up knowing just where each
family belonged. Miss Robinson, the village dressmaker, belonged to
one of the higher layers. Her father had been manager of a department
in the mills. She therefore felt she had her position to consider: 'one
had to be wary, touchy, quick to take offence at fancied slights or
misplaced familiarity. One could pass the time of day with the wife of
one's right-hand neighbour, a market gardener, but not with the wife
of the bricklayer on one's left—a very common person.' At the
bottom, of course, were the really poor, with their masses of children,
a new baby always replacing the old baby. Wainwright the sweep's
family are described as if in a highly professional photograph—one to
balance the great lords and ladies on the wall at the Hall.

> Intensely serious they were, hoarse, wary; forlorn as a group
> strayed from another world and clinging defensively together.
> Their eyes were sharp, bright, hard, rats' eyes above high sharp
> cheekbones, their lips long, thin and flat, their skulls narrow and
> curiously knobbled. They didn't look like other people's children.
> They had hardly any hair: and undersized frames with square
> high shoulders, almost like hunchbacks, and frail legs; and they
> were enclosed in large trailing ragged clothes, swathes of trouser,
> strange adult boots that clapped and flapped as they ran.

If she could have maintained this degree of objectivity she would
have become a much more considerable writer.

Class Tension

Perhaps the tensions were too great for her. Perhaps she was too exposed to the contradictions of her time and situation. When we strike a good potential there is a temptation to expect more than it can give.

Tension in style is caused by the friction of different emotions, one of which is usually fear. Lehmann combined admiration of what was above with fear of what was below. When guilt (social guilt, not the ontological kind, which can act as a releasing agent rather than an inhibitory one) was overlaid, complications were bound to arise.

Tension rarely betrays itself in an overt manner. After all, it is part of the professional writer's skill to make the imposition which he practises as perfect as possible. A manuscript is not written once but a dozen times, and it is rare for the crudely revealing statement to be retained. There have been writers who have written the first draft in the first person to gain immediacy, and then changed it throughout to the third person. The same sort of transformation is being practised continually, though not so baldly. Even so, the odd phrase or prejudice slips through. The rest is seen in tricks of style, and the organic connection between trick and truth may only be uncovered by a special kind of training. When it is accomplished one is inclined to say: So what? One knew it before.

In *Dusty Answer* a newspaper headline is quoted: 'Triple Boating Tragedy'. 'Why were they always triple? What must it be like to be relatives and friends of a triple boating tragedy? But that was a class disaster, like a charabanc death—not general.' Here the inner disturbance ruffles the surface and peeps out. First the natural, human query: what must it feel like? And then the irrational comment on those who refuse to die alone. One doesn't have to think long to realize why class disasters are bigger and perhaps better. But what an odd moment to drop one's guard.

The tension is at its height in *The Weather in the Streets,* which is a continuation of *Invitation to the Waltz,* and follows the later fortunes of Olivia, after a gap which contained an unfortunate marriage. We have the same characters and the same milieu. The strain of contempt apparent in *A Note in Music* is found again. The contempt is rarely expressed openly yet has a savage intensity, and is paralleled by a bitterness that breaks through rather more frequently. The contempt and the bitterness can be and are turned in both directions, as though an animal is desperately at bay. This is a recognisable fact of English middle class life, where envy is masked by admiration. The bourgeoisie adores the aristocracy until it is humiliated, then turns on it fiercely.

Olivia is pregnant by her aristocratic lover, Rollo Spencer. His mother visits her to demand that the relationship should cease. (She doesn't suspect the pregnancy until the end of the interview.) But Olivia must be sacrificed to protect the façade of Spencer family life. 'Façades of virtue and principle, as an example to the lower classes. Anything may go on underneath, because you're privileged . . .' And all the time Rollo's sister Marigold was a 'drunken tart'. Olivia speaks angrily of the attempt to hide everything from Rollo's wife. 'You think it's all right to behave like her—she's so well-bred and ladylike— she must be protected. And it doesn't matter what happens to inferior people like me—we can be ill—we can be worn down—and badgered and attacked—and dropped overboard—so long as *you're* . . .' Very passionate and very true but it masks a truth that is never stated so explicitly: that the accepted relationship between the working class and the middle class is seen to be that of the middle class and the upper class too.

The bitter relationship that Olivia discovers she has towards the Spencer family, with such tragic consequences for herself, has in fact been clearly illustrated in another section of the Spencer family, though more quietly, more bearably. Mary had married beneath herself. Her husband Harry was a natural bore—'but something more separated him from the rest of them' something deeper: Harry was not out of the top drawer . . . Mary—possibly a little past her first hopeful bloom—had married out of, say, the third drawer down: her father's agent? her brother's tutor? her mother's secretary? Relatives had turned the smooth public face of acceptance upon her choice, for the sake of the family, for dear Mary's sake . . .?'

Snobbism

So what it all comes down to is that there is a strong vein of snobbism, not only apparent in Rosamund Lehmann's characters, which she intended, but also showing through her own feeling, which she did not. I hope I am charitable. She said that her daughter Sally was incapable of snobbery in any of its guises *(The Swan)*. Perhaps she wrote this because she knew that she herself was. One feels she would like this to be true of herself, and when snobbery does peep out of her writing it is truly innocent. It is not hers personally, but a product of her class, her family and its immensely privileged situation.

It expresses itself in *Dusty Answer* through a kind of self-admiring dilettantism. Next door to Judith there lived, off and on, four boys and a girl, brothers, sisters and cousins. Judith goes to Cambridge and she hears of them from time to time. Sometimes one of them, Martin, sends news. This is the atmosphere.

Julian he had scarcely seen. He thought he wrote about music for one or two weeklies, but he didn't know which. Also he had heard that he was writing a ballet, or an opera or something; but he did not suppose it was serious. . . . And Roddy. Oh, Roddy seemed to be messing about in Paris or London nearly always, doing a bit of drawing and modelling. Nobody could get him to do any work: though last year he had done some sort of theatrical work in Paris—designing some scenery or some-thing—which had been very successful. He was saying now that he would like to go on the stage.

The astonishing thing is that although Miss Lehmann is undoubtedly a sensitive person, this is the sort of writing that causes a sensitive person's flesh to creep. There is quite a lot of it, too, it is not a momentary aberration. For instance, on a continental tour during a personal crisis, Judith decides 'she must go home, be alone, find work, write a book, something. . . .' This comes from a professional writer who refers to the arts as the spasmodic production of bored people. It is not an excuse to say that these are descriptions of real people. Part of our criticism of a writer must be concerned with what he chooses to write about, what he considers worth bringing to our attention.

Judith's Cambridge is presented through distorting lenses. There is Mabel Fuller, the undergraduate from a humble background. Not one pleasant thing can be said about her. 'Earnestly her eyes beamed and glinted behind their glasses. Presumably she was kind and well-meaning, but her skin was greasy and pink was not her colour; and her lank hair smelt; and when she talked she spat.' The wretched Mabel says: 'I was so set on coming here, it meant so much to me, I want to teach, you know—if my health permits.' Mabel, judging Judith by her clothes, feels she is not a serious student: 'Most girls who come here have got to depend on their brains for a livelihood, so of course no-one's got a right to come here just to amuse themselves, have they?' Judith puts her down as a 'brain-sucker'. To do her justice, she modifies her contempt a little later and feels slightly ashamed. There is really no meeting point, apart from that of physical space: Mabel's life is an unremitting slog, and she should be despised for it, and Judith's is an emotional odyssey and oh, how beautiful! Mabel ought really to be a maid, it might improve her looks, for the maids were flaxen-haired and red-cheeked, and they smiled at Judith. 'Maids were always nice, anyway.' And then, at the other extreme, Jennifer, beautiful, admirable Jennifer, a girl with the right background and a good name, between whom and Judith there was such a strong mutual attraction. 'Christ!' says Jennifer. 'To think only a few days ago I was stalking in Scotland with my angel cousins!' Jennifer breathes Veblen all over us, Mabel can do no better than Tawney.

The range of snobbism in *A Note in Music* is immense. It would not be worth mentioning were it not for the fact that the author gives the impression of approving of most of the manifestations she records, though perhaps a little shamefacedly. Hugh and his sister Clare, visitors from the South in a northern town, are excruciating. She asks him if he mingles much in society. He laughs. 'Not much. I've dined out a few times—met some of the local snobs and magnates—Uncle Lionel's friends—played bridge—that sort of thing . . . I go to the movies with one of the clerks in the office: when he's feeling the devil of a chap he takes me on to the local dancing-hall, and we pick up a partner apiece and drink lemonade and dance divine waltzes with all the lights dimmed.'

The novel starts with Grace Fairfax's memory of the golden southern summers of her childhood—a cosy English August lawn, the garden fête. Now she lives behind a grim façade of tile-and-stucco. Grace and her friend Norah Mackay have settled down into middle-aged dullness, despised by clever young Hugh. Grace is a clergyman's daughter, still aware of her superior origins. She has married a man who holds some kind of clerical post in an office. He was the kind who wanted to keep up appearances. He insisted on dressing for dinner: it 'keeps one up to the mark'. His favourite word was 'gentleman' and a dinner jacket, however ill-fitting, proclaimed his quality, his public school past. Grace tends to make something of a cult of Oxford. Her father had been there and she saw how he harmonized with it, 'bore its stamp'. It was hard to accept their present role, that of a 'provincial couple'. They had one servant, Annie, who had served in more impressive households. One method of 'keeping up appearances' was to restrict conversation to general topics while she was in the room. This practice of 'not speaking in front of the servants' was picked on by the social rebels as a mark of extreme snobbishness—one might call it a deliberate act of alienation from one's fellow-men. It was considered hilarious. Yet would anyone discuss intimate matters in front of people they were not intimate with, whether servants or not? On the whole, it would appear to be a decent sensitivity for the feelings of others. Yet here it is treated as a joke. The underlying assumption (never explicit) was: Why worry about lower class feelings?

The inferior husbands used to give themselves away by odd turns of speech, or unacceptable behaviour, making it perfectly clear that they were not quite-quite. Tom, Grace's husband, betrayed his true nature by using such quaint expressions as 'he thanked me very civilly'. She decided that the word 'civil' did not match the family estates he liked to refer to. Norah's husband, Gerald, was a professor at the university. He had no class, and he didn't know how to ride or shoot or hold a rod. He was referred to as 'an ill-mannered boor': perhaps his brilliance had unhinged him.

The North-South contrast, an important element in English snobbery, as Orwell has pointed out, is in strong evidence in this novel, set as it is in a northern town, with some of the characters longing for the *douceurs* of the South. Grace says to sophisticated Clare: 'I used to live in the South. I think if you're born and bred a southerner you never quite get used to the climate—or anything—here. You may get to love it, but it's almost like living abroad, I think . . . You want to go home.' And again: 'It's all right with the sun. I've been thinking, if all the people could get drenched through with sunlight *once,* the expression of their faces would be different ever after.' She thinks sadly that it has already been spring in the South for a month. 'Here it gets mixed up with summer all in a week or two, and after that it's autumn again.' Clare and her brother Hugh 'had such good manners, both of them: easy, delightful manners from the South'. The views expressed here are, of course, sensible and unexceptionable, but they provide the basis for a sense of superiority that everyone knows exists and that has been expressed in fiction time and again. Perhaps because of those phrases that may unwittingly offend, 'the expression of their faces', 'easy, delightful manners from the South', the northerner has the feeling he is being patronized and reacts with a self-righteous sense of moral superiority.

The latent snobbishness in Miss Lehmann's attitude is to be seen most clearly in her stories, which were collected in *The Gipsy's Baby and Other Stories* and published in 1946. There were five stories and they had all appeared previously in *Penguin New Writing.* Two of them, the title story and 'Wonderful Holidays', are full of rather loaded class references.

'Baby' begins with three evocative paragraphs describing the home and family of Mr Wyatt, a shepherd. They bear comparison with the similar description of the Wainwright *ménage* in *Waltz.*

> Their dwelling stood by itself, with a decayed vegetable patch in front of it, and no grass, and not a flower; and behind it a sinister shed with broken palings, and some old tyres, kettles and tin basins, and a rusty bicycle frame, and a wooden box on

wheels; and potato peelings, bones, fish heads, rags and other fragments strewn about. The impression one got as one passed was of mud and yellowing cabbage stalks, and pools of water that never drained away. . . .

Mrs Wyatt accepted her circumstances in a favourable spirit, and gave birth each year to another baby Wyatt. She was a small crooked-hipped exhausted slattern with a protruding belly and black rotten stumps of teeth. . . .

(The children) had flat broad shallow skulls, sparse mousish hair—foetus hair—coming over their foreheads in a nibbled fringe, pale faces with Mongolian cheekbones and all the features laid on thin, wide and flat. Their eyes were wary, dull, yet with a surface glitter. They were very undersized and they wore strange clothes . . .'

Nearby lived three little girls, one of whom tells the story, who live in a vastly different style. 'Ladies and gentlemen to the front door, persons to the back.' Their superior way of life was expressed by their going to bed early—which, of course, the Wyatts never did. Rebecca tells her story honestly. 'I never thought of the back lane kids as children like myself: they were another species of creature, and, yes, a lower. I imagined their bodily functions must in some nameless way differ from my own.' When the children came to visit them Rebecca noticed how inhibited they were. They showed none of the spontaneous ways Rebecca and her sisters were accustomed to in their equals. They were also much less greedy. You would expect them to be more concerned with stoking up than the pampered young of the middle and upper classes, but they were not.

This is very nearly very good objective writing, but not quite: somehow it just misses. I always get the impression (an impression produced by the writing) when I read Rosamund Lehmann that although she sympathizes wholeheartedly with the poor in their trials and even enjoys their company in small doses (with brother John looking over her shoulder, maybe), she cannot disguise her feeling of, first, superiority, which was a spontaneous childhood reaction, and second, distaste. In the event her attitude is seigneurial.

But her distaste comes to the surface in what seems to me an unacceptable degree not when faced with the Wyatts, who are so far beneath her socially as to be unimportant, but when confronted with the lower middle classes. When Ivy Tulloch, the only child of the head gardener at Lady Bigham-Onslow's, is invited to tea, the wretched child (who is being brought up in the greatest gentility) gets the full force of the Lehmann scorn.

She was a fat bland child with bulbous cheeks and forehead, and we despised her prim smug booted legs and her pigtails bound with glossy bows. She had far more and smarter socks than we, and insertion and lace frills to the legs of all her knickers; whereas we had only one ornamental pair apiece, for parties. She was kept carefully from low companions, never played in the lane, and was made ever such a fuss of by her ladyship.

This paragraph really ought to be treated as a classical text for the expression of English class feeling. Compare the contempt of this with the compassion expressed for the Wyatts. There is a tone here often to be encountered in public-school writing about the council ranks. One gets the impression that these are people trying to compensate for their comforts and elegances by playing the parts of pioneers and backswoodsmen. It is the social equivalent of the comedian who wants to play Hamlet.

A favourite device employed in 'writing down' is to put odd speech into its indirect form, which makes it appear even odder. Someone says jovially, 'I don't know nothing about it', and the middle class novelist tends to write: 'He said that he didn't know nuffink about it'. (It has frequently been pointed out that educated people say *ask* and *love* while the lower orders say *arsk* and *luv*.) Rosamund Lehmann is guilty of this sort of thing. At the expense of a booking-office clerk at a country railway station (in 'Wonderful Holidays') she reports: 'she said regretfully that she couldn't think wherever Mr Hobbs could have got to.' This is mild, but it registers, for it follows the original speech rhythm in a way that would not be done by the orthodox presentation of indirect speech. Mrs Plumley, a cook, is not let off so lightly. 'He hadn't said nothing of where he was off to' are not her actual words but a report of them. This is a form of satire not used against her own class, not because it cannot be done with effect, for it can and often is ('he said he was most frightfully sorry, etc.') but because her animus doesn't run in that direction.

The Reported Speech Trick is also used to some effect in *The Echoing Grove*, where there are several instances. Madeleine reminds Jack Worthington of how he and Rickie had fought at Oxford. The landlady reported finding them locked on the floor in combat. 'So she says to herself: "Then it's murder, is it?" and she lets out a screech, and bless her if you didn't drop your hands off of one another as like as if it was the Sunday joint you'd been caught stealing. . . .' Rickie cannot resist a stream of this sort of thing when he has his long talk with Georgie near the end. 'She was ever so pleased to see him . . .'—

this is mockery, not Rickie's natural language. 'You could have knocked him down', meaning with a feather. Dinah used to read poetry 'and the fact was she did speak it nice'. Rickie uses this mode because he is recounting something told him by Rob Edwards, who is actually referred to elsewhere as 'a working- class character.' Lehmann is the only one of my six novelists who uses such naked terms, holding a section of the population apart as specimens, aware more of differences than of similarities.

There are times in 'Wonderful Holidays' when the public school 'private' humour becomes obtrusive because it is so unfunny to those outside the tribe. One feels that a sense of balance would demand that such usages should be kept to a minimum if a charge of being esoteric is to be avoided. Jane complains that her brother John is always tweaking her Sunday uniform frock (which she has to wear all the time, because her trunk has not yet arrived from school) and saying, 'What ho! for a public schoolgirl.' It is the frequency of touches like this that remove Lehmann's work from any claim to universality. She is, of course, in this story confined by her subject which is about two upper middle class families who are putting on theatricals in wartime to amuse the villagers. Mrs Ritchie says, 'Nerves are getting frayed on the committee. I hoped we could avoid class antagonism by having half gentry, half village, but it seems to be working out the opposite way. What it comes to is, the village feel we ought to be running it all for them. They're alarmed, I suppose, at the responsibility. If we butt in they think we're patronizing and if we retire they think we're snobbish. Both ways they're resentful.' Mrs Ritchie is no doubt sincere but has not enough social awareness to realize that if you see a community in terms of *village* and *gentry,* then there are only two roles open to the latter: the patronizing and the snobbish. Mrs Carmichael, her friend, has her own disasters to relate. Someone has said they have left all the dirty work to a village woman and 'of course we'd all be too stuck-up to come to the Social.' And as if to confirm this, she goes on: 'Now I suppose we'll *have* to go. And if we do they'll feel awkward and be on their best behaviour.'

It would be hard to think of a better example of a fictional theme that demands the universal approach, human compassion and human tolerance, if it is to succeed. Rosamund Lehmann could not bring these qualities to her work. She is stuck so deep in her class that her work is imprisoned by the attitudes generated by class feeling. Whatever her personal desires, whatever her public stance, she is still convinced, like little Rebecca, that 'they were another species of creature, yes, a lower.'

V

Christopher Isherwood—Routine Protest
(First Fiction: *All the Conspirators*, 1928)

The Class System Discovered

Isherwood's family name was Bradshaw-Isherwood. As a young man he knew that he was likely to inherit an estate in the North of England. At Cambridge he was inspected by what he called the Poshocracy and seemed all right. 'I didn't look like a midnight swotter, hadn't pimples or a grammar school accent, didn't wear boots; further enquiries (exceedingly tactful) disclosed a minor county family with the background of an Elizabethan "place".' On leaving Cambridge his family made him an allowance of £150 a year. 'I was adaptable; I could always find my feet. And, on the whole, I quite enjoyed my life in a community where cunning and diplomacy could always so easily defeat brute force.' In the event his adaptability was to be of more value to him than the allowance.

He must have seemed a faultless stereotype of the public schoolboy when he arrived at Cambridge. The Poshocracy could never have had any doubt about him. He was neither a Paul Pennyfeather (from Waugh's *Decline and Fall*) nor a Widmerpool (from Anthony Powell's *Music of Time* sequence). His prep school was St Edmund's at Hindhead in Surrey, from where he went on to Repton. A story called 'Gems of Belgian Architecture', written in 1927 but not published until 1966, in *Exhumations,* contains a description of an Old Boys Day. The Old Boys of the prep school (some of them still very young) speak in a jargon which is quite alien to anyone outside the private educational belt. Here is a sample.

> 'Nobody we know. Four little ticks who've been at Public Schools a term. Come back to tell their friends what it feels like to be bummed.'

'Yes, I did that too. I came down with Dog.'

'How's Dog getting on now?'

'Oh, stenching of money, as usual. He's got a flat in Knightsbridge. Every time you meet him he's driving a new make of car.'

'Is it true he's living with a lady who keeps a hatshop?'

'I hadn't heard it. Quite probably.'

'I'd heard she was an Art Photographer.'

'She'd need some art if she photographed Dog.'

'How's his brother?'

'I've only seen him once. He was playing golf with Pa at Ranelagh in complete Yankee sporting togs. He's very, very nasty.'

His first novel, *All the Conspirators,* is obviously by an immature young man whose knowledge of anything but a small section of the world is extremely limited. If we regard Isherwood as one of the outstanding members of the later *New Writing* group we will naturally look for social concern. In fact, this novel barely touches on the conditions on which Left-wing writers naturally concentrate. Isherwood was at the time far more interested in the exciting new techniques of Woolf, Forster and Joyce, and his main subject was the fate of the artist in bourgeois society. It ends with the artist symbolically confined to a wheelchair. But it was a beginning, for even here Isherwood begins to relate this particular condition to a wider social malaise.

The first hint of criticism, a satirical one, comes when an old friend of the family writes a letter to Philip urging him to return to the desk-job he has left. 'As for your employer—he and I are very old friends (we were at Harrow together!) and I am sure that you would not find anywhere a kinder or fairer man.' But Isherwood belonged to a group that was appalled by such blatant privilege, although old buffers (and young buffers like Waugh, an exact contemporary) took it for granted. In this passage we have the small beginning of something that later was to bulk very large in the work of Isherwood and his friends, the attack on a whole set of relationships that is summed up in the public school system. For the first time in English literature the opinion begins to be expressed that there may be something wrong in the mere fact of being at Harrow.

To use the Marxist jargon that was to become so widespread, Philip was 'alienated'. His alienation was spiritual rather than physical, and it was still a middle-class affair. He was aware that most of the people in his office enjoyed the life, but he detested it and regarded it as the murder of his life. The offices were not really the refuges of public-school men, as was often believed, but were a sort of non-commissioned department which supported the system and accepted occasional crumbs from the table. The public-school men were to be found in partnerships, though some had gone in at the bottom and worked up fairly rapidly—or, to be more exact, slid up. They were valuable and their role was widely advertised. But quite a lot of the more spirited men couldn't stick it—the monotony rather than the hypocrisy—and went abroad. The real work was done by the 'regular clerk type. A navvy wouldn't dirty his hands with it.'

Thus Isherwood's attitude towards his society, or the part of it he knew, was one of intellectual and emotional hatred. Philip found himself a victim. The apologists for bourgeois society are never that, of course. They are the entrepreneurs and the rentiers and they do well out of other people's work.

Towards the end of the novel Philip meets the other type of alienated man, the working man, especially the unemployed man. Philip has left home and is approached by a man who wants to sell him a printed sheet with a poem written on behalf of unemployed ex-service men. 'I dunno where I shall sleep tonight and that's stryte', he says. Nor does Philip, but he at least has some money in his pocket. It begins to rain. The two have something in common. Philip reads the poem. What it says, from the ex-soldier to the civilian, is in effect: We have nothing. You have everything.

One feels in this novel that Isherwood is running hard to keep pace with his own development; that his first contact with the unemployed, and the imaginative response it triggered, came after he had begun writing it. His autobiography, *Lions and Shadows,* 1938, shows how the process continued. It was sub-titled 'An Education in the Twenties'. The education was only partly social, but it is admirable in its honesty and self-criticism. On the whole, Isherwood was a rare bird for his time in sensing so strongly the indefensibility of the class system, although he belonged to the more fortunate section of it. Although there were others who reacted in the same way, their absolute number was small. He didn't know the answers but he knew something was wrong. A sense of guilt bothered him and was partly responsible for his inability to settle to anything for long.

He is worried again by the public schools. What attitude should he take towards them? When at Repton, 'I knew, or had known while I was there, that public-school life wasn't, in my heroic sense, a "test". It was a test, if you like, of social flexibility, of a capacity for "getting on" with one's contemporaries, of slyness, animal cunning, criminal resource—but certainly not of your fundamental "manhood" or the reverse. I *had* known this: did I know it now?' In fact, he was forgetting the inconveniently prosaic truth about the system, and began to erect a cult about it.

With his friend Philip he loved to pretend to be very rich. 'Wearing our best clothes, we would saunter down Bond St, pausing at every second shop, entering a watchmaker's to enquire the price of a gold waterproof wrist-watch, turning up our noses at a selection of seven and sixpenny ties, choosing the most expensive tobacconist's to buy a small packet of cheap cigarettes.' Such behaviour characterizes the young man whose emotion and intelligence are not properly harnessed. When a comparison representing the less fortunate world is at hand, he is appalled and feels guilty. When it is not, he reverts to boyhood type and plays at life. He forgets that others have to pay for the game.

The General Strike, however, brought the falseness of such attitudes to his attention. He called it 'the tremendous upper-middle class lark.' The Poshocrats came down from Oxford and Cambridge to take over. 'Everything was perfectly all right, really. The strikers were all right— except for a few paid agitators controlled by Moscow, and some gangs of professional roughs. The great mass of working class entered "into the spirit of the thing".' When it was over the Poshocrats went back, feeling that nothing more serious had taken place than 'a jolly sham fight with pats of butter'—a skirmish he had been involved in once at Cambridge. 'For the first time, I knew that I detested my own class: so sure of themselves, so confident that they were in the right, so grandly indifferent to the strikers' case. Most of us didn't even know why the men had struck.' Later, when holidaying in the Isle of Wight he half-consciously assumed a half-Cockney twang. This was to win the confidence of working men he used to talk to, for he had alienated himself from the hotel crowd. Nor was he the only one of his generation to adopt this type of protective coloration. One meets them today, aging professional men, going about their work at home and abroad, with this mark now stamped on them indelibly to show where once their sympathies lay.

He felt insecure. He was passing through what he deprecatingly called 'yet another of my pseudo-scientific phases of class hatred.' This particular phase was brought on by the behaviour of the rich in the hotel he stayed at. They infuriated him. In some ways they did not seem to be fully human.

Bathing, for these people, was something rather childish, slightly to be ashamed of, to be got through quickly, just before lunch, so as to leave plenty of time for the ball games which formed the really serious business of the holiday. And so, even while they were in the water, their jokes tacitly apologised for what they were doing; some bathers even behaved with an elaborately parodied childishness, just to show that they were well aware that this wasn't, in any sense, proper adult 'sport'.

Yet he belonged to them. He came from them and could not deny it. Why couldn't he join them? Why couldn't he understand them?

Why didn't I know—not coldly from the outside, but intuitively, sympathetically, from within—what it was that made them perform their grave ritual of pleasure; putting on blazers and flannels in the morning, plus-fours or white trousers in the afternoon, dinner jackets in the evening; playing tennis, golf, bridge; dancing, without a smile, the fox-trot, the tango, the blues; smoking their pipes, reading the newspapers, organizing a singsong, distributing prizes after a fancy-dress ball?

It is possible that Mr Holmes, a schoolmaster whom Isherwood greatly admired, had set a few seeds of social criticism in his mind. Although he appeared to represent no particular political point of view he passed an occasional comment which was all the more influential for its disinterestedness. He once said that dozens of brilliant scholars were rejected by Oxbridge because of their provincial accents. Perhaps this remark settled in Isherwood's mind and later was partly responsible for his experiment with Cockneyism An accent is like skin colour, it cannot be disguised. It is amazing how much else can be disguised or concealed if you set about it with sufficient energy and resource. The family described in *All the Conspirators* have no doubt about their position in the social scheme, but it was as well not to examine the reality. Mrs Lindsay, her son and daughter live in a dingy house in Bellingham Gardens, Kensington. They manage to keep servants. There is also a lodger (whose presence—or, more bluntly, whose financial assistance—makes the servants possible) but she is explained away as an old schoolfriend of Mrs Lindsay. Thus her status is disguised. The parts above the surface are never quite what they seem. The lodger, Mary Durrant, is known affectionately as Currants. She was well trained, but again it was in an area that the public did not see. She felt guilty about taking a bath if she had had one the previous day, it was such a waste of hot water. (Nothing to do with expense, of course.) Dorothy did not like her to use the gas-fire in her bedroom before dinner.

That was one wing of this vast, sprawling middle class. In the same book we meet Victor Page, whose rich uncle invites Victor's fiancée and her mother to his house in the country for a week. This time there is no lack of money, but the ghost of money ruins the visit. Mrs Lindsay is very excited but her host avoids her company. He is a rich man and detests the impoverished genteel class. The house is called Wildlands, and is a Victorian substitute for a country house. It is approached through woods surrounding the lower slopes of Hindhead. The building has two wings, one of which was a billiard room. Colonel Page knocked the other down and rebuilt it as a covered squash court. He felled a good many trees. In front of the house was a flagstaff. The whole thing was a pretence, including the name, for the most untamed creatures in the Hindhead area were stockbrokers. The life was restless and bored, what we have come to think of as 'twentyish'. People are referred to as 'ghastly bores' or 'utter duds'. The young ones drive to London or the South Coast. They go for a gallop and invite people for tennis. One cannot seriously complain of any of these activities, so what was Isherwood getting at? The answer is probably contained in a remark he made about La Paz on his return many years later from a South American journey. Immense fortunes had been made in the city and yet there seemed nothing to show for it. He wrote: 'Leaving aside all ethical considerations, all criticism of means, one must at least demand this of great wealth: that it shall create a style, a sophisticated luxury, a larger way of living—even if only for the few.' And this was what the Colonel Pages of that time failed to do.

Such a society produces its own characteristic figures. The most explicit one in Isherwood's work was a social exhibitionist named Chatsworth, in *Prater Violet,* 1946. He was the head of the Imperial Bulldog Picture Corporation, by whom Isherwood is invited to script a film. Chatsworth is constantly trying to impress—but since everyone sees through him, who is his target? There was no need to impress Isherwood, who was on his payroll. As usual, one must assume he was impressing himself, a familiar piece of narcissism which argues a state of schizophrenia. Fundamental lack of self-confidence is a disease as much as cancer or paranoia. Chatsworth's behaviour was psychologically rather than socially motivated, yet the framework of his society dictated the shape of his neurosis. Even if he has no real audience he must be able to imagine one.

When standing a treat, he orders in an unnecessarily loud voice so that heads will turn. He informs his guests that there was a little place in Soho where he keeps his claret. 'Picked up six dozen at an auction last week. I bet my butler I'd find him something better than we had in the cellar. The blighter's so damn superior but he had to admit I was right.' A superior butler is about as high as you can get in status symbolism. Monte was his spiritual home, he never cared much for Cannes. Monte had a *je ne sais quoi,* something all its own . . . 'Roulette's a damn silly game. Only fit for suckers and old women. I like chemmy, though. Lost a couple of thousand last year.' He congratulated the head waiter on the Crêpes Suzette. 'Give Alphonse my compliments, and tell him he's excelled himself.' He tries to combine the plutocratic with the democratic, with weird results. 'My wife tells me I'm a bloody Red. It just makes me sick the way most people treat servants. No consideration. Especially chauffeurs. You'd think they weren't human beings. Some of these damned snobs'll work a man to death. Get him up at all hours. He daren't call his soul his own. I can't afford it, but I keep three—two for day and the other fellow for the night.' He then produces a red morocco cigar case of beautiful workmanship and tells his guests that the cigars cost five and six each. After talking a lot of nonsense about what he'd like to do in films, with various extravagant claims, he says, 'I bet I know what Isherwood's thinking. He's right, too, blast him. I quite admit it. I'm a bloody intellectual snob.'

Mrs Lindsay, Colonel Page, Chatsworth—each was a blemish on the social body, but it was a body to which he, Isherwood, seemed to belong inextricably. What exactly could one do about it? The personal aspect of the social problem was given fuller treatment in *The Memorial,* 1932 where the unhappy relationship between Eric and his mother is a major theme. It was rooted in his growing social conscience. He was keenly aware of the poverty and injustice he saw all around him and found his mother's complacency unbearable. But there seemed precious little he could do about it.

> Nothing, nothing, he thought—seeing a tram, people shopping. Sane women with baskets choosing fish, or materials for curtains. Sensibility is an invention of the upper class, he had read, had said. Suppose one explained everything to that policeman. Don't get on with yer Ma, eh? After all, some of it could be translated into that language. But he would expect a black eye to be shown him, or a bruise inflicted by a poker.

The Memorial is a Lost Generation novel. The families of the squirearchy find themselves in straitened circumstances after the war and are unable to adapt. There is a tendency for the younger elements to turn to a bohemian kind of life: the atmosphere is one of *après moi, le déluge.* Mary, a squire's daughter, has managed to establish a kind of Left Bank existence quite successfully in her London home, which she has turned into a concert-hall-cum-art-gallery. Her daughter Anne disapproves, especially as she has to move into the music room so that they can accomodate a Central School student until she can find digs. Why couldn't the girl have made proper arrangements beforehand, asks Anne. But nobody ever did that sort of thing here. Planning is out when the future is likely to be unbearable. 'Always these last moment decisions, rushings out to get food, collect people for a party. Always this atmosphere of living in a railway station—just for the sake of living in a railway station.' Perhaps one felt nearer to the masses by pretending one's home was Waterloo.

The shadow of unemployment just touches this book, as it did the previous one, but this time it is more sombre. One is aware of its presence as a social matter, whereas in *All the Conspirators* it made a brief entry towards the end, and then only in individual terms. It has now become as opaque, and perhaps as inhuman, as a mountain range. Eric, from his rich country house background, is occupied in some unspecified social work in South Wales. He describes to politely indifferent well-to-do patrons of the arts the system of food tickets given by the Guardians. Part of the groceries obtained with the sixteen shillingsworth food ticket often had to be handed over to pay the rent. He described to his aristocratic listeners a town where fourteen of the nineteen pits had been closed down and thirteen shops in the main street had shut. Even the Chairman of the Board of Guardians was undernourished. A man who owned four houses was starving because he could get no rent and because, as a householder, he was not entitled to relief. The children were tubercular. Families of eight shared a room. The houses were mostly condemned. People lived on bread and pickles.

The Left Wing movement among writers before the war, often ridiculed today, was completely honourable. The social situation was unbearable to watch (God knows what it was like to participate in) and no decent person could turn aside. But there was little he could do. Writers made a protest, and it turned out to be a routine protest, whose positive results were slender indeed. There was a growing spirit of socialism, to which the writers contributed, but the influence of the individual is not measurable. Contemporary protest (1971) seems thin and pointless when compared with the starvation issues of those days. A writer like Isherwood, and the Isherwood figures that adorn his fiction, could do little more than acknowledge the situation and register a protest. When changes occurred they would be precipitated by forces much more powerful than those possessed by a few magazines and novels. *The Memorial* shows us these forces at work, although the movement is still slow and cumbrous. Lily married into a County family. She classified people by their attitude to the squire. Mr Askew, who kept the paper-shop, was loyal. So was Mr Hardwick, the bank manager. Mr Higham, the grocer, was not. She had heard there was a great deal of socialism in the Derbyshire village since the war. It was symbolized by the new War Memorial, which shocked her. The names of the dead were inscribed in alphabetical order, irrespective of rank. 'That was really disgraceful because in fifty years' time nobody would know who anybody was.' Her own son, Eric, was passing through a communist phase. (Unorthodox views were usually pigeonholed as 'phases' by those who did not approve of them.) He used to quote Lenin and say of the Manchester slums: 'We've no right to live when all these people are starving.' This was called talking 'priggishly'.

In every sphere of action one has to distinguish between the true and the false, which is often by no means easy. In poetry we have the poetaster (often widely praised during his lifetime), in politics the parlour socialist. There is no need to question the sincerity of the parlour socialist, for sincerity is not something as obvious as a hooked nose or even personal generosity. It may take years to discover how sincere one was in a particular area of feeling. Isherwood expressed this in *Prater Violet,* published in 1946 when the great surge towards social justice had at last been accepted on a national scale. Now was the time, a safe time, to decide how genuine one's expressed opinions had been. It began when Isherwood was trying to script a film and discovered that he didn't know how people spoke. Mock Cockney was no longer good enough. What troubled him was that he felt sure that Shakespeare and Tolstoy would have known. 'I didn't know because, for all my parlour socialism, I was a snob. I didn't know how anybody spoke, except public schoolboys and neurotic bohemians.' The same sort of difficulty arose when news of the invasion of Austria by the Nazis came through. Isherwood wanted to say something apt and significant to Bergmann, but found himself tongue-tied.

I knew what I was supposed to feel, what it was fashionable for my generation to feel. We cared about everything: fascism in Germany and Italy, the seizure of Manchuria, Indian nationalism, the Irish question, the Workers, the Negroes, the Jews. We had spread our feelings over the whole world; and I knew that mine were spread very thin. I cared—oh yes, I certainly cared—

about the Austrian socialists. But did I care as much as I said,
tried to imagine I did? No, not nearly as much . . . What is the
use of caring at all, if you aren't prepared to dedicate your life to
die? Well, perhaps it was some use. Very, very little.

These may be impeccable sentiments but they are still as far
removed from a true appreciation of the situation as the earlier ones.
The fact is, Isherwood was in a state of high moral tension which
could only be alleviated by the feelings of guilt. Now guilt requires an
object and in this case it was Isherwood himself, the feeling, thinking
person. It also requires a reference. The first one was poverty and
injustice but when it was discovered that the guilt sensation produced
no noticeable effect on the situation, a new term of reference had to be
found. This time it became a sense of personal inadequacy. From
feeling guilty about the society in which he lived and from which he
profited, Isherwood passed to a new stage where he felt guilty for not
feeling more guilt about society or in a way sufficiently intense to
produce a solution. In fact, outside the writing of fiction, at which he
quickly became expert, Isherwood only knew one thing with any sense
of personal authority—that the middle class, his own class, was
emotionally bankrupt. His next works are about Germany, beginning
in the Autumn of 1930 with a snapshot (*sc.* 'I am a camera') of a
district in Berlin where the houses are 'crammed with the tarnished
valuables and second-hand furniture of a bankrupt middle class'
(*Goodbye to Berlin,* 1939). This was Germany—but it is more than
that, it is that section of capitalist society most advanced in the decay
that is overtaking the whole of it.

Germany released much that was latent in Isherwood's mind. There
he found confirmation of the impressions he had formed about his
own class and its allies in England, but he also found something more,
something that he could never reach in England. Walter Allen in
Tradition and Dream says that 'Isherwood had to go to Germany to
find the working-class he could write about.' In England he had no
entree; in Germany he could be accepted because the main barrier
between him and them was not accent or habit but his foreignness.
Foreigners are always forgiven.

The Political Thirties

Isherwood confessed in a late novel, *Down There on a Visit,* 1962 that
when he was twenty-three he had 'liberal views, in a vague, unthought-
out way.' He had a vivid image of a society that was running to fat, an

image that he tended to introduce into some of his criticism of earlier writers. H.G. Wells hated the 'fatty conscience' of the Big House; 'the peace of the Victorian Age was a sort of fat after-dinner nap on top of many shelved problems and ignored injustices', from an essay on Stevenson. And one feels that Isherwood saw himself falling into the inevitable slot, making the Routine Protest of the decent man.

During the winter of Hitler's Munich *Putsch* and Mussolini's final campaign against democracy, of the first British Labour Government and Lenin's death, Isherwood and his friend Chalmers (*Lions and Shadows*) were utterly ignorant of the political world. Hitler's name was hardly known to a dozen people in the whole of Cambridge. Mussolini enjoyed some popularity among rugger and rowing men. 'The Labour Government and all its works were, for ourselves, comprehended in the withering word "politics" and therefore automatically dismissed as boring and vile.' In his own small world he had had a little experience of authority, enough to sicken him when he looked back from a later and more enlightened viewpoint. At Repton he had the right to cane his fags. He started with the friendliest intentions towards them but soon became peevish, alternated between good humour and bad temper and 'generally behaved like any petty office boss.' He noted that study-holders were encouraged to exercise this privilege.

We get some idea of his approach to politics and its increasing maturity from *Exhumations,* a book of short pieces put together and published in 1966. In an Introduction to the section on Vedanta and the West he said that during the mid nineteen-thirties he would have described himself as an atheist, a liberal, a supporter of the Popular Front and an advocate of armed resistance to fascism, in Spain and everywhere else. He does not appear to have joined the Communist Party though his friend Stephen Spender did on the invitation of its Secretary, Harry Pollitt, 'believing, as many of us did then, in the sincerity of its co-operation with the united front against Fascism and being willing on this account to agree to differ about the justice of the Moscow trials.' Slowly he began to adopt a more cynical view of society, one that was well expressed in a |fable| called 'The Wishing Tree', which was originally printed in *Vedanta and the West,* 1943. Children make a wish at the Kalpataru Tree. The wish is fulfilled but it is only a link in a series of wishes; as they grow older, the children never stop wishing. And it is their elders who teach them what to wish. 'As long as you wish for the right things, you may be quite sure you really want them, no matter what disturbing doubts may trouble you from time to time. Above all, you must wish continually for money

and power—more and more money, and more and more power—
because, without these two basic wishes, the whole game of wishing
becomes impossible—not only for yourself but for others as well.' By
the end of the thirties his approach had become less partisan; the fault
lay not so much in a class, not even in a system, but in an attitude that
was practically all-embracing in the West. By a different route he was
coming to conclusions similar to Galbraith's.

Although Isherwood never gives any suggestion of being a profound thinker he did not remain satisfied for long with the simplicities
of official Left Wing thought. 'A Day in Paradise', which was
published in *The Ploughshare* in 1935, was already slightly unorthodox. It describes a visit to an island in the sun, and how the
hunger and poverty are concealed by the advertising brochures.

> 'The life of the port', we read, 'is extremely typical and
> picturesque'. So we take a snapshot of the most typical of the
> children (he appears to be mentally deficient) pat him, rather
> gingerly, on the head and give him some money. Immediately,
> twenty or thirty others are after us, shrieking: 'Penny! Penny!'
> They become rather a nuisance and have to be shooed off.

Now his feeling of personal guilt intervenes. He writes from the angle
of a decent but naive traveller.

> If, just for a moment, passing through the slums of our native
> town, we are reminded of that filthy lane down by the port; if
> we remember, for an instant, our first dismayed impression of the
> island before the guide-book began to reassure us, of a sinister,
> squalid place where human beings are living as no animals
> should be allowed to live . . . then quickly the image of the
> island, as the travel-bureau and the guide-book present it, will
> slide, like a brightly-coloured magic-lantern picture between us
> and our real memories, and we shall repeat, as hundreds of
> others have repeated: 'Yes, indeed . . . it's a paradise on earth.'

Such writing is liable to make the real Party man squirm. It is not
disciplined, it is too independent in spirit, it probes too much. Anyone
who starts by having misgivings about travel brochures will very soon
express doubts about Party directives. And very soon Isherwood was
writing heresy. He did in fact swing violently to another ideological
camp. The one supremely social act, he affirmed in the concluding
passage of 'The Gita and War', first published in *Vedanta and the
West*, lay in being true to one's inner conviction: 'we can only help
others to do their duty by doing what we ourselves believe to be right.'

Later he was to accuse himself of parlour socialism, as I have already shown. ('Wasn't I a bit of a sham anyway?' he asks in *Sally Bowles*, 1937, where he writes in the first person and uses his own name.) At the most we find in this novella and *Mr Norris Changes Trains*, 1935, a mild indignation. At least he felt it. The men who made no protest at all were the guilty ones.

Mr Norris is set in Germany and has for its background the rise of Nazism and the collapse of the German Communist Party. It naturally has little to say about English social conditions, in which I am primarily interested. But it is written in the first person and gives us information about the psychological condition and growth of its author. County connections are suggested in the first chapter (similar to those in *The Memorial*). There is an aggressive democrat, a female newspaper correspondent who informs everyone that her parents kept a tobacco and sweet shop in Shepherds Bush, as if daring you to think the less of her for it. This is a new type that was emerging—impatient, rebellious, neurotically critical and extremely Left wing in opinion. In contrast Mr Norris represents the downward path, that of the rich young man of the nineties who spends a fortune in two years and is then forced to live on his wits. Mr Norris's advocacy of communism was entirely opportunist, being a way of making sufficient money to live in relative comfort without undergoing the indignity of a formal job. It may have been (perhaps unconsciously) a criticism of the rich men, even aristocrats, who hitched themselves to the Marxist bandwagon during this period. (There is a portrait of one in Anthony Powell's *Music of Time* sequence.) But Mr Norris was not so blatant, calling himself a communist 'in all but name'. He was keeping his lines of retreat open. Bradshaw, the narrator (it is part of Isherwood's family name), drifts into communist sympathies and does some work on behalf of the Party. I think it is important to realize that, judging by the tone in which the book is written, there is no strong feeling expressed, but a sense of decency demands that he should take some action, however trivial, in view of the alternatives. Bradshaw was aware of his position. 'Their passion, their strength of purpose elated me. I stood outside it. One day, perhaps, I should be with it, but never of it.' And so he did translations into English and stuck 'Vote for Thälmann, the Workers' Candidate' stickers on doors and shop windows. This was how, merely because he was a decent, sensitive young man who happened to be in Germany during the rise to power of Hitler, Isherwood became associated with the *New Writing* group.

Many decent, sensitive people were similarly affected. Orwell's political enthusiasms can be largely interpreted as the reaction of outraged decency. Most of the Left wing writers of that time were middle class innocents, and it was their innocence that eventually afflicted them and made them aware of a sense of betrayal. For every convert whose name became news there were hundreds of unsung hopefuls. Isherwood presents one in *Lions and Shadows*, 1938. Madame Cheuret had adopted an attitude of neutrality during the General Strike. 'Oh dear, why do they have to do this sort of thing? It's *so* un-cosy.' Isherwood remarks in parenthesis: 'She would have been considerably surprised if she could have seen herself, exactly ten years later, addressing a co-operative woman's meeting on the necessity for helping the Government in Spain.' This was the sector Isherwood belonged to. They began with a complete lack of interest in, even a positive distaste for, the political world, but slowly came round to conviction and commitment.

Isherwood contrasts the two periods with their associated ideologies, in a much later work, *The World in the Evening*, 1954. In 1926 the older generation were still sitting under the shadow of war—'disillusioned, bereaved, resentful'—trying to warn the rising generation of impending doom and being answered with the 'absurd heartbreaking innocent-cynical confidence of the young.' The latter were much more concerned with jazz, Dadaism, flappers, cocktails and nightclubs. Stephen's novelist wife is reminded of Lady Macduff's son, who answers his mother's question on how he will live now his father is dead with, 'As birds do, mother'. She gave her next novel this title. Her hero says: 'Stop torturing me with these terrible lamentations . . . don't keep trying to drag me into your wretched half-world of mourning . . . I have my own life. If I make a mess of it, it shall be *my* mess. I reject all your warnings, prophecies and omens of doom. I refuse to be intimidated by the past.'

Then comes Hitler, and what a change in orientation! Michael is one of the committed young, fights in Spain with the International Brigade and is wounded. His very presence throws Stephen (now a rich idler, but essentially decent) into an agony of shame. Gerda, the German refugee, whose husband is a prisoner of the Nazis, reacts bitterly against the expression of private feelings, in fiction as well as in life, in the face of so much public suffering. When Stephen asks her if she expects everyone to sit around discussing politics she exclaims, 'Politics! People are taken in concentration camps and beaten and tortured and burned like the garbage in ovens—you call that politics?' Elizabeth Rydal, the novelist, does in fact react emotionally to the situation in her own way. In a letter to a friend she writes: 'Oh, the ghastliness of these times! Mary, don't you smell *pest* in the air? It's spreading out of Germany all over Europe . . .' And later: 'Oughtn't I to be doing something to try to stop the spread of this hate-disease? Oughtn't I to be attacking it directly? But, of course, this very feeling of guilt and inadequacy is really a symptom of the disease itself. The disease is trying to paralyse you into complete inaction . . .'

Down There on a Visit, 1962, again returns to the thirties but this time Isherwood changes his emphasis. Having shown the genuine response to the international situation, he now turns to one which seems in many ways to be unreal. Dorothy was 'one of those upper middle class English girls who had caught Communism like flu. I think she really felt she wasn't worthy of her precious workers; they were purer, nobler, far more spiritually *dans le vrai* than she could ever hope to be.' Isherwood admits that just before meeting her he had himself gone through a short attack of 'worker-worship'. He found himself slipping easily into slogan-language, even after the attack had passed. The truth (what he had seen in China, which he visited with Auden) made it seem 'heartless and vile'. He still talked the language shamelessly on the lecture-platform, where he strutted mock-modestly, playing the hero. Another friend, Mary, managed to be a member of the Communist Party 'in the spirit of a catacomb Christian!' (These remarks are made in a diary purportedly kept during the Munich crisis, by which time Isherwood had presumably modified his earlier views.)

Dorothy's conversation is terribly thirtyish and immature. She brings a young German back to England with her and senses her mother's hostility to this alien influence. 'She was never rude to him—oh no!—she just treated him quite pleasantly but as if he was a servant. Of course, from her point of view, that's exactly what he *is*. She realized, instantly, he was working-class . . . He's working-class, so he's the same as a servant, and she never forgets it for one instant.' It seemed to Dorothy that the Communists were absolutely right: such people (her people!) were the class enemy. It would be necessary to liquidate them at all costs because their way of life was in fact the way of death. Poor Dorothy felt acutely uncomfortable at the thought that she came from them and had been conditioned by them so that everything she thought and felt must be permanently warped by their educational system. She is longing to say, 'Liquidate me too!' When the German boy started an affair with another woman, Dorothy was ashamed of herself for caring. 'I hate and despise myself for minding, but I do. It's all part of this ghastly way I was brought up—this awful bourgeois thing they teach you, about *owning* people . . .'

The most deliberately propagandist of Isherwood's works were his plays, which were written in collaboration with W.H. Auden. Here we can see the approach to politics, that he later came to distrust so strongly, set baldly before us. Technically he was responsible for the plotting and part of the prose but morally he was as responsible for the views expressed in the verse, which was the most vital part of these plays, as Auden. The schoolboy tone prevails throughout. Nevertheless, the immaturity is partly redeemed by the peculiar qualities of Auden's verse technique, with its unfamiliar imagery, its offhand mode of expression and its closeness to ordinary life. Isherwood's feelings about society, which have emerged in the novels which preceded the plays, is admirably expressed in a song in *The Dog Beneath the Skin*, 1935. One of the journalists says: 'All countries are the same. Everywhere you go, it's the same: Nothing but a racket!' He then begins a song which is taken up by the others.

> The General Public has no notion
>   Of what's behind the scenes.
> They vote at times with some emotion
>   But don't know what it means.
>   Doctored information
>   Is all they have to judge things by;
> The hidden situation
>   Develops secretly.

T.R. Barnes wrote of this play in *Scrutiny*: 'One agrees with most of it—it's all very true, but one is bored—the authors have not succeeded in "making familiar things new" '. This comment can be applied to all three plays and need not be challenged.

The second play, *The Ascent of F6*, 1937, bears the fiercest attack on the capitalist socio-economic system. There is a background of political change, seen through events taking place in Sudoland. General Dellaby-Couch, one of the old school, naturally does not know what is happening.

> In your father's time, Lady Isabel, a British Governor was required to rule, not to coddle a native population according to the sentimental notions of a gang of home-bred politicians. The Sudoese hillman has not changed since your father's day: take him for what he is, he's a fine fellow. He's a man and he expects to be ruled by men. . . . Show him the business end of a machine-gun and he'll—

He is interrupted by Sir James Ransom, Minister for the Colonies:

Public opinion has changed greatly, during the past twenty years, with regard to the native populations of the Empire.

While these two dither with their platitudes, Lord Stagmantle, proprietor of the *Evening Moon,* knows the truth and uses it for political ends.

The truth, Lady Isabel, is that the natives of British Sudoland would like us to go to hell—pardon my language—and stay there. The truth is that we've got fifty millions invested in the country and we don't intend to budge—not if we have to shoot every nigger from one end of the land to the other.

Despite his respect for the Sudo virtues, it is the General who massacres a crowd of unarmed natives, and it is Stagmantle, of course, who uses this event to smash the Labour Government.

No offence, General. We were out to smash the Labour Government, you know: and by God, we did! Your little stunt came in handy: any stick's good enough to beat a dog with, you know.

So much for the political situation, in which Lord Stagmantle plays the role of a cunning *éminence grise,* far beyond the capacity of a narcissistic dunderhead such as Waugh's Lord Copper.

Again the cheated public is the apathetic witness of the high tragedy. Middle class dream and middle class reality are contrasted in the lives and speech of Mr and Mrs A., shorthand for Mr and Mrs Modern Everyman. They generate an atmosphere of despair and frustration and there are no signs of any turn for the better. In a moment of vision Mrs A. sees through the shams.

> O, what's the use of your pretending?
> As if life had a chance of mending!
> There will be nothing to remember
> But the fortnight in August or early September,
> The boarding-house food, the boarding-house faces,
> The rain-spoilt picnics in the windswept places,
> The camera lost and the suspicion,
> The failure in the putting-competition,
> The silly performance on the pier—
> And it's going to happen again next year!

She asks her husband why he can't get a better job.

> My job may be small
> But I'm damned lucky to have one at all.
> When I think of those I knew in the war,

> All the fellows about my age;
> How many are earning a decent wage?
>
> There was O'Shea, the middle-weight champion; slouches
>   from bar to bar now in a battered hat, cadging
>   for drinks;
>
> There was Morgan, famous for his stories; sells ladies'
>   underwear from door to door;
> There was Polewhele, with his university education; now
>   Dan the Lavatory Man at a third-rate night-club;
>
> And Holmes in our office, well past fifty, was dismissed
>   last week to bring down expenses . . .

Now and again the A's go to their betters with questions. The answers come pat and clear, sometimes with a touch of acerbity.

> Mr A: Why is my work so dull?
> General: That is a most insubordinate remark. Every man has his job in life, and all he has to think about is doing it as well as it can be done. What is needed is loyalty, not criticism . . .

And again:

> Mr A: Why have I so little money?
> Stagmantle: Ah, I was expecting that one! I'm a practical man like yourself, and as it happens I'm a rich one, so I ought to know something about money. I know there are far too many who have too little. It's a damned shame, but there it is. That's the world we live in. But speaking quite seriously as a business man, I can tell you that money doesn't necessarily bring happiness. In fact, the more you worry about it, the unhappier you are . . .

On The Frontier, which appeared in 1938, makes a powerful onslaught on monopoly. This has always been the weakest point of socialist polemic *vis à vis* capitalism. It is difficult to know which pot is the blacker. Valerian, a great Westland industrialist and monopolist, looks out of his study window and glories in the Valerian works. He muses on the decline of the neighbouring cathedral and speaks in the imagination to one of his workers.

> Run along, little man. Lunch is ready for you in the Valerian Cafeteria. Why so anxious? You shall have every care. You may spoon in the Valerian Park, and buy the ring next day at the Valerian Stores. Then you shall settle down in a cosy Valerian villa, which I assure you, has been highly praised by architectural

experts. The Valerian School, equipped with the very latest apparatus, will educate your dear little kiddies in Patriotism and Personal Hygiene. A smart Valerian Family Runabout will take you on Sundays to picnic by the waterfall, along with several hundred others of your kind. The Valerian Bank will look after your savings, if any; our doctors will see to your health, and our funeral parlours will bury you . . . And then you talk about Socialism.

The model for Valerian is Laundauer, the Jewish business man in *Goodbye to Berlin*. Valerian's last sentence suggests that the authors were aware that there would be very little difference between Valerian Enterprises and Westland Sovcom, yet the target of their criticism remains political. It is never suggested that Mr and Mrs A. are victims of a way of life that is supported with equal enthusiasm by both parties to the political dispute.

This was only a passing phase with Isherwood. In a review of *Grapes of Wrath* he stated that overt political propaganda, however just in its conclusions, must always defeat its own artistic ends. The reason for this is that the politico-sociological case is general and the artistic instance is always particular. It is useless for the author to claim that the misfortunes of his characters are caused by a system, for the reader will reply, with every right, that it is the author who has put them in a particular situation. 'Legally speaking, it was Mr Steinbeck who murdered Casy and killed Grampa and Granma Joad.' Fiction is fiction, not life, and its truths are parallel to, but not identical with the truths of the real world. Although such an argument may be marginal to my main theme, it expresses a very important truth about much modern reviewing and criticism, where the critic bases his stand on the credibility (in his view) of the characters' actions. This is entirely a matter for the author, who has full copyright in his creations. The logical end of fashionable donnish criticism is a kind of intellectual Plotto.

Isherwood wrote about the pre-war political and social situation truthfully and engagingly, if at times a little naively. Since the war he has indulged in a certain amount of hindsight writing, which it is valuable to place alongside the more immediate impressions of the earlier work. The first work of this kind was *Prater Violet*, 1946. Isherwood is his own main character and at one stage reflects on the coming war.

Like all my friends, I said I believed that a European war was coming soon. I believed it as one believes that one will die, and yet I didn't believe. For the coming war was as unreal to me as death itself. It was unreal because I couldn't imagine anything beyond it; I refused to imagine anything; just as a spectator refuses to imagine what is behind the scenery in a theatre. The outbreak of war, like the moment of death, crossed my perspective of the future like a wall: it marked the instant total end of my imagined world.

He had a sense of foreboding which he could not particularize. Isherwood is the only one of my six authors who gives the impression of having lived through my first chapter.

Prater Violet can be read either as an amusing account of film-making or as the private agony of an Austrian caught up in the political vortex of those days. Isherwood is helping Bergmann with the script of a silly Ruritanian comedy about a flower seller and a prince. Bergmann sudenly decides that the tale is immensely significant and symbolic, and the characteristic dilemma of the intellectual in those days is spread before us. Rudolf, the prince, represents the would-be writer or artist all over Europe. His economic background is bourgeois. He is accustomed to comfort. He takes a romantic interest in the proletariat. He comes among the workers in disguise, and under false pretences. He flirts with them. Without warning his world collapses. He loses his investments, he has to face the realities of unprivileged life. He is declassed and must find a new class for shelter. This had not yet happened in England, but it will. However, he finds he is unable to cut himself free of his background.

> He wants to crawl back into the economic safety of the womb. He hates the paternal, revolutionary tradition, which reminds him of his duty as its son. His pretended love for the masses was only a flirtation, after all. He now prefers to join the ranks of the dilettante nihilists, the bohemian outlaws, who believe in nothing, except their own ego, who exist only to kill, to torture, to destroy, to make everyone as miserable as themselves—

Stodgy Old England

The England of the period between the two wars was in a state of stagnation. The impression of stagnation was greatly emphasized in the eyes of visitors from the more mobile, more restless continental countries which were suffering from wounds not yet inflicted on England. There was still a further exaggeration of emphasis when the newcomer encountered a member of Isherwood's own group, the complacent, still comfortable country house gentry. When Isherwood went to Germany he had to make an adjustment that was not demanded from most Englishmen. Looking back across the Channel, he soon saw England with continental or German eyes. England looked like a traditional family sitting round the fire making toast and warming their toes. He made little of it at the time but it seeped in, and later it emerged in the hindsight novels.

There is very little direct contrast in *Goodbye to Berlin*. There is no need of it because the reader will supply it himself. When it is expressed it is in traditional terms—for example, the reputation of English girls. Sally is an unusual English girl (it would be truer to say that she does not coincide with the continental notion of an English girl, which is as false and misleading as the English view of the French girl). Fritz tells Isherwood that Sally is an English girl who sings at the Lady Windermere, adding 'Hot stuff, believe me!' Isherwood, as a cultured Englishman, holds the continental view of the English girl (it is polite fiction, and is rarely found among the lower classes) and dutifully replies: 'That doesn't sound much like an English girl, I must say.' Sally is as aware of the prevailing myth as anyone else and even tells Fritz that she has a French mother—probably an invention, but a necessary one to build up the image she requires. Whether Sally and Isherwood believe in their own fables is uncertain. Of course, since the war the myth has been shattered. English girls are now regarded by foreign men as the most available of all Europeans, with the exception of Swedes.

If the English girl is well behaved and nicely brought up, the Englishman wears a bowler, carries an umbrella and is always accompanied by a dog, which he loves far more than any girl. One of the film men in *Prater Violet* is a dandy named Ashmeade, whose umbrella is always neatly furled. One advantage of the national stereotype is that you will always find someone who resembles it; one is enough, he will do for the whole nation. Ashmeade is sufficient to set Bergmann a-generalizing.

> You see, this umbrella of his I find extremely symbolic. It is the British respectability which thinks: 'I have my traditions, and they will protect me. Nothing unpleasant, nothing ungentlemanly, can possibly happen within my private park.' This respectable umbrella is the Englishman's wand, with which he will try to wave Hitler out of existence . . .

Of course, there is more hindsight wisdom after the event here. The egregious Chamberlain had left his mark.

But it was in *Down There on a Visit,* published in 1962, at a time when Isherwood felt English society had improved out of recognition, that he expressed himself most forcefully on the subject of English stolidity. He observes his fellow-countrymen as he returns to England by Channel steamer before the war:

> How compactly the English sit, confronting their visitors: here we are, take us or leave us—this is where you'll do things *our* way, not yours. Byron saw the last of them here. So did Wilde. You say Goodbye to them for ever and go away to fame and death among the dagoes, and they couldn't care less. Oh yes, when your name has been a household word for the past two generations, they'll concede that they used to know you—slightly. But they'll never really admit that they were wrong about you or about anything. They are indomitable, incorrigible, and so utterly self-satisfied that they no longer have to raise their voices or wave their arms when they address the lesser breeds. If you have any criticisms, they have one unanswerable answer: you can stay off our island.

It is an odd characteristic of the English that though they, as a body, know themselves to be the Chosen People of the modern world, their intellectuals tend to fall over backwards to prove it otherwise. This situation has, it is true, been modified considerably since the war. It probably has a lot to do with Splendid Isolation and Britannia Ruling the Waves, which she no longer does. But in the past no people were more contemptuous of foreigners and no set of intellectuals were more ready to see the beam in their own eyes before examining the mote in others'. It was a kind of equilibrium. Both had their foolish sides. To refuse to eat French food on the grounds that it is inferior to English is, in cultural terms, heretical, and one to which few intellectuals would subscribe. Yet Isherwood, now serving as our representative English intellectual, is quite capable of transmitting that unthinking old piece of nonsense that the English countryside has ceased to exist. He takes Dr Fisch, a refugee, for a motor tour of England, to see the 'real' England. Predictably he writes: 'The country as far as Derby isn't country at all, but a suburban building estate as yet undeveloped; petrol pumps, tudor cafés, cattle which seem as out of place as animals in a zoo.' It is perfectly easy to understand why Isherwood trots out this conventional wisdom, which is not even true today, despite the building and 'development' that has gone on over the last thirty years. It is the statement of a person who pretends to love Nature but doesn't really care—and that, regrettably, is the situation of a large section of the essentially urban English intellectual class, despite their rural retreats and hideyholes. Isherwood had early associations with Derbyshire and he worked in London (when he was in England), and thus he judged England by a thin line of tarmac or rail that stretched between the two. I once remember reading an even more stupid statement by A.J. Taylor to the effect that the nearest countryside available to an Englishman is to be found in Mexico. And so it will seem if you spend too much time in the Oxford-Paddington express.[1]

The English attitude to politics before the war was equally stolid—unimaginative if you are of one persuasion, or heroic if you are of the opposite. In *Down There On A Visit* Isherwood quotes from a diary supposedly kept during the Munich crisis. The following extract describes an English Sunday. Foreigners, of course, are in a panic.

What stodgy stolid-faced horror! The church-bells clanging to each other across the estates of some fascist bastard of a retired colonel, where the gamekeepers still fire at trespassers with shot-guns loaded with salt. Sunday lunch at the pub: roast beef and stewed plums and pink soap-cheese—served with that weary English air of 'Well, I suppose we've got to eat'—in the rapidly chilling parlour before a smoky fire. The Sunday papers seem even more ominous than in town. There was an article by Garvin called 'The Way'. (It should have been called '*I* Am the Way'). The crowd in the bar on Saturday night—to whom Hutton's record test-match score of 364 is still the most important event of the month. And yet these people are quite ready to fight if Czechoslovakia is attacked. You feel how united they are—not by a leadership or a political belief but by a common absorption in cricket, football pools, the pictorial press.

In some future age, a Chinese historian will study us and say, 'But I don't understand—how *could* such people have cared what the Nazis did?' But somehow they do care. They care with their own kind of passion, which neither the Nazis nor any other foreigners will believe in, until it's too late.

This is an example of The Diary as Art, immensely popular during the 'thirties. It should be compared in tone with the flat, bald diary which Orwell kept and which has since been published, often to the

---

1. For a sane appraisal of England by someone who has taken the trouble to look at it, see William Golding's *The Hot Gates,* especially 'Digging For Pictures.'

great disappointment of literary types. But the sentiment is the same in each case: these people don't seem to care yet they will resist and finally win through. It occurred to me that Isherwood's diary was wise after the event. In a private letter he told me that it was only slightly expanded and rewritten from a personal diary kept at the time. It was quite accurate about political events and his own reactions and moods.

All for Youth

The last section ended with a paradox. So far as Isherwood is concerned, he knew that a radical change was to come in the tone of English society. Today young people give the impression of caring much more than their parents did about what is happening to and among others. This, as one might expect, is very much to his liking. 'I am an American citizen', he wrote to me, 'but I often come over here and indeed feel that the England of 1970 is very much more "mine" than the England of 1938! I mean, it is more the country I used to want it to be.' He made a statement along the same lines to Edwina Coven, who interviewed him for *She*.

> I just feel more in contact with the young generation than with my own age group. They are implementing the things we wanted when we were young and it's as simple as that. We talk the same language. Youth's defiance of the establishment is something that I sympathize with and comprehend.

And in the Foreword to the paperback reissue of his first novel, *All the Conspirators*, in 1967 he said that the motto of the book had been: My Generation—right or wrong! He was self-consciously applying the stream-of-consciousness technique but only to the youthful characters, irrespective of whether they were to be admired or not. The older ones did not merit it. But the odd thing about Isherwood is that his sympathies have remained with the younger generation of each decade. He has refused to become an old fogey, which is to the good; but on the other hand, he has given the impression of never maturing, so that while the youthful enthusiasms of his own youth give the impression of sincerity, the youthful enthusiasms of his later life sound forced. The later work of Snow and Bowen may not always be superior in literary skill to their early work, but they always give the impression of a developing mind. Isherwood, to the contrary, gives the impression of standing still—at times, even, of being in retreat.

The post-war Isherwood always manages to work in a realistic sexual reference, which he waves like a banner: the wetness of masturbation or the groaning of intercourse. None of the others do this. Elizabeth Bowen manages to give the impression that she remains fully adjusted to the society she finds herself in (so distant from that of 1924) whereas Isherwood, who started later, has to announce his citizenship. In the thirties he took a look at his society and didn't like what he saw. He described it objectively and left it to the reader to make his decision. In *A Meeting By the River,* 1967, he treats homosexuality not as a sexual deviance but as an emblem of rebellion. Patrick loves a young man but breaks with him because he has a wife and two children.

He urges the young man to examine his own feelings and asks if it is impossible for him to love a woman.

> First ask yourself frankly, am I against heterosexual love simply because it's respectable and legal and approved of by the churches and the newspapers and all those other vested interests I hate? Sometimes I've worried about you, Tommy, fearing that you'll waste much of your wonderful vitality in defying organized Society—such a hopeless fruitless occupation!

Yet this is the kind of attitude that Isherwood often appears to be displaying himself. Either he is determined to shock the respectable sections of society or he expresses himself with such gaucheness that this is the effect he produces. A contemporary critic, W.W. Robson, has even suggested that Isherwood may be 'morally too imbecile to realise that the behaviour he describes is shocking to normal people' (*Modern English Literature,* 1970). It is in fact possible that Isherwood has lost touch so completely with the audience he used to delight that he is no longer capable of judging their responses.

He describes the new way of looking at life in *The World in the Evening* as 'High Camp'. The argument is put forward by two homosexuals, who are naturally treated with the greatest sympathy as normal parts of the landscape. High Camp is a new vision, in itself a twist from the traditional ways of looking and feeling. It has an underlying seriousness but it is necessary to make fun out of it (not of it), which is why it sometimes seems heartless. (This can happen to such an extent that George Steiner once confused Camp with laughing about concentration camps. He did this because Camp involves Black Humour and it is just conceivable that such humour might be derived from the spectacle of life in such camps—but this would be a perversion we could not possibly associate with Isherwood, though there are members of the movement who derive fun from individual, sexually motivated sadism.) One of the men says to the other, 'You're expressing what's basically serious to you in terms of fun and artifice and elegance. Baroque is largely camp about religion. The Ballet is camp about love.' What is needed, he says, is Quaker Camp. One day a genius will create it and it will enable us to comprehend the moral and spiritual side of existence.

Isherwood has seen, in his own view, three dominant stages of youthful attitude towards life: the cynical, pleasure-seeking spirit of the twenties, the serious, socially-conscious approach of the thirties, and now the post-War emergence of High Camp. He feels that the latter is not only a product of the second, but is a valuable one.

Vedanta and Society

Isherwood is differentiated from my other novelists by the profound change of direction which took place during his career. From being a socially-committed Left-winger writing of his environment with superb control he has become a disciple of the Hindu mystics writing with a considerably reduced grasp of his subject matter. It would be very interesting to know what has produced the decline in quality. On the surface, as he moves from what he obviously considers the less profound to the more profound point of view, we might reasonably expect a rise in quality. There are various possibilities. Perhaps his talent was capable of coming to terms with the lesser but failed when faced with the higher. Perhaps it is a decline in talent which might have happened anyway. Perhaps the new approach is not, after all, more profound. Perhaps Isherwood has been attracted by a philosophy which he fails to comprehend in its fuller meaning. There would be nothing remarkable in this as most Westerners, however sincerely they are attracted by Eastern thought, rarely manage to come to terms with it without in some way setting up a conflict with the still untouched, unregenerate parts of their natures.

Isherwood probably made the first step on the Eastern path through a leaning towards pacifism. The fellow-traveller of the thirties was naturally not pacifist (the tone was set by the communists who have never regarded pacifism as anything but surrender to the class enemy), but Isherwood was probably alarmed by the menace of the coming war. The idea that another world war would destroy civilization was a familiar one in those days. If his first resistance to war was utilitarian it was soon followed by resistance on a deeper, moral level. Yet he always remained tolerant and in an essay entitled 'The Gita and War' wrote that we must respect the warrior, Arjuna, because it was his earthly role. Perhaps a more radical change of belief was from a faith in the workings of the personal will to one in a mystical determinism. The last sentence of his essay on 'Vivekananda and Sarah Bernhardt' reads: 'All we *do* know is that their meeting, like every other event in this universe, did not take place by accident.' Which is a very far cry from the beliefs underlying *The Memorial*.

In 1948 he wrote an introduction for *Vedanta for the Western World,* a collection of essays by Eastern and Western writers. In it he gives an imaginary conversation between an uninitiated Isherwood and a teacher. Isherwood asks about his duty to the community and the claims of social service, and gets this reply:

> As soon as you start thinking and acting in the way I have shown you (i.e., loving the Self, the Atman, in other words, becoming aware of Reality), your life will be nothing but social service. You will be more available to your neighbours than ever before, because you will be less egotistic. You will do your duty to the community far better, because your motives will be less mixed with vanity and the desire for power and self-advertisement. You think you love some of your neighbours now. You cannot dream how you will love them all, when you begin to see the Reality within each human being, and to understand his absolute identity with yourself. What is it that your neighbour needs most? Isn't it just that reassurance, that knowledge and peace which are the objects of your search? How can you transmit them to others, until you have won them for yourself? By helping yourself you are helping mankind. By helping mankind you are helping yourself. That's the law of all spiritual progress.

Vedanta believes in many existences, here and elsewhere. An accumulation of good karma will cause the individual to be reborn in something that may be described as 'heaven' whereas bad karma is a sort of 'hell'. But there are time limits and when the karma is exhausted people are reborn on earth. Human life is the only condition in which one can create fresh karma. Elsewhere one merely enjoys or suffers the effects of one's earthly actions. At this point Isherwood tries to effect a reconciliation between the socialist and the mystic, between his early self and his reborn self. 'The socialist may disapprove of my attitude, but I thoroughly approve of his activity. I do not believe that it can produce any permanent material improvement in this world; but it is spiritually constructive, and that is all that finally matters. Right action is the language of spiritual progress.'

Isherwood's best account of his new beliefs is to be found in a little book entitled *How to Know God: the Yoga Aphorisms of Patanjali*, which he translated with the help of Swami Prabhavananda, with a commentary, and which appeared in 1953. Here I am mainly concerned with the social aspect of the beliefs, although these must be seen in their wider context. The most important difference between Yoga and modern Western psychology is that the latter does not recognize the existence of the Atman, the Godhead within man. In other respects the two approaches have a great deal in common. In Patanjali's terms, Yoga is an effort to separate the Atman (Reality) from the non-Atman (the apparent).

The power of the Word, for good and evil, has been recognized by mankind since the dawn of history. Primitive tribes enshrined it in their taboos and secret cults. Twentieth century cultures have prostituted it to the uses of politics and commercial advertisement. Verbal delusion is especially common in our society. In political speeches the delusion is often double, as the speaker believes the words correspond to one reality and the audience connects them with another; both are wrong. Instances are 'the spirit of democracy' and 'the American way of life' which are encountered constantly in newspapers and over the radio and have a wide range of meaning over the population as a whole.

We have to train the mind to concentrate, but this must be accompanied by non-attachment.

> If we try to concentrate while remaining attached to the things of this world, we shall either fail altogether or our newly acquired powers of concentration will bring us into great danger, because we shall inevitably use them for selfish, unspiritual ends. Our own epoch is witnessing a terrible demonstration of the consequences of this second alternative. Twentieth century man has concentrated upon science and technics without unlearning his attachment to nationalistic power; and so he has the secret of atomic energy—a secret which, in proper hands, would be harmless and beneficial to all, but which, in his present unregenerate state, may destroy him. The danger, as many of our more serious thinkers have pointed out, is not in the fission of the atom, it is in the human mind.

The doctrine of reincarnation is unpalatable because it makes us responsible for our condition. We prefer to blame God, or our parents, or the environment, or the political system. 'If we have been born physically or economically underprivileged we are provided with a permanent grievance, which permits us to spend a lifetime sulking and cursing our fate, and with a permanent excuse for all our own weaknesses and failures.' As a corollary of this, religious teachers are often accused of preaching passive acceptance of an unjust status quo. But Patanjali tells us not to be contented with the lot of others. Such contentment would be mere callous indifference. 'Rather, as members of a community, we have a positive duty to help less fortunate neighbours toward better and fairer living conditions.'

Yoga is also criticized because it is said to control occult powers which it never uses for the general good. But Yogi warn against the use of these powers and Sri Ramakrishna referred to them as 'heaps of rubbish'. As the powers are rarely exhibited there is also a good deal of scepticism about them but they are in fact latent within all of us and could be developed through constant practice. Western man has made a different choice, however. He has preferred to concentrate on the production of mechanical rather than pyschological power. As a result we have the telephone where we might have developed telepathy, we have the helicopter instead of levitation, and television instead of clairvoyance. Many of us regret the materialism that is expressed in such a choice and yet, for once, we may have been wise. Uncontrolled occult power might have brought us to a condition even more calamitous.

Novelists should never write about their philosophies—in their fiction, I mean. The philosophies should inform or colour the fiction. On the whole Isherwood's new beliefs are not too intrusive, yet at the same time they are not fully integrated into the action. In the brilliant pre-war novels, *Mr Norris Changes Trains* and *Goodbye to Berlin,* he never told us his views as an author (views were attributed to characters including one named Isherwood, but that is a different matter) yet we were never in doubt as to where his sympathies lay. In the post-war novels he is never crudely propagandist but some of the characters scarcely exist as credible flesh-and-blood people; they are mouthpieces—usually controlled and reasonable, but still mouthpieces. In general they give the impression of being the kind of people who keep Art Diaries, brimming with self-revelation.

The novel in which his new beliefs are presented most vigorously is *A Meeting by the River*. Oliver becomes a monk in a Hindu monastery near Calcutta, as the result of a meeting in Germany with a Swami who is now dead. At first he tries to tell the leading Swamis of the monastery how they can become more efficient. He discovered that the dye for the monks' robes was prepared by rubbing a rock against a wet piece of marble, which slowly produces a small amount, greasy and full of lumps. He points out that a lot of the dye gets washed out each time the cloth is washed, so it has to be dyed again. Why not arrange with a chemical firm to mix a large supply of fast commercial dye? It will be easier and quicker, it will ensure a uniform shade, and it will last longer. Mahanta Maharaj is amused but doesn't snub him—as, it is suggested, he merits. What would be the point of this innovation? It would save time. The Swami murmured, 'Ah yes, time—', and no more was said about the matter. With the best will in the world one finds it difficult to be impressed by this incident. Two traditions are contrasted and one doesn't even trouble to justify itself. It knows. But the man brought up in the Western tradition finds the attitude unbearably smug, for he knows that not far from the monastery is the most hopeless city in the world and he finds it difficult to excuse the squalor, the misery and the suffering by reference to eternity. He also knows that this monastery, or others of the same type, have been here for thousands of years. 'Ah yes, time . . .'

Oliver feels the same pricking of conscience. 'I told him without making any bones about it my opinion of people who try to save their own souls while neglecting the ills of their neighbours' bodies. That was how I saw the human situation then, and it seemed awfully simple to me. You only had to choose between social service and private selfishness . . .' His brother Patrick follows him, led by a fascination he scarcely understands but partly to save Oliver from sacrificing himself. 'We went into all this thing about the Red Cross and the Quakers and how the Swami had made him see that the Western concept of social service is fundamentally unsound, because it's based on judgment by results and a belief that social conditions can be permanently improved. . . .' Oliver says such a view is idiotic. Patrick says Oliver's opinion is asinine: 'Of *course* conditions can be changed permanently, for better *or* for worse—by blowing up the world, for example!' In this argument Patrick represents the early Christopher Isherwood, still unregenerate; so, in a sense, does Oliver, because he is a person who is being discarded. Patrick finally admits that he can see some sense in what Oliver is getting at but deplores his sloppy phraseology.

In this novel Isherwood never comes near giving a convincing idea of what Oliver is looking for. There is a defeatist air about the writing, as though the author knows full communication is impossible. Thus he concentrates on the tension between the brothers, which is good sense when we consider that he is writing a novel and not a thesis. But unfortunately Isherwood appears to have lost (let us still hope it may be temporary) his earlier talent for making a character come to life. He is writing within the traditional framework of the novel, there is no trace in his work of *nouvelle vague* or anti-novel, and so his success or failure must be measured by his ability to create men and women who give the impression of reality. Oliver and Patrick, and all the characters in the post-war novels, sound tired and probably look pale. Instead of meeting them in their physio-psychological selves we hear Oliver telling us what Hindus believe:

> . . . all one's work should be done symbolically, as though it was some kind of religious ritual which has no practical usefulness, only intrinsic spiritual significance as an offering to the Supreme Being or whatnot—in other words, what's important is one's attitude to the performance of the action itself, not to its results— success and failure are regarded as equally irrelevant.

There was a time when Isherwood was equally impressed by socialist thought. He did not, however, lecture us in his novels, which were good. He left it to the plays, which were not.

VI

Nancy Mitford: The Uncrossable Bridge
(First Fiction: Christmas Pudding, 1932)

The Family Background

John Crosby, the resident American humorist on the *Observer*, once called her 'that relic of the thirties'. She herself, in a postscript to 'Portrait of a French Country House', 1961 *(The Water Beetle)*, says that the English regard her as 'their chief purveyor of fairy tales'. Each claim has its element of truth: the satirical aristocrat was a genuine phenomenon of the period between the two wars, and her tales are as significant and amusing as *Goldilocks and the Three Bears*.

Socially she is a very special kind of person for in one way and another, through the great Abercorn-Devonshire-Marlborough complex she is related to just about everyone except me. Her extended family includes Lord Bicester, Lord Balniel, the late John Kennedy, Harold Macmillan, Lord Astor, Viscount Hampden of Lazards, the Earl of Lucan, Sir Max Aitken of the *Daily Express,* the late Sir Winston Churchill, Viscount Cobham, the Dukes of Buccleuch, H.C.B. Mynors, John Hare, Viscount Boyd of Guinness and Lord Kindersley (also of Lazards). There wouldn't be time to recount all the interests. Some of the relationships might be distant but all would have to be acknowledged, however distasteful some might seem.

Her fiction, except in a very specialized sense, is not autobiographical, but there are parts of it which could well be, as a reading of her sister Jessica's *Hons and Rebels* makes clear. Take, for instance, *Love in a Cold Climate*, 1949, which begins:

> I am obliged to begin this story with a brief account of the Hampton family, because it is necessary to emphasize the fact once and for all that the Hamptons were very grand as well as

rich. A glance at Burke or Debrett would be quite enough to make this clear . . .

The Hampton family was very ancient, Burke making it a bit more ancient than Debrett. 'Tall, golden-haired barons, born in wedlock and all looking very much alike, succeeded each other at Hampton, on lands which had never been bought or sold, until, in 1770 the Lord Hampton of the day brought back, from a visit to Versailles, a French bride, a Mademoiselle de Montdore . . .' Her name was taken as the title. The son was 'enormously rich, he spent enormously.' He acquired a splendid collection of art objects after the Revolution, including many pieces from the royal establishments and others looted out of the Hôtel de Montdore in the rue de Varenne. He pulled down the plain house at Hampton (built by Adam) and took to England stone by stone a Gothic *château*. He also built Montdore House in Park Lane and a castle on a crag in Aberdeenshire. There were coal mines in Northumberland, valuable and extensive house property in London, one or two docks and two million pounds sterling in the estate.

Thus the heirs of Montdore managed to combine the two most important aristocratic strains of Western Europe. Polly, the only child and contemporary heir, used to enjoy reading the *Tatler*. 'Heavenly *Tatler* day', she would say. 'I'm in and Linda's in, but not you this week.'

It was naturally a High Tory background. Jessica said that 'participation in public life at Swinbrook (the Mitford home) revolved around the Church, the Conservative Party and the House of Lords.' Mother was a staunch supporter of Conservative Party activities and campaigned at each election. 'Crowds of placid villagers were assembled on the lawn at Swinbrook House to be harangued by our uncles on the merits of the Conservative Party, and later to be fed thick meat sandwiches, pound cake, and cups of nice strong tea.' The family always had a booth at the annual Oxfordshire Conservative Fête. As usual in the aristocratic world, the family fortunes were declining, though Jessica's account of Mediterranean holidays, coming-out parties, planned World Tours, etc., etc., give little indication of the hardships actually undergone. The family had a slogan which described the decline since grandfather's day: 'From Batsford Mansion to Asthall Manor to Swinbrook House to Old Mill Cottage'. One of the most attractive features of this family was its rollicking, self-mocking humour.

In her Preface to *The Stanleys of Alderley* (a selection of family letters from 1851 to 1865) Miss Mitford relates how she was taken at the age of four to see Blanche Countess of Airlie, who asked how the child was progressing in French. When her mother confessed that instruction had not yet started, the old lady proclaimed in an awful voice: 'There is nothing so inferior as a gentlewoman who has no French.' As a household, the Mitfords had no time for the French but in later life Nancy learned to appreciate, and even over-value, their good points.

There is a recurring apoplectic figure in the novels (Uncle Matthew in the *Love* novels and General Murgatroyd in *Highland Fling*) who is, on Jessica's authority, a not too exaggerated portrait of their father, Lord Redesdale, who died in 1958. Jessica wrote: 'I developed the theory that he was a throwback to an earlier state of mankind, a missing link between the apes and *homo sapiens*. My mother confiscated my allowance for calling him "the Old Sub-Human", but he didn't really mind.' She once proposed measuring his cranium to see how it corresponded with the measurements of that old fraud, Piltdown Man, and then turning the results over to Science. 'How would you prefer to be catalogued?' she asked him. 'Would you like to be known as the Swinbrook Man, the Rutland Gate Man or the High Wycombe Man?' Farve, as they called him, loathed the younger generation, especially the literary and artistic. He called them 'sewers' and Evelyn Waugh (who became a close friend of Nancy) was one of them. Farve did not believe in 'discriminating' in the modern fashion, and this applied to foreigners more than anyone else. 'In fact, he was in general unaware of distinctions between different kinds of foreigners. When one of our cousins married an Argentinian of pure Spanish descent, he commented, "I hear that Robin's married a black".'

Adjustment to the world outside Swinbrook was not easy. The girls were given a hint in 1926 when they naturally did what they could to repel the Bolshies in the General Strike. Nancy and Pam, then in their early twenties, established a canteen in an old barn on the highway, about two miles from the house, and took alternate shifts in serving tea, hot soup and sandwiches to scabbing lorry drivers. They discovered for the first time that lorries ran all night, and every day one of them had to get out of bed in the small hours to keep the service running. Nancy received a great shock of reality when, after several rows, she got permission to study art at the Slade, and went to live in a furnished bed-sitting-room in Kensington. She went back home after a month. After only a week the room was knee-deep in underclothes for there was no-one to put them away. Jessica's shock came when she married and set up house and discovered that you have to pay for electricity.

Only a person of extraordinary resilience could have adapted to alien conditions so efficiently as Nancy Mitford has done. Above all she was saved by her superb sense of humour. I shall have occasion to refer to this and to illustrate it again and again in what follows, but before ending this section I would like to draw attention to the one subject (apart from France and the French in her later work) that draws a lyrical response from her. This is hunting, the aristocratic sport (despite what so many of its apologists have to say for it, defending it in a democratic age). When she touches on hunting, although only briefly, her tone changes from the satirical to the lyrical, as in *Pigeon Pie,* 1940 and in this passage from *The Pursuit of Love,* 1945. (She is writing about the Radletts who loved animals, used to unstop fox earths and cried about their suffering—but could not resist hunting).

> It was in their blood and bones and in my blood and bones, and nothing could eradicate it, though we knew it for a kind of original sin. For three hours that day I forgot everything except my body and my pony's body; the rushing, the scrambling, the splashing, struggling up the hills, sliding down them again, the tugging, the bucketing, the earth and the sky. I forgot everything, I could hardly have told you my name. That must be the great hold that hunting has over people, especially stupid people; it enforces an absolute concentration, both mental and physical.

There is a similarly lyrical reference to the sport in her study of Madame de Pompadour. She stated that court existence would hardly have been possible without hunting.

> It is the fashion now, among those who have never hunted, to regard it as a dull and cruel sport. Dull it is not, and for cruelty cannot compare with the long, awful journey to the gruesome slaughterhouse, against which no voice is ever raised. A day on horseback in the immeasurable forest, with its rides starring out, each ending in a blue distance, and its varying carpet of leaves and flowers: the smell of earth and horses, the cold rain on a warm face, the distant horn when the hunt seemed lost, the kill by a lake, with wild swans circling overhead, the tunes, unchanged in those woods since Charlemagne, which the hunters play over the dead beast: the gathering cold and darkness of the ride home, the lighted warmth of the arrival, the relaxed nerves and physical well-being—these things once enjoyed can never be forgotten.

It is clear that Nancy Mitford is a rather complex personality. Born in the heart of privilege, she experienced a childhood which was as intellectually restricted as that of a slum child. When cast into the outer world she rapidly formed her opinions, surprisingly enlightened ones, about what was just and what was feasible. A natural gift for satire was accompanied by a keen native intelligence. And yet, when her career as a whole is surveyed, one has a feeling of disappointment. A clue to what happened may be found in one of her volumes of the Stanley letters. Many of these are from a thoroughly unpleasant young man named Johnny, who delights in calling Indians niggers and insulting them whenever the opportunity arises. This Miss Mitford excused as boyish fun. Johnny had two brothers, Henry and Lyulph, who were radicals. Henry was also an eccentric who became a Muslim. It is the orthodox Johnny, whose opinions are fundamentally so like those of a well-behaved bank clerk of the period, whom she admires. In fact, in some respects Miss Mitford seems as essentially earthbound and conventional as Evelyn Waugh. In his teens Johnny indulged in a few escapades but quickly settled down to the dreariest orthodoxy. There is a code of behaviour which delights on first acquaintance because of its freedom and gaiety; we are all invited to laugh and clap our hands at privileged antics, but it must also be understood that these are not to continue too long, should never be integrated into an unorthodox way of life, and should never be indulged in by people below a certain social level. It is a simple 'wild oats' philosophy, and implicit in it is the recognition that two seasons of the wild should be succeeded by a life-time of the tame. And who is to do the taming? Those we laughed at while young. They are suddenly, miraculously, disclosed as wise.

An Unreal World

What appears to the rest of us as the unreality of Miss Mitford's early family life was especially in evidence in her first novels. They are satirical, but one feels the satire is not really so far removed from the actuality as might be supposed or as is generally true in this type of writing. It is easy to trace the influence of her friend Waugh, especially the Waugh of *Vile Bodies,* which appeared two years before *Christmas Pudding.* It is an account of the capers of the idle fashionable rich, amusing yet trivial. The word 'satire' is used, perhaps too glibly at times, about such works, for much depends on the author's intention and to what extent it shows. *Vile Bodies,* in the final impression, gives a critical view. It is hard to see *Christmas Pudding* as anything but a romp. Most of her shafts are spent on the older

NANCY MITFORD: THE UNCROSSABLE BRIDGE 171

generation of fuddy-duddies. The young are glamorous and realistic. The former have the money and don't know how to use it properly; the latter, who need it, don't have it. Sally Monteath is 'trying on a dress for which, unless a miracle happened, she would never be able to pay.' The drifting aimlessness of artists and writers resembles the early work of Anthony Powell. A horror is expressed of living in the country. Sometimes one is compelled to but at the price of sheer boredom. 'I don't know. After all, hundreds of people live in the country, I believe, and presumably they must occupy themselves somehow. Besides, it's patriotic not to go abroad now.' It is really a wish-fulfilment literature aimed at a readership rather more ambitious than those that used to find their fulfilment in Annie S. Swan.

One may have to live in the country because the only way out of poverty's worst moments is to stay with rich friends. These often live in the country—perhaps that's why they're rich, they have nothing to spend their money on. The idea of taking a job is not explored until her third novel. The Monteaths go down to Gloucestershire. (When they were in similar trouble on another occasion they went to Scotland.) 'Do you realize', says Sally, settling into the corner of a first class carriage, 'that from this moment we literally shan't have to put hand to pocket for six whole weeks. It's a beautiful thought.'

Noel Foster in *Wigs on the Green*, 1935, suffered the indignity of a job but not for long. He received a legacy (the gentleman's way out) and for the last time he looked round the office 'which for the last two years had been his prison.' To proclaim his new state, he treats a friend to an expensive dinner at Boulestins and ostentatiously produces a roll of ten pound notes from his pocket while fishing for his handkerchief. An aunt had left him £3,314. It is not much, by the standards of the best people, but it gives him a chance. He sets off to woo Eugenia Malmains, England's richest heiress. He fails, however, and later returns to his old job with Fruel and Whitehead. But in between came the inevitable frolic.

But social unreality is to be seen at its most intensive in *Highland Fling*, 1936. It begins with Albert Gates coming down from Oxford and going to the Ritz. 'He knew that there would never be any danger for him of settling down to a life of idleness; the fear of being bored would soon drive him, as it had done so often in the past, to some sort of activity.' Once again we see boredom as the main driving force of work or activity; rarely interest, never conscience. While he is at the Ritz a friend, Walter Monteath, comes in with Sally Dalloch with the news that they have just got engaged. They are, of course, desperately poor. Sally thinks her family will stump up £500 a year, and Walter has an equivalent amount. 'Besides, why shouldn't I do some work? If you come to think of it, lots of people do.' This is another recurring phrase: 'lots of people do', so why not us? But it is mock-humorous, a rueful admission that the chosen people have been let down by whatever gods are supposed to protect them. Walter's job lasted three days. 'I can't tell you what I suffered for three whole days. It was like a P.G. Wodehouse novel, only not funny at all, or perhaps I've no sense of humour. To begin with, I had to get up at eight every morning . . . Then, my dear, the expense! I can't tell you what it cost me in taxis alone, not to mention the suit I had to buy—a most lugubrious black affair.' The food at a restaurant called Simkins was so dreadful he had to go to the Ritz to recover. Those three days had cost him thirty pounds. So 'they struggled along as best they could on a joint income of one thousand a year.' To add to the horror, they lived in a tiny flat with no servants except an old woman and a boy who came in daily. During the first year of married life they spent double their income. Sally had to sell nearly all her jewellery. The usual romp developed when they looked after a very aristocratic, ancient and philistine house party in a Highland castle during 'the season'.

The coming of war gave Miss Mitford a chance to adapt her sense of fun to an entirely new situation. We are still concerned with a crazy aristocracy in *Pigeon Pie*, 1940, but the war situation (even if it is a phoney one) presented a wider scope than the previous one. Up to date Miss Mitford had concerned herself with sitting targets. The war situation made it necessary for everyone to do some kind of work, or at least, to pretend to. It was, in a sense, a minor social revolution or, to be more precise, a minor mental revolution within a small social group. Lady Sophia Garfield was accustomed to being driven in a Rolls-Royce by a chauffeur. She was the only child of a widowed peer who lived in seclusion, with neither telephone nor radio, in the North of Scotland. She was descended from Charles II and 'was enough of a snob to feel that this equivocal connection put her on a superior footing to Heatherley, whether he was American or German, neither country having, so far as she could remember, existed in Charles II's day.' She married Luke Garfield, an ex-diplomat who worked in the City. Sophia radiated 'an atmosphere of security and of the inevitability of upper-class status quo.' As she drives to London just before the outbreak of war she remembers her first meet, 'the autumn woods and the smell of bonfires, dead leaves and hot horses'. This is the only non-satirical idyllic passage in the whole novel. It reads like a passage strayed from another book.

When war comes her friend Rudolph (he is also her lover) says she must get a job. 'There is only one justification for people like you in a community, and that is that they should pull their weight in a war. The men must fight and the women must be nurses.' Her enemy, Olga Gogothsky (who used to be known as Baby Bagg) mentions with a shudder that in Russia the aristocracy were given over to the peasants to do as they liked with. Sophia said there must be something wrong somewhere: 'If the Duchess of Devonshire, for instance, was handed over to the peasantry to do as they liked with, they would no doubt put her in the best bedroom and get her a cup of tea.' Whose fault was it if the peasants behaved like demons? This is typical Mitford: despite her mockery of aristocratic imbeciles, despite that rather odd reference to a peasant's 'best bedroom', she was convinced that the British aristocracy were fundamentally wiser than any of its European counterparts. Hence its continued existence into 1940.

One of Sophia's friends is Fred, who is in the Cabinet. He had been to Eton, but considered himself to be in the closest contact with the man in the street, 'which was strange, considering that, except for the High Street, Windsor, and The Turl, he had hardly ever been in a street.' But business people were a different matter. Sophia had to meet and entertain them because of her husband's position in the City. 'About twice a week he obliged her to entertain or be entertained by insufferably boring business people, generally Americans.' She was not very good at it. 'He said that she treated the wives of these millionaires as if they were cottage women and she a visiting duchess. He said they were unused to being treated with condescension by the wives of much poorer men, who hoped to do business with their husbands.' In fact, she thought of them as a different species, like Rosamund Lehmann and the working class. The worst charge that could be made against a person was, as we have seen, that he was a bore. The two leading spies of this story, the Eiweisses, 'were known to be bores, on both sides of the Atlantic'. Germans were stupid, anyway. There is a reference to 'Bloomsbury's yellow front', presumably a jibe (and not unmerited) at the *New Statesman and Nation,* as it then was.

Despite her aristocratic background, Sophia rejected Nazism and was not taken in by Ribbentrop. (It is more likely that she rejected the Germans as a race; Rudolph said explicitly he was joining up to fight the Germans, not the Nazis.) Sophia said that if Chamberlain and Hitler came to an agreement and there wasn't a revolution as a result, she would emigrate. She thought the British Empire was worth fighting for. She was extremely insular (in so many ways the likeness with Waugh can be traced, but there were also outstanding differences which will be mentioned later). 'She loved England and never thought abroad was worth the trouble it took getting there.' When she hears that the Boston Brotherhood (a religious organization her husband belongs to) are holding a big dinner party at their house, with a hundred guests from every European country, she has to go out: ' . . . think of it. I mean the whole point of the war is one doesn't have to see foreigners any more.' Fred, who is now an ex-Cabinet Minister, 'used to join with her in blasting abroad, its food, its manners, its languages, its scenery, and the horrible time one had getting there.' When Fred changed his ways and talked of Federal Union, she misunderstood: 'it will be an awful bore having to rule over those fiendish foreigners, and I rather doubt if we can be bothered. Perhaps we could make the French do it for us.'

Despite the fun, there is a ground bass of cynicism running through the novel though it is too cheery and light-hearted to cause real offence. Fred talking about his Ideals is an example. If he ever regained Cabinet rank, he said, he would follow Them, not just go from one day to the next. Federal Union would be the thing. He tries to explain everything to Sophia but she is so muzzy after a good meal she can't take it all in. He outlines the scheme again and she says, 'Well, if it means the whole world is going to be ruled by the English, I'm all for it.' He explains again, taking enormous trouble—then a friend comes across and she introduces Fred as Sir Frederick Union. But on the whole, she is not to be taken in. When she is told that some terrible event will happen on Friday, as a result of the spies' schemes, she wonders what it could be: 'The assassination of some public man, for instance; although it was difficult to think of any public man whose assassination would not greatly advance the Allied cause . . .'

The Pursuit of Love, 1945, and *Love in a Cold Climate*, 1949, represent a great advance in literary skill. One can probably account for this in two ways: first of all, the characters are real, even though their actions and conversations may be just as insane as those in the earlier novels; and secondly, and perhaps deriving from the first point, there is a human sympathy and compassion in the writing which never appears in the earlier works. It is naturally difficult to illustrate such features by quotation as they are products of a total reading. The story of *The Pursuit of Love* is told by Fanny, who will one day receive £15,000 p.a. She is looked after by an aunt and spends part of her time at Alconleigh. The description of the Alconleigh estate and family illustrates the qualities of aristocratic permanence, incon-sequence and indifference with conviction. 'The table is situated, as it was, is now, and ever shall be, in the hall, in front of a huge open fire of logs.' The inconsequential behaviour of its inmates reminds one of occasional aristocrats in the work of Elizabeth Bowen. Linda attempted suicide when she was ten by eating a basket-full of yew-berries. She was 'discovered by Nanny and given mustard and water to make her sick. She was then "spoken to" by Aunt Sadie, clipped over the ear by Uncle Matthew, put to bed for two days and given a Labrador puppy . . .' Aristocratic indifference was exhibited after Fanny's mother ran away when she was only a month old 'and subsequently ran away so often, and with so many different people, that she became known to her family and friends as the Bolter; while my father's second, and presently his third, fourth and fifth wives, very naturally had no great wish to look after me.'

Meanwhile Linda's younger brother Bob never had his nose out of Debrett, his favourite book. He once told Lucille that *les origines de la famille Radlett sont perdues dans les brumes de l'antiquité*. (That was the family name of the Alconleighs.) These people are no longer merely figures of fun. They may well be absurd at times but their absurdity has acquired a credibility that had been completely lacking before. In fact, if the British aristocracy had really been like those portrayed in the earlier novels they would have disappeared before the French. I have already mentioned Mitford's conviction that the British aristocracy possessed a natural wisdom and common sense denied to its continental counterparts, and we find Fanny expressing similar sentiments in this novel. The strength of the English aristocracy (unlike the French) was that it was able to throw off its ancestors with the greatest of ease. Loyalty was to the land, not to a pedigree. 'Uncle Matthew had no doubt a large income, but it was derived from, tied up in, and a good percentage of it went back into, his land. His land was to him something sacred, and sacred above that was England.'

The aristocratic families are described with a stricter regard for truth, and less urgency to raise a laugh at any costs. As a result, wit tends to replace humour, which is a gain, for humour, though by no means inferior, requires greater delicacy of treatment. When it is laid on too thickly, as in *Highland Fling* or *Vile Bodies* the result can be exhausting—even boring, which is the major crime. The contrasting descriptions of the homes of two country lords give the reader an impression of documentary accuracy. Lord Alconleigh was a back-woodsman.

Alconleigh was a large, ugly, north-facing Georgian house, built with only one intention, that of sheltering, when the weather was too bad to be out of doors, a succession of bucolic squires, their wives, their enormous families, their dogs, their horses, their father's relict and their unmarried sisters. There was no attempt at decoration, at softening the lines, no apology for a façade, it was all as grim and bare as a barracks, stuck upon the high hillside. Within, the keynote, the theme, was death.

The latter was a reference to the interior decoration of warriors and animals, halberds and pikes and ancient muskets, heads of beasts, glass-topped cases holding medals, badges, penholders made of tiger's teeth, the hoof of a favourite horse, telegrams announcing casualties. Lord Merlin, on the other hand, was a worldly aesthete.

Merlinford nestled in a valley of south-westerly aspect, among orchards and old mellow farmhouses. It was a villa, built at about the same time as Alconleigh, but by a very different architect, and with a very different end in view. It was a house to live in, not to rush out from all day to kill enemies and animals. It was suitable for a bachelor, or a married couple with one, or at most two, beautiful, clever, delicate children. It had Angelica Kaufmann ceilings, a Chippendale staircase, furniture by Sheraton and Heppelwhite; in the hall there hung two Watteaus . . .

And there were no heads on the wall.

But if Mitford's treatment of reality is more acceptable in these two novels, there can still be no disguising the fact that the life she described was still a long way removed from that of the general population. The Radletts were always on the peak of happiness or were drowning in despair: they loved and loathed, laughed and cried, lived in a world of superlatives. There was nothing unusual in this, but the consequences were exceptional. They would go as far as they dared in teasing their father (Old Sub-Human), and sometimes he pounced in retaliation. 'Had they been poor children they would probably have been removed from their roaring, raging, whacking papa and sent to an approved home, or indeed, he himself would have been removed from them and sent to prison for refusing to educate them.' The Radlett girls, like the Mitfords, were not allowed to go to school because education was a waste of time. What they got was smuggled in by mama, with the help of a well-stocked adult library.

In *Love in a Cold Climate*, 1949, we have yet another example of that astonishing fear of poverty and eventual ruination suffered by some very rich people. Fanny (for this book is a sequel to the previous one) noted that although fortunes seemed so secure in those days it was quite normal to think that everything would soon be lost. The Radlett children lived under the shadow of the workhouse because although Uncle Matthew had about £10,000 a year gross to play with he had a financial crisis every two or three years and was quite certain in his own mind that he would end up on parish relief. Whenever he had such a crisis he used to buy a new motor car, as if to stress the unreality of his world. Lady Montdore also dreaded poverty, and tried to stop Polly marrying Boy by pointing out the abject poverty they would be reduced to. 'One's only got to look at the hopeless, dreary expression on the faces of poor people to see what it must be.' When Fanny broke with this society and married a don, Lady Montdore referred to their suburban Oxford house as a 'horrid little hovel.'

This wonderland of poverty was further explored in *The Blessing*, 1951. There is a suggestion that Sigi should be sent to Eton, so he is taken there to case the joint and meets Miles Boreley; Miles is tremendously impressed by a boy named Badger-Skeffington. He says the family is *nouveaux riches*.

> 'Now hold on, Miles that's not true. I often see Bobby Badger at my club, he's frightfully poor, it was a fearful effort to send the boy here, I believe.'
> 'Yes, I know, Uncle Hughie, the point is they are *nouveaux riches* and frightfully poor as well. There are lots like that here. Their fathers and mothers give up literally everything to send them.'
> 'Oh dear, how poor everybody seems to be, in England', said Grace. 'It's too terrible when even the *nouveaux riches* are poor.'

Grace, who married a Frenchman and lived in France and became a Francophil, is under the impression that everyone in France is rich. What it could mean is that the English rich are taxed more highly than the French—and no other people count.

Then some people's money is better than other people's money. In *Cold Climate* Lady Montdore was disgusted (and perversely pleased) when Linda Radlett's engagement to Anthony Kroesig was announced. 'What a silly girl, well, she always has been in my opinion. No place. Rich, of course, but banker's money, it comes and it goes and however much of it there may be it's not like marrying all this.' Lady Montdore was a great believer in 'all this', which meant position allied to such solid assets as acres, coal mines, real estate, jewels, silver, pictures, incunabula and so on.

Position meant privilege and the ability to carry out one's wishes. Uncle Matthew, for instance, insisted on attending the Bench on one occasion to make sure that a certain ruffian should get several years and the cat. Too many of his fellow beaks had curious modern ideas about justice, and he felt compelled to wage war on them, fortunately assisted by a retired Admiral in the neighbourhood. One must also be in a position to pull strings. Of course, everyone does this, but some people can manipulate much more influential strings than others. It's the only way to be successful, comments one of the characters. 'Luckily for me I like important people best and I get on with them like a house on fire, but even if they bored me I should have thought it my duty to cultivate them, for Montdore's sake.'

Who and what are unreal? A brief answer would be that they are those whose attitude, if persisted in for more than a short period and who are not cushioned by others (or other systems), would suffer personal disaster. Cushioning is the secret. An individual or a class whose responses are unreal may never suffer if he or it is protected. Mitford comes from such an unreal milieu. She recognized its unreality and at one stage tried to break with it, but at the same time she recognized other unrealities in other sectors of society. In *Christmas Pudding* she portrayed a bohemian set, consisting mostly of art students. 'All Marcella's arty friends lived in basement flats decorated with tasteless frescoes. There were hardly any chairs, but the floor was covered with the semi-recumbent forms of dirty young men in stained and spotted grey flannel trousers and dirty young women with long greasy hair.' One of the young men was holding forth in praise of timber camps, which were triumphs of organization and a wonderful opportunity for city clerks to enjoy outdoor life. And at the other end of the social range she noted the remoteness of Oxford.

> Nobody who has not lived in a university town can have any idea of its remoteness from the world. The dons live like monks in a cloister, outside time and space, occupied only with the daily round . . . there were some rich, worldly dons whose wives dressed at Dior, and who knew about Paris and embassies, a tiny minority on the fringe of the University—in every way; they did not even live in the town itself as we did . . . (*Don't Tell Alfred*, 1960)

It must have been difficult at times to know if there were such a thing as reality, and especially to know where it was to be found. Turning from the narrowness of life in a 'university town' (this has ceased to be a meaningful contemporary expression), she looks to embassies as a kind of lifeline. Professor Tweedledum may well have considered Sir Alfred Tweedledee a colleague in the great wide world, but others might have considered them as having more resemblance to fellow-members of a club.

The Value System

Miss Mitford's attitude to her class has exhibited ambivalent features yet fundamentally she has remained an aristocrat, convinced of the aristocratic virtues. She has also, throughout her work, tried to evaluate the aristocratic virtues, which is more than Waugh ever did, except in the most perfunctory way—and it might be suggested that this was because Miss Mitford as least knew what she was talking about at first-hand. We have a picture of the kind of aristocrat who is to be admired in Lord Montdore who was 'so much the very type of English nobleman that those who believed in aristocratic government would always begin by pointing to him as a justification of their argument.' The toughness of the English aristocracy is frequently stressed. At a ball given at Hampton Lady Montdore and her sister-in-law, Lady Patricia, exulted in it. 'Do you remember how, in the war, people used to say we should never see this sort of thing again, and yet look! Only look at the jewels!' They frankly enjoyed their privileges. One of them, sitting in a luxury car on a wet day, says: 'I love being so dry in here and seeing all those poor people so wet.' This was animal pleasure rather than sadism, a state in which honesty is rivalled by lack of imagination. The English aristocracy has managed to preserve itself by not over-indulging in thoughtless sadism.

The coming-out ritual was an accepted part of the system. Polly said, 'It was all very dull, this coming-out seems a great bore—do you enjoy it, Fanny?' Some of the girls did but, whatever their feelings, it was not something you questioned. Fanny couldn't answer Polly's question, she just knew that girls had to come out, and that was that. It was a stage in their existence like public school for boys, which had to be endured before real life could begin.

Nothing could be more natural than that the aristocracy should believe in luck as the dominant factor of social life. In *The Blessing* Grace leaves her husband, after much provocation, when she finds him in bed with another woman. She complains to her father who laughs and says what rotten luck— for the husband! Grace replies that lives can't be built entirely on luck, whereupon he gives her a little lecture on the basic principle of life in wonderland:

No good saying that, as they always are. Luck, my darling, makes the world we live in. After all, it was by luck you met Charles-Edouard in the first place (bad luck for Hughie): by luck that he came back from the war safe and sound; by luck that you had that clever|little|Sigi—by luck, indeed, that you got your mother's large blue eyes and lovely legs and not my small green eyes and bow legs. Luck is a thing you can never discount. It may be unfair, it generally is, but you can't discount it.

It was really quite logical that someone holding Nancy Mitford's views about a select class should launch the U-non-U game on the world. There had been an earlier essay in social classification during childhood, which was incorporated into *The Pursuit of Love*. The Hons were the Radlett secret society, and anyone opposed to the Hons were Counter-Hons. It was simply a reflection of the society the children were brought up in, with some qualifications. The battle-cry was 'Death to the horrible Counter-Hons!' Fanny was a natural Hon because her father was also, like Uncle Matthew, a lord. But there were many honorary Hons, people who were granted membership through merit and not descent. Linda once said, 'Kind hearts are more than coronets, and simple faith than Norman blood.' Here, unwittingly, the girls were acting out the principle which made the English aristocracy a more resilient social force than the French. Fanny was not really sure whether they believed in the principle ('we were wicked snobs in those days') but they subscribed to the general idea. As a consequence Josh, the groom, was head of the honorary Hons; he was greatly beloved and 'worth buckets of Norman blood'. Linda continued to categorize people in this way for the rest of her life. When she left Tony to run off with Christian, a communist, she said to Fanny: 'we are surrounded by comrades all day, and they are terrific Hons . . .'

The U-non-U affair was given publicity in a small book entitled *Noblesse Oblige: an Enquiry into the Identifiable Characteristics of the English Aristocracy,* 1956. It was edited by Nancy Mitford, who also contributed an essay on 'The English Aristocracy'.[1] Her social analysis is today much more interesting than the often irritating trivia of U and non-U. The essay begins:

> The English aristocracy may seem to be on the verge of decadence, but it is the only real aristocracy left in the world today.

1. Originally in *Encounter,* with Prof Alan Ross's 'U and Non-U', which set the nonsense off.

The rule of primogeniture has kept together the huge fortunes of English lords and it has fortified the class system.

> Most of the peers share the education, usage and point of view of a vast upper middle class, but the upper middle class does not, in its turn, merge imperceptibly into the middle class. There is a very definite border line, easily recognisable by hundreds of small but significant landmarks.[1]

Mitford then expresses horror at the idea of certain solecisms which may be encountered in a wider society. One must endure 'many embarrassing modern situations', such as the ejaculation of 'cheers' before drinking, or 'it was so nice seeing you' after saying goodbye. 'In silence, too, one must endure the use of the Christian name by comparative strangers and the horror of being introduced by Christian and surname without any prefix.' One's only comment can be: Poor Nancy! 'The dreadful Bye-bye has been picked up by the French, and one hears them saying *bon—alors bye-bye mon vieux*. It makes me blush for my country.' Such stupidity negates the value of what might have been a minor piece of sociological enquiry.

She has, nevertheless, in some respects an idealized view of English society (despite its horrors!) which she attributes to the good example of the aristocracy. Their effort is unrelated to money. This has communicated itself to the English with the result that 'their outlook is totally different from that of our American cousins, who have never had an aristocracy. Americans relate all effort, all work and all of life itself to the dollar. Their talk is of nothing but dollars. The English seldom sit happily chatting for hours on end about pounds. In England, public business is its own reward, nobody would go into Parliament in order to become rich, neither do riches bring public appointments. Our ambassadors to foreign states are experienced diplomatists, not socially ambitious millionairesses.' One could shoot a few holes in this if one wished but it has elements of truth. At least it appeals to acceptable values, which is more than most of Waugh's statements on behalf of the aristocracy used to do.

She remarks that the English have brought tax evasion within legal limits to a fine art.[2] Death duties can be avoided altogether if the owner of an estate gives it to his heir and then lives another five years.

1. This view is directly opposed to the orthodox one, that the English class system does not possess clearly defined boundaries.

2. Since she wrote this, M. Chaban-Delmas has shown that the French are equally capable.

The crippling effects of supertax can be overcome in various ways, especially by aristocrats because they are impervious to a sense of shame: 'shame is a bourgeois notion', she asserts.

Her interest in the minutiae of social behaviour which eventually led to the U-non-U conception can be traced in some of her earlier work. There is a letter in the collection, *The Stanleys of Alderley,* which she edited in 1939, from Johnny Stanley to Lady Stanley, dated Calcutta 20th May 1860, which reflects exactly the same attitude as she was to hold a century later.

> Campbell Beale and Hill are no friends of mine, the two latter are snobs—they talk of Lord Hay for Lord W. Hay, wear net neck-cloths, they talk about gentlemen and say dresses for gowns, they always want to give their nasty hot arms to ladies on every occasion . . .

Apart from the shift in meaning which the word 'snob' has undergone, this has the very tone of contempt of the U-battalions. Even as a child Nancy Mitford had this preoccupation, although then (to judge by information given by sister Jessica) intonation was her target. She once made up a poem illustrating the main 'refainments' of a govern-ess's speech:

> Ay huff a löft, as ay lay on may ayderdown so
> söft (tossing from sade to sade with may nasty cöff)
> ay ayther think of the löft, or of the w-h-h-h-eat
> in the tröff of the löft.

She was not, of course, the only person to find amusement in the exaggerated linguistic contortions of those who wish to assert membership of a higher class—always without success. Nor is there anything perverse in noting different speech usages—Elizabeth Bowen did it in *The Death of the Heart,* 1938, when Portia goes to stay with Anna's old governess at a seaside town and is distressed to find one of her host's daughters calling the living room 'the lounge'. The practice only becomes absurd when one idiosyncracy is for some reason regarded as superior to another idiosyncracy. Only two years later is a similar observation in Miss Mitford's *Pigeon Pie,* when Heatherley tells Sophia that her bulldog may be returned under her eiderdown. Sophia corrected the word mechanically to 'quilt', but it is the author's comment which changes an observation into a prejudice. 'She despised the word eiderdown.'

Perhaps Uncle Matthew was responsible after all. Nancy may well have laughed at him (in effect, her father) but he was too strong a personality to be ignored. There is a strong U-outburst in *The Pursuit of Love*. Uncle Matthew was against education, and he was able to give his reasons.

> Education! I was always led to suppose that no educated person ever spoke of notepaper, and yet I hear poor Fanny asking for notepaper. What is this education? Fanny talks about mirrors and mantelpieces, handbags and perfume, she takes sugar in her coffee, has a tassel on her umbrella, and I have no doubt that, if she is ever fortunate enough to catch a husband, she will call his father and mother Father and Mother. Will the wonderful education she is getting make up for all these endless pinpricks? Fancy hearing one's wife talk about notepaper—the irritation![1]

Aunt Emily defends education but nevertheless feels it her duty to put Fanny right about notepaper, which should be called writing-paper. Other faults of Fanny are that she says lunch, *en*velope and puts the milk in her tea first. Matthew also despised the expression week-end. An interesting point is that all of this goes towards the building up of Uncle Matthew as a figure of fun; some years later a similar list of faults, partly overlapping, is presented as evidence of social solecism.

It is not surprising that when Miss Mitford started her studies in eighteenth century French court life she found plenty of comparable material. Thus in *Madame de Pompadour*, 1954:

> As in all closed societies certain words and phrases were thought impossible. *Cadeau*, which should be *présent; je vous salue; aller au français* instead of *á la comédie francaise; champagne* instead of *vin de champagne; louis d'or* for *louis en or*. *Sac* was pronounced *sa, tabac, taba* (as it still is) *chez moi, cheu moi, avant hier, avant-z-hier*, and so on. It was all quite meaningless, and so was much of the Court etiquette which had come down through various dynasties and whose origins were long since forgotten. An usher opening a door stood inside it when certain people passed through, and outside for others. When the Court was campaigning the *Maréchal des Logis* allotted rooms. On certain doors he would write; *pour de Duc de X* whereas others would merely get *le Duc de X;* people would do anything to have the *pour*. The occupant of a sedan chair must stop and get out when meeting a member of the royal family. The occupant of a

1. It will be recalled that a similar catalogue had been given by L.P. Hartley eight years earlier in *The Go-Between*.

carriage, however, must stop the horses and not get out; people who got out of their carriages showed ignorance of Court customs. The Dukes were allowed to take a *carré*—the word *coussin* was tabu—to sit or kneel on in the chapel, but they must put it down crooked; only Princes of the Blood might have it straight.

And in her *Voltaire in Love*, 1957, we are given some of the precepts of the Baronne de Breteuil for the benefit of her children: do not blow your nose on your napkin (she explains that although such advice might be considered unnecessary, she had actually seen the Montesquiou brothers blow theirs on the tablecloth); break your bread, do not cut it; smash an egg-shell after eating the egg; never comb your hair in church; be careful how you pronounce the word Monseigneur, it is different according to whether he is a Prince of the Church or of the Blood. Many of these admonitions are full of good sense, but it was the categorization that delighted the author.

There was one person who deprecated her activity in this matter: this was Evelyn Waugh. Did he feel it gave too much away? In his 'Open Letter' to the editor of *Noblesse Oblige* he said that to describe Uncle Matthew was one thing but to act as a guide in these matters was 'mischievous'. Twenty-five or thirty years ago the phrases dubbed U came more naturally to most ladies and gentlemen than the non-U variety, but fashionable usage is in constant transition. If the Finns and her disciples wander through the English world with her lexicon, they will assuredly drop bricks. 'For habits of speech are not a matter of class but of society and on the whole English people do not congregate exclusively or by preference with their social equals.'[1]

Snobbery

The word 'snobbery' has undergone a slight shift in meaning during the past hundred years, as will be seen by reference to Johnny Stanley's letter quoted in the last section. For him a snob was a person who wished to give the impression that he belonged to a superior class

1. There were naturally many who were merely irritated by the vogue, "After all, it was in this putatively new and egalitarian world that thousands of persons were induced to waste their time deciding, in tones of owl-like solemnity, whether they must forgo the word 'mirror' for the compound 'looking-glass', and whether they must henceforward ridiculously refer to a built-in electric fire with a shelf above it as a 'chimney-piece' ". P. Hansford Johnson, *Cork Street, Next to the Hatter's*.

in society; to us it means a person who imagines he is superior to others because of wealth or privilege. Miss Mitford has wobbled considerably on this point but has in recent years declined into snobbism. T.H. Pear, an academic of unusual subtlety, says that her humour 'is possibly meant to be caviare to the general' (*English Social Differences*, 1955). Whether it is meant to be or not, it probably is. And David Pryce-Jones has written that 'she will probably prove to be the last writer in Europe to have made use of a duke or a marquis, unselfconsciously, as a fictional hero.' Such a remark is as rash as that of those newly elected members in 1945 who howled that there would never be another Tory government, but at least it reflects the climate of our time. Despite the humour, she writes uphill.

There are not many indications that she ever disapproved of snobbery. (After all, snobbery is found in all circles; I am here concerned with the snobbery of the 'Best People'.) The only explicit statement that can be construed in this way is to be found in her essay on Augustus Hare, which first appeared in *Horizon* in 1942, in which she deplored his 'besetting weakness', which was to exhibit the most servile reverence to anything connected with the aristocracy. But even this is suspect, for it is an example of the older type of snobbery. After all, Hare died in 1903.

Snobbery is most obtrusive in *Love in a Cold Climate*. There are one or two instances of aristocratic snobbery. Lady Montdore, for instance, always called her husband 'Montdore' to those she regarded as her equals, but to border-line cases such as the estate agent or the doctor he was Lord Montdore, even His Lordship. She never called him my husband, 'it was all part of the attitude to life that made her so generally unbeloved, a determination to show people what she considered to be their proper place and keep them in it.' She was also cheered when she learnt that some ladies were so poor that they had to live in Chelsea. There was something about that part of the world that roused her to the worst degree of uncharitableness. In bringing Polly out she was determined not to take her about much in the debutante world—'all those awful parties, SW something.'

But what roused Nancy most of all, speaking through Fanny, was Oxford. She married a don and at first looked forward to a new world, perhaps exciting, probably intelligent. She soon felt disabused. The leader of the little section of Oxford society she moved in was Norma Cozens, wife of the Waynflete Professor of Pastoral Theology. The Cozenses lived in 'the very worst kind of Banbury-Road house, depressing, with laurels.' The front door was opened by a slut and inside the hall visitors got mixed up with a large pram. It was very cold but the other ladies were décolleté to the waist behind, and had bare arms. 'Their dresses were in shades of biscuit and so were they.' The hearth was not laid for a fire but had a piece of pleated paper in the grate. The naked ladies did not seem to be cold, Apart from there being no fire, the room was terribly cheerless. The hard little sofa, the few and hard little armchairs were upholstered in a cretonne of so dim and dismal a pattern that it was hard to imagine anybody, even a Boreley, actually choosing it . . .' Norma was a Boreley, from the local squirearchy. 'There was no carpet on the floor, just a few slippery rugs, the walls were of shiny cream paint, and there were no pictures, objects or flowers to relieve the bareness.' She was introduced to three other couples, dons and their wives. 'They were ugly and not specially friendly, but no doubt, I suppose, very brilliant.' The food was so terrible that she felt very sorry for Norma, feeling something must have gone wrong—but she had many more such meals later. 'It probably began with tinned soup and ended with dry sardines on dry toast, drunk with a few drops of white wine.' The custom of leaving the men after dinner was adhered to, while the men enjoyed the only good item on the menu, excellent vintage port. The men only reappeared just before it was time to go home.

The men all knew Lord Montdore slightly but none of the women knew Lady Montdore. They all spoke as if they knew her quite well, but as if she had done each of them personally some terrible wrong. She was not popular in the county because she turned up her nose at the local squires and their wives as well as at the local tradesmen and their wares, ruthlessly importing both her guests and her groceries from London. And so Fanny came to feel herself on Lady Montdore's side against 'these hideous people'. The Boreleys and their circle naturally had their prejudices of contempt, like Lady Montdore, things 'they could not stick', such as foreigners, well-dressed women and the Labour Party. Although they could not abide the Radletts, for obvious reasons, Lord Merlin was quite a different matter. 'Dinner with Lord Merlin was recognized at Oxford as being the very pinnacle of human happiness.'

In later years Miss Mitford lived in Paris. She was there during the student riots of May 1968 and her diary was published in the *Spectator*. They upset her so much, a spring of social contempt seemed to be touched off and her reactions were irrational and hysterical. She objected to the name of the student leader, whom she called Cohen-Bandit, adding the comment that the name fitted his behaviour. One wonders how conscious this mistake was, for his name was Cohen-Bendit. But once she had made this association, she found the practice irresistible. Writing from a lofty *ancien régime* angle she had in her first entry: 'People's names are so often suitable: Montgomery, Alexander, de Gaulle, Wilson, Brown and so on.' Apart from the vulgarity of the common name gibe, does she consider William Douglas Home to be automatically a better writer than Anthony Powell? And how should we classify a Heath: as a murderer, a band-leader or a Tory prime minister? And does Mitford suggest elegance, acres or a gathering of old ladies? Admittedly this is tedious, but who started it?[1]

I don't think snobbery is an unforgivable sin—we all indulge in it, one way or another, so if we are to be prudish who would 'scape whipping? To do her justice, in her introduction to her translation of *The Princesse de Clèves* Miss Mitford said that 'like many intellectuals she was at heart a snob'—meaning Madame de Lafayette. This might be considered as a confession, if not an apology. She once heard a superior voice on the radio saying '. . . a *Daily-Telegraph*-Nancy-Mitford kind of snob.' She did not rush to arms but quietly accepted the charge, adding that in her opinion snobberies do more good than harm.

Philistinism

She grew up in a philistine atmosphere in which artists in particular were almost certain to be 'sewers'. This is unduly reflected in the early novels, where the sole aim seems to be to raise a laugh. The social criticism is too glib to be of value. Lady Bobbin's opinion of modern artists in *Christmas Pudding,* for instance, is regulation stuff. 'Some of these artists, you know (if you could call them artists, which, person-ally, I don't) would be different beings after a day's hunting, do them all the good in the world, take their minds off those hideous atrocities that they pretend to like. Diseased minds, that's what they've got, diseased minds in unhealthy bodies.' This sort of thing has been done better elsewhere, with more human understanding and psychological subtlety, notably by Anthony Powell in *From a View to a Death.* I mention it here for the record.

In this respect *Highland Fling* might well be accused of indulging that disreputable Gallic and non-English custom of shooting sitting targets. There is hardly a page in which some wretched aristocrat is

1. Here I must admit a humiliation. I went to the London telephone direc-tory hoping to find pages of Mitfords, thus proving them to be as plebean as Atkinses or Calders, but there were only three, and one of them was a Brigadier.

not popped off and prepared for the pot. For example, the guests at Dalloch Castle are marshalled into Lord Craigdalloch's study to listen to the wireless. After Grieg, it is announced that Miss Sackville-West would give readings from T.S. Eliot. 'Tripe!' said the general, and turned it off. He then began to arrange the next day's shooting. Monteath, a poet, and Gates, an artist, are despised because they don't shoot. 'Just as well, from the look of them', is the predictable comment. General Murgatroyd asks if that 'fella Gates' were an aesthete. Monteath said he hoped they all were, whereupon the General snorted and told Captain Chadlington how he had once played a salmon for two hours. On another occasion Gates starts reading *The Testament of Beauty* during a shoot and mischievously suggests that the General has read it. Not surprisingly he has never heard of it, although it is by the Poet Laureate himself, and therefore part of the Establishment. The general has an answer ready: 'I expect it's immoral stuff, anyway. Kipling ought to be the Poet Laureate, to my mind.'

But if the old guard are philistine, the younger set can be idiotically pretentious. Gates tells Lady Prague that the Dutch School was one of the many sins against art that have been perpetrated through the ages. Lady Prague herself dismisses a beautiful wax model as a 'dust trap'. The ordinary Society art-lover is typified by Lady Brenda. 'She reads few novels, but a great many "lives" and "memoirs". Her favourite novelists are Galsworthy, Masefield, David Garnett and Maurois. She loves "modern pictures, especially flower pictures", and admires some of John's portraits, but thinks Orpen the finest living artist. She has never been to the Tate Gallery, but always means to go.' Gates says that she is so overbred that there is no sex or brain left, only nerves and the herd instinct. 'There are so many like that in English Society, a sufficiently uninteresting species.'

That was in 1936. Fifteen years later, in *The Blessing,* the target has changed completely. It is no longer the traditional taste, formed by the nineteenth century, but the new aggressive Left wing orthodoxy which takes a beating. Miss Mitford had been through the new twentieth century fashions and come out on the other side, so to speak. Ed Spain was a leading London intellectual, known to his contemporaries as the Captain or the Old Salt. A product of Eton and Oxford, he had bought an old suburban playhouse called the Royal George. He attracted a band of faithful followers, clever young women all more or less connected with the stage and all more or less in love with the Captain. One of the Captain's main problems was to know where to put the grand young men of literature and the arts at a first night. His own box only held four. 'Neither he nor the crew were ever likely to forget the first night of *Factory 46* when Jiri Mucha, Nanos Valaoritis, Umbro Apollonio, Chun Chan Yeh and Odysseus Sikelberg had all graciously announced their intention of being present. The situation was saved by Sikelberg getting mumps, but only at the very last minute.'

Miss Mitford really let herself go on the Crew. One feels there is more than normal satire here, there is a good dose of bitterness working itself out. Possibly it is the disillusionment and weariness felt by many writers, artists and critics these days when they finally realize that what they had believed to be aesthetic emotions and motives turn out to be propagandist or even pathological. Here is the Crew.

> They looked very much alike, and might have been a large family of sisters; their faces were partially hidden behind curtains of dusty blonde hair, features more or less obscured from view, and they were all dressed alike in duffle coats and short trousers, with bare feet, blue and rather large, loosely connected to unnaturally thin ankles. Their demeanour was that of an extreme sulkiness, and indeed they looked as if they might be on the verge of mutiny. But this appearance was quite misleading, the Captain had them well in hand; they hopped to it at the merest glance from him, emptying ash-trays and bringing more bottles off the ice. The Royal George, if not always a happy ship, was an intensely disciplined one . . . the Crew added but little to the gaiety of the party. They sat in silent groups combing the dusty veils over their faces and thinking clever thoughts about *The Book of the It*, *The Sheldonian Synthesis*, *The Literature of Extreme Situations* and other neglected masterpieces.

Then who are the Philistines? The Crew despised Grace and made no effort to conceal it. They saw life through Marx-coloured spectacles and to them Grace was the personification of the rich bourgeoisie, whom they despised. As a younger Grace would almost certainly have joined in the baiting of General Murgatroyd and his circle, there is an element of poetic justice here. In fact, each generation of rebels tends to become the next generation's reactionaries.

Political Excursions

Nancy was genuinely appalled by Fascism and wrote a novel, *Wigs on the Green,* 1935, which tries to kill it with mockery. Eugenia Malmains is based on her own sister, Unity. She stands on an upturned washtub on Chalford village green and harangues a dozen aged yokels.

> 'Britons, awake! Arise, oh British lion! The Union Jack Movement is a youth movement, we are tired of the old. We see things through their eyes no longer. We see nothing admirable in that debating society of aged and corrupt men called Parliament which muddles our great Empire into wars or treaties, dropping one by one the jewels from its crown, casting away its glorious colonies, its hitherto undenied supremacy at sea, its prestige abroad, its prosperity at home, and all according to each vacilating whim of some octogenarian statesman's mistress . . .'

But there she had to stop because Nanny, the traditional upholder of social morality among the aristocracy, called her to order. We are left in no doubt of Miss Mitford's opinion of such puerilities. But the novel never rises above this level of knockabout comedy. Nor was there anything new in Eugenia's criticism of Parliament. There had been similar heavy-handed ridicule of the House of Lords in *Highland Fling*. 'The girl's a lunatic but she's not stupid', said Jasper of Eugenia. There is a hint here of Nancy's bewilderment at the conduct of her often admired sister. Jasper later remarks portentously, 'Perhaps you are not aware that Social Unionism is now sweeping the world as Liberalism swept the world of the eighteenth century.'

It is not quite clear what is meant by Social Unionism. Perhaps nothing specific is meant by the term. In any case, the reference to liberalism in the eighteenth century is scarcely accurate. Nancy Mitford never became a very knowledgeable politician though she was at times a passionate one. It seems likely that the threat of Fascism roused her political conscience, but such arousal was by no means a guarantee of socialist faith. Like many other aristocrats, she expressed loathing of the commercial spirit, and to this extent resisted the spirit of monopoly capitalism. But it is natural for an aristocrat to abhor the system that has destroyed it over most of the world's surface. Aristocrats are as keen on money as anyone else, but when they are sufficiently secure (as they were in their heyday, when group valuations were established), they have no need to care about money. In *The Pursuit of Love* Linda, the daughter of the backwoods peer, Lord Alconleigh, married Tony Kroesig, a financier's son, to the consternation of her family. Later she tired of him and left him but in the meantime the commercial spirit came in for some hard knocks.

> Inwardly their spirit was utterly commercial, everything was seen by them in terms of money. It was their barrier, their defence,

their hope for the future, their support for the present, it raised them above their fellowmen, and with it they warded off evil. The only mental qualities that they respected were those which produced money in substantial quantities, it was their one criterion of success, it was power and it was glory. To say that a man was poor was to label him a rotter, bad at his job, idle, feckless, immoral.

This kind of emotionalism made the working class seem the natural allies of the aristocracy. Both were in opposition. Then there is a kind of upper-class simplicism which insists on equating the real poverty of the working class with the imagined 'poverty' of those whose dividends are not as productive as they used to be.

Tony made no bones about his hatred and distrust of the workers. While full of grandiose schemes for the improvement of conditions among 'capitalists', he believed that the man in the street should be covered by machine guns. This was not possible owing to the weakness in the past of the great Whig families, so the ordinary man 'must be doped into submission with the fiction that huge reforms, to be engineered by the Conservative party, were always just round the next corner.' With their minds concentrated on the constant acquisition of wealth, their taste was deplorable. The Kroesig home, The Planes (in Surrey, which the Radletts, like Elizabeth Bowen's Lady Naylor, did not consider 'the country') was horrible. It was an overgrown cottage with large rooms, low ceilings, small windows with diamond panes, uneven floorboards, furnished in neither good nor bad taste but in no taste at all, not even comfortable, with a garden that 'would be a lady water-colourist's heaven', herbaceous borders, rockeries and water-gardens carried to the perfection of vulgarity, a riot of huge and hideous flowers, each bloom twice as large and three times as brilliant as it should have been and if possible of a different colour from that which nature intended. It was only bearable in winter when the snow merged it with the landscape; in other seasons it rivalled glorious Technicolor. Nancy Mitford must have felt this was the portrait of a Fascist. He was the Enemy. And so (it could be worked out by a kind of social algebra) this made her a Socialist. *Faute de mieux*, in all probability.

The rich have a vague idea at the back of their minds (but it is constantly there) that if they behave too outrageously socialism will take hold. For example, in *Christmas Pudding* Lady Bobbin declares herself against unlimited champagne at parties because it was 'just the very sort of thing that breeds socialism in the country.' Nancy, like Fanny in the *Love* novels, grew up against this kind of background, which she later learned to laugh at—but laughing at an attitude certainly does not eradicate it. Fanny completes the transition from backwoods girl to modern intellectual by marrying a don with the result that she describes herself as an intellectual pink, the two of them 'enthusiastic agreers with the *New Statesman* . . .' Nancy herself apparently gained a reputation among her set for being too advanced. In his 'Open Letter' Waugh chides her gently for living 'so remote from the scene you describe' and adds a much stronger reproof, that she has become a socialist.

What exactly was entailed by her socialism? It is treated tangentially, never in anything but a chatty way, in the novels—if we are to assume, as I think we may, that Fanny bears a close resemblance to the author. In all probability her socialism was of a kind that would have aroused no comment in a less privileged environment. Jessica supplies a little information in *Hons and Rebels*. Nancy was an elder sister and had pro-Labour friends, but Jessica found them disappointing. She probably expected something romantic, even Byronic, from them. 'When they discussed politics they seemed to support socialism, but as far as I could see they never really did anything about it. I felt they didn't take anything very seriously. They tore down old standards on every hand, they jibed and satirized and talked fast and long, but that seemed to be about all.' It sounds like the familiar adolescent game. Anyway, Nancy couldn't campaign for the Labour Party because it would upset her parents and also be frightfully boring! No doubt her socialism received a jolt when a Labour Government began putting socialism into practice, just as many Communists felt obliged to leave the Party when the Russians behaved consistently over Hungary in 1956. During the past thirty years there has been a fairly large group of butterfly socialists and communists with extremely frail wings. Their original reasons for affiliation are individual and varied, and can often be traced to the nursery. Perhaps the most successful presentation of the type in fiction is Anthony Powell's Erridge Lord Warminster who was an aristocratic Left Winger until the actual taste of war socialism sent him scuttling to his retreat.

There is a suggestion in *The Blessing*, 1951, that Miss Mitford found the democratic cameraderie of the new world acceptable and even amusing. The relationship between Grace Allingham and her Nanny (who later becomes Nanny to Grace's son, Sigi, for aristocrats and nannies provide parallel dynasties) is, at a superficial glance, remarkably close. It is the consequence of the war situation, when an ex-farm labourer sleeps in the next bunk to an ex-public school prefect —at least, for a time. Here is a fragment of conversation between Grace and Nanny:

> 'Run me a bath darling. I'm going out to dinner with that French-man."
>
> 'Are you, dear? And what's his name?'
>
> 'Bother. I never asked him.'
>
> 'Oh well', said Nanny, 'one French name is very much like another, I dare say.'

It doesn't amount to much. It is probably rather daring, like jumping into the river fully clothed after an all-night party. Rather oddly, the intimacy to be found in Waugh among people of backgrounds which differ just as widely is much more respectful, on both sides.

Nancy Mitford's brief encounter with socialism and her acceptance of democratic values does not really impress for long. It is one thing to be sorry for the poor but quite another to accept an improvement in their condition. There are a lot of factors involved, both economic and psychological. There is a brief hint in *The Pursuit of Love*, 1945, that her concern with these matters is basically trivial. I have drawn attention before to the completely different standards of poverty ac-knowledged by the rich for themselves and for others. This ambivalence is always to be encountered among those whose avowed principles in such matters are not completely sincere. Linda tends to speak of the idle rich young men in London who had been pensioned off by their relations in the same terms as she uses for the genuine unemployed. But if there is only a hint in this novel, by the time *Don't Tell Alfred* appears fifteen years later it has become a whine. Fanny's boys run away from Eton and take jobs as packers in a razor factory. Northey, Fanny's private secretary, comments that they 'were getting £9 a week which, incidentally, makes skilled secretarial work in embassies seem rather underpaid . . .' We are not told how much more a skilled secretary in an embassy ought to get, but there is a suggestion that some sacred privilege has been upset. It is when the taxi-drivers are considered, however, that the *ancien régime* suddenly and viciously brandishes its fist. Uncle Matthew had an arrangement with a taxi-driver, who spent his off-time in a shelter which Nancy calls sarcastically the Rest and Culture Hall. She is convinced that the cabbies did themselves well there and comments in parenthesis: 'I often feel pleased to remember this when waiting in a bitter wind for one of them to finish his nuts and wine.' Once upon a time the cabby probably had nothing to drink; now he has a cup of tea. Once upon a time Nancy Mitford was sorry for his condition; now she writhes at the thought of his nuts and wine. Such a remark is on an exact level with the complaints quoted by Priestley (see my first chapter) of pre-war miners drinking champagne.

Foreigners

Nancy Mitford was brought up in an environment that took it for granted that foreigners were inferior to Englishmen. Uncle Matthew is the chief exponent of this point of view and he is still going strong even in her last novel, *Don't Tell Alfred*. Discussing travel agents, he calls them bandits who take people's money and give them ten days of hell in exchange. Then he adds: 'Of course, going abroad in itself would be hell to me.'

In a previous incarnation Uncle Matthew had been General Murgatroyd. First of all he hated Roman Catholics and Negroes above all others, but the first World War put the Germans ahead, The General once nearly fell into a trap but 'suddenly, just in time, I realized that he was a filthy Hun so of course I turned my back on him and refused to shake hands' (*Highland Fling*, 1936). Net result: 'Never shake hands with niggers, Catholics or Germans if I can help it.' Albert Gates opposed this attitude vehemently but somehow failed to make himself understood for Lord Prague joins in the discussion and congratulates him: 'That is the proper spirit, Mr Gates. Down with the Huns! Down with the Frogs! Down with the Macaronis! Down with Uncle Sam! England for the English!'

Linda, growing up in this milieu, unthinkingly reflected it. She took no interest in politics but was 'instinctively and unreasonably English'. She knew that one Englishman was worth a hundred foreigners. She blotted her copybook by marrying a man of German descent who thought in social rather than national terms: one capitalist was worth a hundred workers. Another of the girls, Polly, was sensible enough to marry an Englishman but foolish enough to spend her honeymoon in Spain and then Sicily. 'The horror of abroad!' she exclaimed. In Spain they were always two hours late for every meal. Italian cooking was too oily.

In the family xenophobia could be turned on like a tap. No wonder that Nanny was highly suspicious of the French in *The Blessing*. There are some English who admire France but they are not to be trusted. Grace says to Charles-Edouard, 'Papa loves France'. He replies, 'I'm sure he does. The Englishmen who love France are always the worst.' It is true that the francophil (and the anglophil, for that matter) is rarely popular with either side. This uncertain foundation is even felt by the francophil himself for Grace's father, Sir Conrad Allingham, says, 'I don't like the idea of Grace marrying a frog, to tell the truth.' What it amounts to is that the francophil adopts the French as a subject for study and examination, but this does not mean he wishes for a closer association any more than an egyptologist wishes to set up house on the Nile. Mrs O'Donovan, however, was shocked by Sir Conrad's statement. 'They both belonged to the category of English person, not rare among the cultivated classes, and not the least respectable of their race, who can find almost literally nothing to criticize where the French are concerned.'

Grace had early reservations but soon finds herself charmed by the French and the fascination continues to grow. In this one feels she resembles her creator. While everyone else was saying the French were not what they used to be (after the second war), she could find no fault in them. She loved the servants for their efficiency and loyalty, the aunts for being clever and serious, and the young for being pretty and light-hearted. She discovered that she would have liked to have been born French. In fact, the attitude towards France becomes obsessional in a slightly sick sense. Uncle Matthew's influence was still at work, but it had been turned on its head. The critical sense appears to be absent, as it had always been with Uncle Matthew, whose criticisms were not judgments but prejudices. On the other hand, attitudes towards France have always been exaggerated or unreal, going to one extreme or the other, like those of the Irish to the English. Sir Conrad gives his personal view why most English people hate living in France. 'I always think it's got a great deal to do with French silver. They don't realize it's another alloy, they think that dark look means that it hasn't been properly cleaned, and that makes them hate the French. You know what the English are about silver, it's a fetish with them.' This is a sublimely aristocratic theory— the rest of the population doesn't exist.

There is an argument between Grace and Fanny about the respective merits of the French and English in *Don't Tell Alfred*. Grace, married to a Frenchman, is the francophil. She says the English always pride themselves on growing flowers but it all boils down to michaelmas daisies and chrysanthemums.

Have you ever noticed it's just those very things the English pride themselves on most which are better here? Trains: more punctual; tweeds: more pretty; football; the French always win. Doctors: can't be compared, nobody ever dies here until they are a hundred. Horses, we've got M. Boussac. The post, the roads, the police—France is far better administered—

The argument continues on this unreal level, Fanny replying with justice, newspapers, digestives, Cooper's Oxford marmalade, etc. In this kind of contest the more trivial victories are the decisive ones. It starts as a joke and is meant as a joke, but it gets tedious. Bearing in mind previous anglo-french references which were just as stupid, one begins to smell an obsession and wonders if, behind the laughter, is a fairly sizeable inferiority complex.

The Younger Generation

Elizabeth Bowen accepts them; Christopher Isherwood seeks affiliation; Nancy Mitford is greatly disturbed by them. At times *Don't Tell Alfred* shows signs of turning into a rant against the young. They lack respect for their elders—presumably the kind of respect Nancy had for hers. Alfred talks to Valhubert about the younger generation. Valhubert had had a 'good war' (enough to make the young squirm with embarrassment)—but what did they care?

> They don't care a fig for liberty, equality, fraternity or any of our values—still less for their King and Country. The be-all and end-all of their existence is to have a good time. They think that they could have rocked and rolled quite well under Hitler and no doubt so they could. The black men affirm that we are in full decadence. Nothing could be truer if these boys are typical of their generation . . . The barbarians had better take over without more ado. We made the last stand against them.

Valhubert, to do him justice, says Alfred takes everything too tragically. It might be argued that this novel shows the young passing through a transition stage, but Miss Mitford gives every evidence of being worried. Everything was once so much better. 'I thought with a sigh what an easy time parents and guardians had had in those days—no Teddy Boys, no Beards, no Chelsea set, no heiresses, or at least not such wildly public ones; good little children we seem to have been, in retrospect.' There is a twinkle in the eye of this nostalgia.

But there is no general agreement in detail, only in the general proposition that things are worse than they used to be. Fanny, for instance, is alarmed by the lack of frivolity among the young—in direct opposition to her husband's conviction that they have been corrupted by mindless pleasure-seeking. Her sons find Northy old-fashioned, and she supposes it is because she is as frivolous as a character out of the twenties. Philip says the young make him despair of the female sex: 'I'd sooner marry a Zulu woman of my own age than one of these gloomy beauties in red stockings.' Later he complains of the 'horse-tail girls' who don't like any of the things he's interested in, least of all sex. 'They join up with the Teds and the Beats and wander about Europe with them, sharing beds if it happens to suit; three in a bed if it's cheaper like that (shades of Sir Charles Dilke) and probably nothing happens! Sex is quite accidental.'

The young aristocrats seem to take to this new way of life like ducks to water. Here is a picture of Basil. 'Side whiskers, heavy fringe, trousers, apparently moulded to the legs, surmounted by a garment for which I find no word but which covered the torso, performing the function both of coat and of shirt, such was the accoutrement of an enormous boy (I could not regard him as a man), my long-lost Basil.' Fanny noted that her children regarded people in their thirties as 'old sordids, old weirdies, ruins, hardly human at all', whereas her mother (known as the Bolter, because of her sexual enterprise) was regarded at sixty-five as a contemporary. Basil had adopted a new mode of speech which consisted in superimposing (when he could remember) cockney or American slang on the ordinary speech of an educated person. 'Old Grandad found that Granny's money is earning a paltry four or five per cent on which she pays taxes into the bargain. Now that's not good enough for him, so 'e scouts round, see, and finds out about this travel racket—oh boy, and is racket the word? 'E lays down a bit of Granny's lolly for premises and propaganda, etc., etc.,' The other line for aristocratic youth is showbiz. These two represent new lines of exploitation of the naive, the slow-witted and the merely moral. Fanny's boys (who have escaped from Eton) explain that 'members of the Showbiz were the aristocracy of the modern world; that Yanky was its King and that Yanky's gentlemen-in-waiting had the most covetable position of any living teenagers'. Yanky Fonzy was a pop singer, naturally.

David, who is going to China with a wife who never speaks (she is a bishop's daughter), while leaving behind a Chinese baby they have adopted, is a foretaste of the Hippie. He is the Western Zennite. They had no visas, they were looking for Truth. When told he might end up in gaol he replied loftily that Truth flourished in gaols.

We are the bridge between pre-war humanity with its selfishness and materialistic barriers against reality and the new race of World Citizens. We are trying to indoctrinate ourselves with wider concepts and for this we realise that we need the purely contemplative wisdom which comes from following the Road.

David says he hates the bourgeoisie. 'In Zen I find the antithesis of what you and father have always stood for.' And of course: 'Time does not exist. People who have clocks and watches are like bodies squashed into stays. Anything would be better than to find oneself in your and Dad's stays when one is old.' This boy, David, had taken a first in Greats. Alfred simply doesn't know what to make of him. Fanny says, 'I remember, when the boys were little, you used to say if they don't revolt against all our values we shall know they are not much good . . . I hope when they see me coming into a room they will look at each other as much as to say: here comes the old fool. That is how children ought to regard their father.' Davey, Fanny's uncle, agrees there are no standards of behaviour any more.

Miss Mitford's attitude towards the young, or this type of young, seems to oscillate between exasperation and a grudging understanding, if not sympathy. Fanny (who I assume is as close to being a mouthpiece for Miss Mitford as we can reasonably expect) says that her sons, both brilliant, have given way to complete mental laziness. While David grows a beard and decides to walk to China in search of Truth, Basil lies face downward all day on a Spanish beach. But she thinks it is a phase and they will come out of it. 'They are nothing new—my cousins and I were quite idiotic when we were young. The only difference is that in those days the grown-ups paid no attention, while we concentrate (too much probably) on these children and their misdoings.' David explained to his father: 'Zen forbids thought.' Alfred looked sad, such words were the negation of his life's work. 'It does not attempt to be intelligible or capable of being understood by the intellect, therefore it is difficult to explain. The moment you try to realize it as a concept, it takes flight.'

There is also a reaction against work, which may have prompted Fanny to regard the whole movement as an expression of organized laziness. The boys leave Eton to take jobs as packers at £9 a week. Fanny says they are being educated so that they can find more inter- esting jobs.

> 'Yes, that's what we've heard. We don't believe it. We think all work is the same and it's during the time off that you live your life. No use wasting these precious hours preparing for jobs that may be far worse than packing when we shall be old and anyway not able to feel anything, good or bad. As it is we get two days off and our evenings.'

There is considerable irony here. Nancy Mitford (Fanny) had not been formally educated because her father (Uncle Matthew), was opposed to it as waste of time. Being a girl of intelligence and intellectual curiosity, she educated herself. Fanny married a don for full measure. Their offspring regarded education as a hoax.

They were told they should think of the future. 'Why must we? All you oldies thought and thought of the future and slaved and saved for the future, and where did it get you?' The answer, in father's case, was to Paris. 'And what good does that do him? How many days off does he get? How does he spend his evenings? Who is his idol? . . .' 'In any case, it's now we want to be enjoying ourselves, not when we are rotting from the feet up at thirty or something ghoulish.'

There is material here for consideration of some of the most important aspects of modern life: the age gap; work and leisure; the purpose of living. Miss Mitford does not face up to them, however. The reader feels she is aware of the issues and is prepared to treat them seriously, but not in this book. Yanky deserts the boys, they decide packing is a bore, and begin to dress normally again. It had been, after all, a phase. There is little doubt that they are now desk-squatters wearing dark suits, constantly on the telephone, doing what they call work for sixteen hours a day, and eating and drinking rather more than suits their metabolism.

VII

C.P. Snow—The Long Climb
(First Fiction: *Death Under Sail*, 1932)

Poverty and Money

Although Lewis Eliot's career (which resembles Snow's own fairly closely in its social aspect) is superficially that of the climb from rags to riches, there are very few rags in *Strangers and Brothers,*1940. His family belonged to that vast undefined grouping which lies between the working class and the lower middle class and contains large chunks of both, simply because there are no clear borders. But we are given very few glimpses of this world, and what there are belong chiefly to *Time of Hope,* 1949. Lewis lived in a street with 'entries' leading to the back doors and with neat, minute gardens in front. His own house had three storeys instead of the usual two. Not far away his aunt's house had a Builder and Contractor sign. His father's people were typical artisan, forming a lower middle class thrown up by the industrial revolution. Before his father went bankrupt they employed a servant girl. For three years he had his own small business; previously he had been employed as a utility man in a small boot factory at £250 a year. His wife (Lewis's mother) lent him her savings of £150 and Aunt Milly (his sister) lent him the rest. Following a pattern very common in English life, his mother felt herself superior, if not to the man she married, at least to his milieu. Her own family came from the agricultural areas and market towns of Lincolnshire (Hartley's country). They were not more prosperous than the Eliots, they were not even more genteel, but they fundamentally despised the industrial world. His mother's pride expressed itself in numerous small ways, such as refusing ever to give Lewis margarine, even after his father's bankruptcy.

But Lewis is much less concerned with his background than with the world he intends to conquer (though his ambitions are not expressed.) He is going to make money (though he is never crude enough to say so.) This attitude towards life is evident even before Lewis Eliot is invented. It is given a good airing in *The Search*, 1934, where young men from Snow's own milieu are beginning the social climb. Sherriff has just enjoyed a holiday. 'I've discovered people I've never really met before: natural simple people. People who've had enough money to live comfortably, and who've made a decent shape out of their lives. And I'm coming to think they get their values straighter than people like us ever will have.' Ominous. Miles and Audrey are not impressed. Sherriff is really referring to the Stanton-Brownes—he is friendly with the daughter. They are a military family, 'very nice', but the girl is insipid, talks mainly about cars, interspersed with giggles and snorts.

All the same, Miles appreciated money. He had had none as a child. Security is the suburban ideal and most of the people he meets seek it, financial and emotional. Hunt tries to pin Sherriff as a type: he imagines he is, at different times, a Selfless Scientist, a Bohemian or a Don Juan; he would like to be a professor because it would impress himself; but fundamentally what he's after is a pleasant house in its own grounds in a pleasant suburb with a nice wife. The author speaks: 'The desire for security (of which money can often be the symbol) decides much of the pattern of our lives; and it is only rarely that we can dismiss it altogether, and even then we are not rid of it for long.' Literature has had little to say about it for it is unpicturesque (but Snow forgets the romantics). One is often irritated by an author's indifference to how people live and where the money comes from, and it is in supplying this need that writers like Gissing and Orwell have a special value. (Snow predictably brings in Dostoevsky at this point.)

In the sequence we soon discover that Lewis Eliot, in his quiet way, has a considerable regard for money. Naturally, it is never stressed for the essence of Eliot is the avoidance of emphasis. His mother felt the shame of her husband's bankruptcy keenly. 'I shall be ashamed to let people see me in the streets. I shan't be able to hold up my head' —yet she carried it off. She had great courage, borrowed money from the doctor, sold bits of jewellery and was even prepared to go to a moneylender. Quite naturally, Lewis felt he was at a disadvantage, especially when he met men at the Bar examinations who came from rich families. 'With that start, what could I not have done?' He had to make an effort and endure a strain they never knew. 'I felt a certain rancour.' Yet on reflection he felt there were certain disadvantages.

His rivals had known successful men all their lives and it took away their confidence. They were always being compared with uncles who had done well. Sheila, his first wife, came from a much richer family than his, that of a country parson who was a member of the Athenaeum. She had often talked of breaking away and 'doing something' but she never did. He used to tease her about 'the sick conscience of the rich', a phrase that is as evocative of Snow as the more famous 'corridors of power'. It was in fact, he reflected, a bad time to be born rich: 'the callous did not mind, nor did the empty, nor did those who were able not to take life too hard', but he knew half a dozen among his contemporaries 'who were afflicted by the sick conscience of the rich' (the phrase is first used in *Time of Hope*). But for Lewis Eliot there was at this time no question of being rich; the first ambition was to make sure of a decent livelihood.

But the rich fascinated him. In the appendix to *The Masters*, 1951, 'Reflections on the College Past', Eliot/Snow returns to their predicament. 'By the thirties, the conscience of the comfortable classes was sick: the sensitive rich, among my friends, asked themselves what use they were . . .' Some of them escaped into academic life, taking it for granted that it was valuable—and in fact the scientists were admired like no other professional men. 'In England, the country with the subtlest social divisions (Pilbrow said the most snobbish of countries), Oxford and Cambridge had had an unchallenged social cachet for a long time; even Lady Muriel, although she did not feel her husband's colleagues were her equals, did not consider them untouchable . . .' Wealthy men could be confident of their social use and still retain their position among the smart.

Finally, in *The Conscience of the Rich*, 1958, Snow makes money his main theme. This is an important novel because it marks a significant moment in our social history. Thackeray and Trollope showed the rich in undiluted confidence. They are still there in Galsworthy but showing signs of stress in Madox Ford. Here they are breaking. It is not only bad conscience that saps their assurance but also the presence of a Fifth Column.

Snow's treatment of character and personality is rarely impressive because it is far too analytical for the purposes of the novel. There are long stretches of boredom in his work when we are told in detail what a character thinks about himself and his friends. We are lectured, the personality is not depicted through action, conversation or stream of consciousness. But when he has a story to tell he forgets the analytic urge and the characters come to life. His method is never impressionist, of course, but unself-conscious presentation of consecutive detail blots out temporarily the rather donnish pedestrianism of his normal method. In this respect *The Conscience of the Rich* has at times the kind of staid excitement one feels while reading, say, Belloc's *Mr Clutterbuck's Election,* but benefits from Snow's superior skill in projecting human motivation and reaction in individual terms.

Mr March, the rich man, is one of Snow's most successful characters because he shares, as a personality, the weakness that Snow exhibits as a writer. This study could easily be the work of an intelligent Marxist, portraying a man whose personality has been fragmented and alienated by the unnatural demands of capitalist relationships. He is staccato and dictatorial, and his innate humanity has been inhibited by a lifetime of false values. In this novel Snow resembles no other writer more closely than Steven Marcus!

Charles March is disinherited and muses not so much on the loss of luxury as on the loss of freedom. 'There are times when it's valuable for a doctor to be independent of his job. He can do things and say things that otherwise he wouldn't dare. Some of us ought to be able to say things without being frightened for our livelihood, don't you agree?' This perhaps is a later discovery on Eliot's part, even if it is made for him. Earlier he had been envious of wealth in the conventional way. While they were both barristers Charles got on faster because of his connections. 'The plaintiff knew one of Charles's uncles, and Hart himself; Hart, who had married Charles's cousin, suggested that young March . . .'

Lewis was always treated like one of the family, but could not escape the awareness of his own relative poverty, especially his origins. As the butler took his overcoat for the first time Lewis thought it was probably the cheapest he had received for years. On one occasion the family joked about the servants, who didn't think much of the new type of guest, particularly when compared with those that had come in the old days. Lewis was envious of Charles's good fortune, not his success, though we are not told how he distinguished between them. 'My envy kept gnawing, as sharp, as dominating, as neuralgia'. In natural gifts there was not much between them. 'In everything but natural gifts he had so much start that I was left at the post.'

The Marches had been bankers and had made their money in the previous century. No individual March had ever been enormously rich. There had probably never been a millionaire among them. But most of the fortunes at the dinner-table (when the family gathered for its Friday night assemblies) would be between £100,00 and £500,000. Another extremely rich Jewish family was the Holfords, who had appeared in England in 1860 with the name of Samuel, hypenated themselves to Samuel-Wigmore within ten years, and dropped Samuel by the end of the century. They had made a fortune from cigarettes, and Lord Holford could have bought up the entire March family, as could Schiff, another Jewish millionaire who appears towards the end of the sequence.

Charles is eaten up by social conscience. He is admitted to the Bar, but this does not satisfy him, and he starts training as a doctor. This infuriated his father. Mr March was 'solid in the rich man's life of a former day' and regards his son's reasons as sheer perverseness. Charles marries a distant member of the family who is a member of the Communist Party. She and Charles believe the world will improve if people will work for it; Mr March does not. Most of the younger Marches affected a left wing radicalism which Eliot couldn't take seriously. It was based on nothing more solid than guilt. He had been poor and felt the need for a better society in his own experience. But none of the upper-class, public school Party members are any more impressive than Charles and his wife. She works for a newsletter edited by Seymour. With this character Snow's touch is tremendously sure. 'I shan't have time for your moral sensitivity', he parrots in an attempt to conceal his own dishonesty. He publicized scandals and when he didn't have them he fabricated them. This was a moral outrage to Charles. Our last view of Seymour occurs when he indulges in an arrant piece of snobbery of the type that well-born communists seem to specialize in. He says with great confidence that a guest at the club is Lord Kilmainham; he is an income-tax accountant. There is an acerbity in this portrait that one rarely finds in Snow. Undoubtedly conscience is an important matter.

The Social Roundabout

The centre of gravity of Snow's social range is the professional class, especially within the Civil Service and the universities.

The first book, *Death Under Sail,* 1932, under its mask of detection, bears that familiar English note of experience-brings-acceptance. The first pages follow the theme of 'there ain't no justice'. The narrator, an oldish man, spends a holiday on a yacht with much younger people. There had been times in his life when he doubted whether there was the slightest justice in this world of ours (but it is not a very strong emotion) 'which is arranged so casually and so haphazardly that one man can divide his year between languid days in a yacht and still more languid days by the side of the Mediterranean, while another spends fifty weeks a year in Oldham and the other two in Blackpool.' But as he gets older he learns to accept. His doubts grow less. There is no arrangement that would work better than this 'uneven balance'. If the world of leisure and comfort were swept away, too much would be lost. He hears the beautiful Avice laugh, and thinks how her charm would be irretrievably lost in a drab workaday routine. Idlers like Philip and Tonia contribute to the colour of life; if they went it would mean 'the destruction of a world'. And the injustice seems to be partly eliminated by the career of a man like William, who is one of the party, who had made his way armed with nothing but his wits: 'ten years before he had been working fiercely, intensively, in a Birmingham secondary school.' It is the complete detective writer's ethos.

Finbow, the amateur tec, provides a jarring note, though not a serious one. He says to Ian, 'People like William may not be as pleasant to live with as kindly old dodderers like you and me, but they're a devil of a lot more use in the world.' This is one of the cruxes of our society: efficiency or decency? It exercised Orwell immensely and it lies at the heart of the outlook of writers such as Waugh and Mitford. They had no doubt of the answer; Orwell wrestled with himself, and came down on their side (probably a surprise to all of them); but Snow, after doddering in Sayers-fashion, plumps for efficiency.

Finbow divides people along class lines into sheep and goats. Neither accent nor manners are a test. Both can be picked up and assumed with a fair amount of ease. The sheep are the products of the minor public schools, the goats are the rest of 'this democratic state of ours'. The real difference depends on habits formed in early life. Sheep take exercise as a religious rite and look upon it as a moral duty. A goat takes exercise because he wants to and he doesn't feel conscience-stricken if he doesn't play a game for a month. The sheep live crowded together for a large part of their schooldays, and get used to taking their clothes off in each other's presence. 'Neither of us at school would have thought of putting on a bathing-costume when we went for a swim'. (Snow here aligns himself, through the narrator, with the sheep.) The goats live at home, where physical things are much more private. 'They do *not* get into the habit of removing all their clothes.'

There are two schools of contempt here, operating in an orthodox (and, it must be confessed, tiresome) way. It is doubtful if anything more of value can be said about public school and state school along these lines. (Admittedly, this was forty years ago but the subject had already been given a good airing.) Two years later, in *The Search*, social contempt is reserved for neither people nor classes but for inadequate disciplines, if they deserve the name. 'These Economic Men of yours', says Audrey, 'gutless, heartless, adjusting their demands of bowler hats very neatly to the supply. There never were such men outside a text book . . .' Part of Audrey's trouble was that she despised her course (History) but went on with it. In fact, Snow and Snowmen often find it difficult to restrain their contempt for what other people study. In *Last Things*, 1970 there is a sharp outburst against the function of criticism.

But these early books may not be regarded as important in the Snow canon, although *The Search* could be fitted into the *Strangers and Brothers* sequence without difficulty. In the first of the sequence (to be known in future as *George Passant*, 1940) we are recognizably among the lower middle class, and to a greater extent than in any of the novels that follow. We see Passant and his group through the eyes of Lewis Eliot, who is one of them.

> We were poor and young. By birth we fell into the ragtag and bobtail of the lower middle classes. Then we fell into our jobs in offices and shops. We lived in our bed-sitting rooms, as I did since my mother's death, or with our families, lost among the fifty thousand houses in the town. The world seemed on the march, we wanted to join in, but we felt caught.

The characteristics of this class are well caught and presented. George said he was no good at 'social flummery'—important as a distinction, for there are those who indulge in social flummery, others who will excuse it as a necessary part of a bearable social context, and even some who regard it as the essence of man's social life. No-one could expect it from George, starting where he did: 'you can't expect me to, starting where I did' was a phrase that caught Eliot's imagination. Dinner with his boss (Eden) was an ordeal in which the right dress, the right fork and the proper tone of conversation presented moments of shame. He admits that he has never got over his social handicaps and is shy in respectable society. He is the major influence in Eliot's early life. Jack Coterie, from the same class, was the direct opposite. He took on the colour of whatever world he lived in. 'If he remembered his home and felt the prick of a social shame, (he) just invented a new home and believed it, for the moment, with a whole heart.'

English society is one where the process of aristocrat-making still continues. Tacitly we, as a nation, seem to believe in the role of an aristocracy. The hereditary principle is no longer trusted and is in fact dying out, but an aristocracy is still considered a valuable social force. Thus within the English social context ambition tends to express itself as aristocratising, an ugly word which I do not intend to use again. It might seem strange, on reading *George Passant* for the first time, to be told that the making of aristocrats, with all the self-consciousness and self-confidence of that class, is to be one of the major themes of the sequence. There is no sign of it at the beginning. But by the time we come to *Homecomings,* 1956, for example, the pattern is becoming clear. The new aristocrats are meeting and mingling with, not always happily, the old aristocrats. There are many environmental factors to come between the two groups, though merging will be inevitable. The old aristocrats went to a variety of schools and thought nothing of it; now it had to be Eton, 'with the disciplined conformity of a defiant class. With the same conformity, those families were no longer throwing up the rebels that I had been friendly with as a young man.' Bevill and Lufkin were interesting contrasts. Bevill was matey but did not care for business men. He kept on amiable terms with them because it was a principle of his life. Lufkin, who had made his way by scholarships and had joined his firm at seventeen, felt for politicians like Bevill something between envy and contempt, but softened by a successful man's respect for another's success. This ambivalence came out in his attitude towards the House of Lords. 'The main advantage about these tinpot honours —which I still think it's time we got rid of'—(having it both ways, as so often)—'isn't the pleasure they cause to the chaps who get them: it's the pain they cause to the chaps who don't.' He thought Lord Lufkin an awful name but when Eliot suggested it might be changed he said, 'No. We're too late for that. It's no use rich merchants putting on fancy dress. It's damned well got to be Lord Lufkin.'

One result of the English decision to persist with an aristocratic system is that the class has become remarkably varied, a characteristic that was not found among the historic aristocracies which actually prided themselves on their restriction of entry and conduct. The British aristocracy is as difficult to describe as the Church of England. We have already seen illustrations of this in the world of Nancy Mitford. In Snow we see the aristocracy in process, still forming, and quite unpredictable except for its unpredictability. Pilbrow (in *The Masters,* 1951) would have made a good red Lord, we are told. Was he then an ex-trade union official promoted to represent the Labour cause in the Lords? Not a bit of it. He is in fact much closer to Powell's Lord Warminster.

Though he came from the upper middle classes, was comfortably off without being rich (his father had been the headmaster of a public school), many people in Europe thought of him in just that way. He was an eccentric, an amateur, a connoisseur; he spent much of his time abroad but he was intensely English, he could not have been anything else but English. He belonged to the fine flower of the nineteenth century.

It may be asked why I introduce Pilbrow at this point if he is not an aristocrat? I introduce him as an example of English confusion in this area: he had the style of an aristocrat but had not the title. Later we will meet Lord Luke of Salcombe who had the style of a bureaucrat but had the title of an aristocrat.

The New Man who intends to become an Aristocrat will choose a wife accordingly. (There are, naturally, mistakes and fall-outs and mistimings.) Anthony Burgess has pointed out that part of Eliot's first wife's attraction lay in her being a member of a higher social class, and adds that hypergamy, or marrying above oneself, is a recurring theme in modern British fiction (Anthony Burgess, *The Novel Now*, 1967). The women are of the greatest importance in the process of aristocrat-making. They can help by their charm and sympathy; they can repel or scare off by being bitchy; they can lose the game by gaucherie or ineffectiveness; with a dozen other possibilities. They are well to the fore in *The Light and the Dark*, 1947, where Lady Muriel lords it over everyone within reach. (She is *there;* her strategy is to keep others at a distance.) She was at her most crushing when discussing women of the lower orders, especially when they were trying to catch men. (Rosalind was throwing herself at Roy.) 'She's not a lady. She's not even gently bred. No lady could do what this woman is doing.' Lady Boscastle agrees about the behaviour but reminds her that they have known similar cases—but she is interrupted by Lady Muriel. 'It was not the same. If a lady did it, she would do it in a different way.' Lewis discovered that although Lady Boscastle was exquisite and 'travelled' and much more cultured and sophisticated than the genuine Boscastle ladies, she was of middle class origin. This could never be changed. Lady Muriel loathed her.

Lady Muriel becomes indignant over Rosalind who at one point appeared to be throwing herself at Roy's friend, Udall. 'I understand that the lower classes are very lax with their children', she says. 'If that young woman had been my daughter she would have been thrashed.' At times like these one becomes weary of Eliot's gutlessness and subservience. He never stands up for his own kind and accepts any insult they may receive. At the best of times he is a negative character and one wonders why so many important people like him, confide in him and invite him to their homes. It is true, he is merely a working part in the novel scheme but Snow might have made him a more credible personality. This is a major flaw in the series and it is one area in which *Strangers and Brothers* compares ill with Powell's *The Music of Time,* where the narrator, Nicholas Jenkins, though quiet and reserved, is positive and personable. It is also hard to accept Lady Muriel in mid-twentieth century. She reads exactly like the author of a nineteenth century aristocratic memoir. However, Snow wishes to make his point and is prepared to drag in characters out of libraries as well as from streets and drawing rooms. Rosalind is more real. She is from the same town as Roy and Lewis and her origins are lowly, but she has got on in the world and makes a satisfactory living as a designer. One of her functions is to say, when invited to lunch with the Boscastles and feeling dreadfully nervous, 'What am I going to say to them? I've never met people like this before. I haven't any idea what to say'. Which she does. There are times when one feels the sequence might be renamed *People Like This.*

Homecomings, 1956, is less enchanted, partly because it takes us back to George Passant, who is real. He has not made the splash he should have, considering his innate ability. This point was seized upon by his Civil Service interviewing board. He put it down to his lowly origin, with no-one to advise him how to get ahead. (Eliot, of similar origin, got ahead but was in no position to advise his mentor.) Osbaldiston argued that Passant's family was probably not as poor as his, yet he had forged ahead. But nothing could compensate Passant for his poor start. He was infuriated more by rich radicals than by aristocratic Tories. The rich radicals got the best of both worlds. When Davidson, the art critic, was dismayed by the imprisonment of Sawbridge for selling atomic secrets to the Russians, Eliot was detailed to explain the case to him. Passant's reaction was explosive. 'If one of my relations had been uncomfortable about the Sawbridge case or any other blasted case, are you going to tell me that that old sunket Bevill would have detailed a high civil servant to give them an interview? But this country doesn't use the same rules if you come from where I did instead of bloody Bloomsbury.' Passant's political passions were still rooted in the East Anglian countryside, where his cousins were farm labourers: like most rooted radicals, he distrusted upper-class ones, feeling they were less solid than reactionaries such as Bevill.

Eliot himself was irritated by Davidson. 'I was irked by the arrogance of men of decent feeling like Davidson, who had had the means to cultivate their decent feelings without the social interest or realism to imagine where they led.' The world they had hoped for had not come, they had been wrong, and when things went wrong they had shown less character than the despised men of the right. Men like Bevill and Rose had been Municheers but when war came they were stauncher than 'the irregular left'. The left had been right about Nazism and war but wrong in nearly everything afterwards. Eight out of ten of Eliot's professional acquaintances moved to the right in opinion.

Kinds of Snobbery

It is obvious that if the socially dominant class is as varied in character as an Oriental sea-port, then many different kinds of snobbery will flourish. The traditional kind, arising out of social pretension, underlies *The Search,* with its theme of young scientists trying to establish themselves. Sheriff pretends he went to a public school when in fact he went to a secondary school in Portsmouth. His family had a boarding house in Southsea, which he kept quiet about. Miles said his own school had not yet adopted the fashion of aping the minor public schools. But none of this was important— there was no tension between them because they were united by their intellectual pursuits, not divided by social pretence. Audrey, who marries Sheriff, discovers the truth. 'He'd like to have been born in the upper-middle class. Why, God knows.' This suggests that Audrey was an inverted snob if nothing else.

The Light and the Dark has been Snow's main vehicle for the presentation of snobbery. The Master's wife, who was Lord Boscastle's sister, was a fearful snob. This is our Lady Muriel of the previous section; she was every bit as interested in social niceties as any middle class lady but she did it on a grander scale. The family had been solidly noble since the sixteenth century, which is a long time for genuine descent, as Snow remarks. They had been barons for two centuries and had managed to become earls after 1688.

Lady Boscastle was worried about her son because he showed no sense of vocation, but like a Waugh aristocrat he was saved by the war, behaving with impeccable gallantry. Snobbery as a vocation was over, but Lord Boscastle was unable to accept such a heresy.

Mrs Seymour was a cousin of Lady Muriel. Her husband had not been much of a catch though Seymour was 'someone one could know.' Everyone was discussed in these terms. The Dean had married an Eggar, 'whoever they may be' (Lady Muriel). Her brother, Houston Eggar, was in the Foreign Office. 'I shouldn't have thought that the Foreign Office was especially distinguished nowadays', said Lord Boscastle. 'I've actually known one or two people who went in', he added, as though straining our credulity. It was agreed that someone was obliged to become civil servants and look after the drains. Lord Boscastle had a special language of nuance with which he placed people socially. Nothing else mattered. Roy Calvert played up to him: 'Should you have said that the Foreign Office was becoming slightly *common?*' Boscastle thought that would be going rather far but he would never have considered it himself and hoped his son wouldn't. Roy pushed his game a little further—Lord Boscastle's son might pick up an unfortunate accent, perhaps that was why FO people learn foreign languages, to cover their own? Boscastle held that the mishandling of policy towards Italy (over Abyssinia—it was hypocritical nonsense) was due to the increasingly middleclass constitution of the Foreign Office. Houston Eggar, the middle-class diplomat, betrayed his own species of middle-class snobbery. He had hoped for a C.M.G. in the Honours List and only got a C.B.E. Lady Muriel didn't know because she never read as low in the list as that. Tom Seymour's girl had married this Eggar—'it's a pity that one doesn't know who he is', says Lord Boscastle.[1] His niece, Joan, caps it by saying the truth is he doesn't know who his grandfather is. Boscastle liked Calvert and paid him a back-handed compliment: 'I must say that if I'd met Calvert anywhere I should really have expected to know who he was.'

Now this is pretty feeble stuff and (like everything connected with Lady Muriel) seems to have come straight out of handbooks of etiquette and the memoirs of noble families. It doesn't ring true. Similar passages in Elizabeth Bowen impress by their conviction; in Nancy Mitford they are turned to satiric account. The only passage where Snow manages to transcend the pedestrian in all this is the one relating to Eggar's C.B.E., which is a good joke. Apart from that, one gets the impression that this is the portion of the sequence that is intended to 'deal with' the old aristocracy—just as *The Conscience of the Rich* is intended to 'deal with' the conscience of the rich and *The Sleep of Reason,* 1968, is intended to 'deal with' sadistic crime

---

1. This seems to have taken Snow's fancy. 'He's a man called Underwood. I don't know who he is', says Lord Hillington in *In Their Wisdom,* 1974. It is explained that this means none of Underwood's family had had any connections with Hillmortons in the past.

—in the latter case with much more success, because the seminar happens to be about something he knows at first-hand: the lower middle class.

He also knows dons at first-hand and shows it in *The Masters*. Again, there is quite a lot of chat about titles but it is donnish chat about titles—the titles they haven't got and would like to have, in many cases. Nightingale refers to a potential benefactor of the college as 'one of these business knights'. Chrystal said he was none the worse for that, which was echoed by Pilbrow, who went on: 'I've never been much addicted to business men, but it's ridiculous to put on airs because they become genteel. How else do you think anyone ever got a title? Think of the Master's wife. What else were the Bevills but a set of sharp Elizabethan business men?' Winslow was wealthy 'and it was in his style to say that he was the grandson of a draper; but the draper was the younger son of a county family.' Lady Muriel was intensely snobbish, as we have seen, but he was the only one of the older fellows whom she occasionally, 'as a gesture of social acceptance', called by his first name. Pilbrow was convinced that 'snobbery will make this country commit suicide'. While things got worse in Europe, the leaders of British society were just sitting by and dining in the best houses. Nightingale attacked Jago's candidacy for the Mastership through his wife. 'He jeered at her accent and her social origins: "the suburbs of Birmingham will be a comedown after Lady Muriel." '

The New Men, whom one might expect to be immune to such a disease, were as bad as any. They may not be so obtrusive as an older generation, but scientific interest was not sufficient to smother social values. Martin's wife, Irene, illustrated the manoeuvres of the genteel poor in *The New Men*, 1954. She couldn't bear to be overlooked: 'It's much more dismaying if you've been taught that you may be poverty-stricken but that you are slightly superior'. She exaggerated her misfortunes—her father lived on a pension from the Indian Army and some of her relations might have been called county. 'In secret, Irene kept up her interest in the gradations of smartness among her smart friends.' But Mrs Drawbell came from a lower level. She was satisfied merely to have a member of the aristocracy in her house. For her the glory of Bevill was that he was the grandson of a peer, not that he was a cabinet minister. When Bevill takes Eliot to his club, the latter muses that if only his mother could have known, she would have felt she had not lived in vain. One wonders to what extent Eliot's own feelings are being foisted on to his dead mother. In fact they sat in a room remarkably like that to be found in the gamekeeper's cottage she had been brought up in. Success can corrode the sense of social reality and at times Lewis Eliot drops into a familiar type of insincerity. He opposes his younger brother's marriage. Martin says he hopes to get a post in a provincial university. ' "If you thought of marrying", I said, "you couldn't very well manage on that".—"I suppose it has been done", he replied.' One is reminded of Eustace's reply to Lady Nelly's remark that when she married her husband hadn't a penny—'I mean, about a thousand a year'. And Eustace says, 'It doesn't seem very much' (*Eustace and Hilda*, by L.P. Hartley).

Finally, in *The Affair*, 1960, we are given examples of the inverted snobbery that is the inevitable concomitant of positive snobbery. Dawson-Hill, the lawyer who was brought in with Eliot to help in the adjudication of the Howard case, loved to speak of the nobility he was familiar with, but usually managed to do it deprecatingly. He told a story about a weekend at a ducal house. 'The ostensible point of the story was the familiar English one, dear to the established upper-middle classes—the extreme physical discomfort of the grand. The real point was that Dawson-Hill had been there.' Crawford loved the story and approved of Dawson-Hill for having been there. Then there was Ince, a social fraud.

> Instead of wanting to be taken for something grander than he was in fact, he seemed to be aiming at the opposite. He was actually a doctor's son, born in the heart of the middle classes, educated like the quintessence of the professional bourgeoisie, middling prep-school, middling public school. He insisted on behaving, talking and often feeling as though he had come up from the ranks. Just as with the other kind of social mimic, one listened to his speech. Beneath the curious mixture of what he thought, often not quite accurately, to be lower-class English or happy-go-lucky American, one could hear the background of an accent as impeccably professional as Arthur Brown's.

Upper-class left-wingers are common enough, and conscientiously call each other Des and Pat and Bert and punctiliously leave the 'Esquire' off envelopes. But the Inces were not political, they did not 'go to the people'. They didn't vote, they were not making an intellectual protest, they just felt freer if they cut their class ties. To complete the irony, Lester Ince married a very rich woman and lived imperially.

Success and Ambition

Frederick R. Karl lists among Snow's strengths as a novelist 'his ability to catch people on their way up.' He is among other things the historian of the Long Climb to eminence, one which he performed himself and described many times in his fiction. In *Time of Hope* he analyses the situation of the lower class boy who possesses social ambition.

The first fact of importance that must be grasped in such a situation is that the family are entirely ignorant of how society works, and therefore how to get ahead. The first big test comes when the boy is ready to leave school: what kind of job should he take? No boy he knew had ever taken a scholarship to the university, and those of his teachers who had degrees had got them externally through London or Dublin. Lewis Eliot's Aunt Milly wanted him to become apprenticed to one of the big engineering firms, but his mother was shocked to the marrow at the thought that he should become a manual worker. Yet when he got his job in the Education office his aunt sneered at it as a white-collar job. Aunt Milly was a woman of great energy, but she had little outlet for it; most of it she put at the service of the temperance cause. In a family of this type one had to be prepared to face opposition to social advancement. For Aunt Milly a really important job was out of the question. If you left the ranks of the manual workers you would probably spend the rest of your days as a junior clerk, and even that would be pronounced *clurk,* the final indignity.

Much of Eliot's determination to get on in the world was the result of George Passant's influence, though Passant himself was incapable of rising far. He announced vehemently that he was a socialist, and demanded what else he could possibly be, with his background. Lewis agreed, and backed it up by speaking at I.L.P. meetings. One side of their socialism was idealistic: George in particular believed

> with absolute sincerity and with each beat of his heart, that men could become better; that the whole world could become better; that the restraints of the past, the shackles of guilt, could fall off and set us all free to live happily in a free world; that we could create a society in which men could live in peace, in decent comfort, and cease to be power-craving, avaricious, censorious and cruel.

But there was another strain, that of sheer class envy. Once the two of them looked through the windows of a middle class club and watched a few elderly men, prosperously dressed, sitting with glasses at their side in the comfortable room. George was infuriated and demanded to know by what right they sat there as though they owned the world.

Lewis felt 'sheer, rancorous envy, the envy of the poor for the rich, the unlucky for the lucky', even when he was advancing in his career. His well connected friends found everything too easy, as we have seen when considering Charles March. But unlike George, Eliot did not rage vocally. He was even able to be amused at Sheila's upper class notions, e.g., that the poor always want to eat fish and chips. She was prostrating herself before the millions, enjoying the romance of slumming. Eliot even gained some inner strength from his inferior social position. When he took his exams he felt a surge of confidence, a feeling of contempt for those who 'tried to keep me in my proper station'. Fundamentally, his socialism was entirely conventional and utilitarian—when he had the chance he was content to join 'em, not beat 'em. He was a born climber. He saw the cars driving up to the big houses of the rich, women swept past him leaving their perfume on the air—one day he would entertain in such a house. When he was first taken to one of Martineau's 'Friday nights' he did not feel envy but pleasure at being inside a comfortable middle class house for the first time.

As we concentrate on the struggle to rise socially there is a tendancy to forget that Eliot did not come from the lowest social level. This is brought out in *The Affair* when, at a party, Eliot talks to G.S. Clark, a Fellow who really had started at the bottom. It had not been easy. (To do both Snow and Eliot justice, neither of them has ever demanded pity or admiration for their struggle. There were others who deserved it more.)

> He came from Lancashire, his origins were true working class. It was very rare, I had thought before, for anyone genuinely working class to struggle through to the high table, though a sprinkling had come, as I did myself, from the class just above. In the whole history of the college, there could not have been more than three or four who started where he did.

Ambition is quite unashamedly one of the main themes of this sequence. It also occurs prominently in the pre-sequence novel, *The Search*. While still young Miles reads a paper to the Royal Society; he hopes to be a Fellow by the time he is thirty-five. 'Walking away from the Royal Society, I was enjoying the prospect of my ambition coming nearer. Soon, quite soon, five years or less, I should have had my chance to lead a scientific attack.' This was the real motive power.

Also in this novel Snow asserted that genius could never be blocked. Anything even a little below it might.

> As far as I knew, I had not seen anyone with the promise of greatness fall into obscurity. That is, I thought almost always a man as gifted as Constantine would come through, whatever the luck; and in fact Constantine's own early career was a record of complete discouragement. But scientists of calibre just a little below the genius were being lost every day. The Austins, the Fanes, the Desmonds—I could replace them, I knew, by men who had gone frustrated into industry or teaching, and I should gain by the transaction. And as for the lesser figures, those who never get to the top, it seemed to be a matter of sheer chance who stays and who goes.

All the same, Miles did not think this was a satisfactory situation. There was too much trial and too much error. Luck must always play a part, even a big part, but it shouldn't decide altogether. He compared the careers of men he had known and found himself asking: "Why ever did *he* fail and *he* get on?"

Money was important, as we have seen, but once you had accumulated enough to be called rich you discovered other factors came into play. Roy Calvert's grandfather had risen from the artisan class and made enough money out of boots to send his son to a public school. His father became really rich and by 1934 must have been worth £300,000. He was much richer than some who lived in greater style. From the time he was twenty-one Roy had an allowance of £1500 a year. Roy deliberately made fun of an eminent surgeon who was receiving an honorary degree. The real iniquity lay in the fact that although he earned £20,000 a year he was not used 'to being made an exhibition of.' The rich liked to think of themselves as a class apart but it was often difficult. Lady Muriel was surprised to find that Eliot was taking a holiday in Monte Carlo. 'She had all the incredulity of the rich that anyone should share their pleasures.' She found some consolation in the thought that he would find his hotel very expensive. Lady Boscastle tried to take him in hand. He was wearing a soft shirt when it should have been stiff. When he said he found it more comfortable she called the excuse 'untravelled', her final word of blame. The chief aim of civilization was not comfort. (She didn't say what it was but it was probably finding something to do with your money that you couldn't do without.) She compared Eliot with Roy, who couldn't do anything untravelled if he tried. She advised him to patronize Roy's tailor and barber. From below money shines like a Grail; when you get it you find a mystique is brought into play—it's like Part II of a course.

This was a pretty sophisticated discovery, and compares oddly with the rather naive approach to wealth and fame that is presented in the anonymous *New Lives For Old*, 1933. First of all, there was Callan, the young scientist who had helped discover the rejuvenation process on which the novel hinges, and then regretted it, largely out of his hatred and fear of sex, and became an eminent Professor in Cambridge. 'In thirty years he had been successful, and like most men, he was the better for it', writes the youthful C.P. Snow hopefully. But we are given an extremely unappetising picture of what success had done for Kittigrew, the Prime Minister. He is always making such remarks as 'I have promised to lunch with Sussex' (the Duke of Sussex). A casual reference to Oxford is thrown in. Kittigrew had been born in a Glasgow back-street and had taught in an elementary school until he was thirty-five. For him it was a perpetual adventure to live at ease among people who were born at the top. Kittigrew had been doing this for years, and the glamour never died for him. These people still 'remained something different from their ordinary, not very intelligent, not very cultivated, selves.' It was incredible that Kittigrew, who had lived on a pound a week when he was twenty, should spend the summer on the steam-yacht of a millionaire duke. It was a dream come true.

Politics

During his youth Lewis Eliot called himself a socialist. He belonged to the school of George Passant, who was more concerned with values and moral codes than with economic and administrative techniques. In 1933 Snow published *New Lives for Old* anonymously. It is virtually a thesis on revolution.

In this novel a period of reckless luxury in the midst of abject poverty is followed by revolution. 'Great cars carried parties from heavy dinners to light comedies. Economists could still see no way out of the chaos in the world.' Billy Pilgrim, a Fabian, disapproved of the situation intellectually and revelled in it with the rest of him. He was quite honest. Honesty is to know what one feels, not what one ought to feel. When he sees crowds in tails and gorgeous dresses enjoying themselves, he doesn't think of starving mobs in Glasgow. But in the long run the starving mobs count.

The existing order, with its country house parties, was pleasant but had not long to live. Secure, middle-class England would be swept away—to be followed by what? Callan, the young life-hater who helped discover the rejuvenation process, and later became an eminent Professor of Biology at Cambridge, rejected Communism. If there is a justification for humanity, it lies in the individual mind, which Communism stifles. Vanden, the novelist, held the same view. He said that Communism would destroy consciousness, which he described as 'consciousness of motive, awareness of one's emotions and those of the people around one, perceptions of the reasons behind the actions that human beings do'. Pilgrim, who had been Callan's superior in the rejuvenation discovery, felt that a few people were beginning to discover true consciousness: 'a handful of people are realizing at last what men are like and why they act as they do and why they give names for their actions which are nothing like the real names. A few people have become more "conscious" than anyone has ever been in the past.'

But there were no signs that capitalism could save itself. If the financiers and politicians could have united for defence, if the more powerful of them could have forgotten nationality and their immediate gains, then they might have carried on. They should have said, 'We will live on a half, a quarter, a tenth of what we've had in the past, and instead we'll abolish the grosser wastes and the bitterest discontent.' It would have been the intelligent action of a man who gives away most of what he has to preserve the necessities.

In this novel Snow comes closer to the feeling of 1968 than in anything written later. The revolution that takes place is dated 1964-5. It is badly written (compared with the briskness of *Corridors of Power* it is horribly sluggish and tedious to read) but it has considerable insight. Revolution was inevitable—the trigger was the refusal to let the poor enjoy the benefits of rejuvenation by keeping costs high, unlike in Russia, where they were given to all. The government were caught napping, but inexcusably—a series of strikes and riots had given sufficient warning. The revolutionaries are represented as being communists—Snow naturally sees the situation in terms of the 1930's—but the movement he describes bears less resemblance to a communist uprising than the kind of semi-aware discontent that lay behind the student riots of 1968. Pilgrim and his friends were determined that the revolution must fail—despite their sympathies and their contempt for the government, they dared not risk chaos. They must save the day and then start to build sensibly. This expresses the feelings of many people today, that contemporary society is unsatisfactory, but it would be retrogressive to destroy it entirely.

Nevertheless, the final impression is a muddled one. In the face of the revolution the government appeared to turn Fascist; elements from the O.T.C.'s, the Territorials and a middle-class organization called the Blueshirts came to the government's assistance. 'This is the only time in my life I've been grateful for the automatic reactions of the English middle classes', says Vanden. Pilgrim admitted he would support the stupidest kind of reaction rather than communism. The only effect of his desire for progress was that he would take the inevitable path a little less readily. And he had been a Fabian for over seventy years!

We see Snow in the traditional (and honourable) dilemma of the social democrat. The socialist side of him wanted a social revolution (he would prefer it not to be violent), the democratic side of him wanted to preserve the political freedoms. Those who sneer at the ineffectiveness of social democracy usually have little concern for political liberty, for reasons which are rarely clear unless they think in terms of a new ruling class and gamble on their membership. It may be true to say, as did Clark in *The Affair*, that the Eliots and the Getliffes have really been liberals all their lives. To many this would be no recommendation but they come from both sides of the political fence. Clark's argument is that they think their attitudes are detached and based on personal conscience. 'In the long run, anyone who has been as tinged with liberal faiths as you have is bound to think that by and large the left is right, and the right is wrong. You're bound to think that. It's the whole cast of your minds.' In the case of the young scientist, Howard, who was under suspicion of academic fraud, the Eliots and Getliffe were determined to think he was a victim because all their prejudices, their life histories and their *Weltanschauung* conditioned them to find a victim of injustice. Distrusted by the right and scorned by the left, such people live in an uneasy no-man's-land of politics. This situation is not stressed, however. It is one we can deduce. But there is very little direct speaking on political matters in these novels.

Snow certainly considers himself to be a political writer, but his conception of political writing is unusual in English fiction. He is interested in decision-making, not with raw material—the likeness is with Trollope. In *The Two Cultures*, 1963 edition, he writes in the additional chapter called 'A Second Look':

I have written, both in novels and essays, more about politics, in particular 'closed' politics (that is, the way decisions are really taken in power-groups, as contrasted with the way they are supposed to be taken), than most people of our time.

But this is disingenuous. Snow is allowing his sojourn in rarefied political quarters to corrode his judgment. No-one really knows how decisions are made, but many people know what the Prime Minister said to the Head of the Civil Service or what the Emperor said to the Lord Chief Justice or what the King said to the Court Jester. To mumble about 'closed politics' brings us close to in-talk about palace revolutions. Decisions are not fundamentally made by well-fed men in the Ritz and Snow knows it. But it is extremely flattering to imagine you have greater insight than other people and even more satisfying to say so in public, with the certain knowledge that a thousand others will gravely nod their heads and say, 'He's right, you know.'

Snow/Eliot has moved in and out of politics all through his life, but this is not to be wondered at. He himself says, in *Last Things,* where an attempt is made to say the final word about just about everything:

> Living in our time . . . you couldn't help being concerned with politics—unless you were less sentient than a human being could reasonably be. In the thirties people such as Francis Getliffe and I had been involved as one might have been in one's own illness.

But then he explains that it is 'closed politics' that he is really concerned with, and that these had increased during his lifetime. He described them as the politics of small groups, where person acted upon person: you saw it wherever people were in action, whether it was in committees, cabinets or colleges as well as the Vatican or the Politburo. Such activities had become more, not less, influential in Eliot's time. Many more people had become half-interested in power groups, in how decisions were made.

The most thorough-going and consistent attempt to 'deal with' the political scene is to be found, of course, in *Corridors of Power.* In this connection I cannot possibly do better than quote from Anthony Burgess's *The Novel Now,* partly because it coincides completely with my own belief and partly because such a viewpoint can hardly be better expressed. Burgess finds in the novel

> . . . a more reverent attitude to politics than most of us can assume: politicians, most of us feel, are to be satirized rather than taken seriously.[1] The passage of Sir Lewis Eliot through the wonderland of high life—country house parties, dinners in pent-houses, fateful teas at the Athenaeum—is treated with an awful

1. Snow takes strong exception to satire. (Footnote added).

gravity: the rulers have all the life and the ruled have ceased to exist.[1] But it is hardly possible to pretend that the enormous tensions which hold society together and move it through history can be very seriously affected by the fortunes of individual politicians: even today the communicator has more real power than the executor. It is, in fact, one of the revelations of the whole sequence that few of the men of power shown are really aware of the sources of their beliefs and attitudes; mostly they seem to believe that they themselves have made them, in the sense that their experience of life has taught them accurately all they need to know—after all, are they not successful?

When Snow forgets his cabals and considers the political situation in more realistic terms, he professes optimism. Terms like optimism and pessimism are abstractions but at least they represent things that matter to the common man: are things going to get better or worse? At the end of an introduction written for *The Public Prosecutor,* a play by the Rumanian, Georgi Dzhagarov (1963), he writes: 'It is right to be optimistic about the social condition; it is wrong, if you are going to put the proper safeguards into a legal system, to be optimistic about the individual condition.' Perhaps the first part of this statement is a kind of whistling to keep up his socialistic courage; certainly it is hard to find any strain of optimism in his fiction.[2] It appears to be a literature without values. Things happen and are accepted, and there is rarely even a breath of criticism from the author.

Snow's behaviour during the Daniel-Sinyavsky trial period was equivocal and caused much distress among British writers, who felt the moral urge to protest even if, in Snow's view, protest brings no noticeable benefit. It is doubtful if a swan in Russia as an official guest did any good either. His introduction to this play suggests a mild disapproval of what is happening to the individual in a communist society. One reads the play and discovers a most severe indictment. Snow seems to be playing down the human suffering, with his irritating air of olympic wisdom, while Dzhagarov is obviously extremely concerned. Then why did Snow sponsor it? Did he have a twinge of guilt about his comfortable Anglo-Saxon Panglossism? It seems at times that Snow has succumbed, with barely a backward

1. Like his universities—all dons and no students. (Footnote added).
2. Perhaps this needs qualification. It is social optimism that is missing. Personal optimism abounds. The emotional flavour negates the overt statement.

glance, to the comforting allurements of the power scene, the secret knowledge of the professional politician and the bureaucratic apologist. In his concluding book, *Last Things,* he throws the cause of social progress and amelioration to an unreal creature named Muriel (a different Muriel from the lady of that name we have already met). She is a rich man's daughter, she lives in considerable luxury with Eliot's son Charles, and she is one of a group, mainly students, who are involved in protest. She tells Uncle Lewis her ideals.

> This country, America, the world she knew, weren't good enough: there must be a chance of something better. The institutions (they sometimes called them structures) of our world had frozen everyone in their grip: they were dead rigid by now, universities, civil service, parliaments, the established order, the lot. One had to break them up. It might be destructive: you couldn't write a blue-print for the future: but it would be a new start, it would be better than now.

He doesn't believe her. Nor, surely, can many readers. But the reasons may be different. The approach of Muriel and her friends is a qualitative one, and Snow has long ceased to show any concern for political values. To the rest of us Muriel may well have sympathetic aspirations, but tactically she seems to provide little more than a student variant of closed politics. Not much nutriment for the masses.

New Values, Changing World

Snow is notoriously a writer who expresses concern for society but is extremely cagey about what he considers valuable in society. This has become increasingly the case as he has grown older and become more involved in public matters. In *The Search,* published as early as 1934, there is a more positive attitude towards social values; they are the orthodox left-wing values of the day. Miles is pessimistic about civilization and is certain it will crash. Certainly this is a very delicate undertone and is rarely discernible, but it is there, though not expressed with great conviction. However, Miles does say it is necessary to hold by humanism and social democracy, just as if no disaster is likely. It is necessary to hold by the faith but we must throw away the views of human nature which led to it.

> They were ineffectual because their human beings were ideal; we may be ineffectual, but our human beings must at least be

real. We want a liberal culture: but it has got to be based on human beings driven by their fears and desires, human beings who are cruel and cowardly and irrational, with just a streak of aspiration . . .

Miles gives up science to write political invective, but we are given next to nothing of his views on politics. (Rulers without ruled, dons without students.) His book, *The Gardarene Swine,* is obviously about the coming disaster but there is not a single paragraph (in the novel) devoted to a current political topic. There is a vague approach to pacifism, but the subject is so muted it is hard to believe that it has replaced science in his scheme of priorities. On what are priorities founded?

The same vagueness characterizes *George Passant.* George is a progressive, he is a rebel against the existing moral and social codes, but what he would put in their place is extremely vague. Getliffe, his defending counsel in the trial, makes a speech which infuriates him. He presents him as the helpless victim of a world he never made. One is reminded of Arthur Miles in *The Search,* telling his wife that the old moral certainties have gone. Getliffe says to the jury: 'It was easy to believe in order and decency when we were brought up. We might have been useless and wild and against everything around us—but our world was going on, and it seemed to be going on for ever.' There is a similar blurred effect when Jack is brought before the School Committee—this time George is defending him. The Principal says: 'Some of your protegees[1] are inclined to think on unorthodox lines?' George replies: 'No doubt: I shouldn't consider any other sort of thinking was worth the time of a serious-minded man.' But what were they thinking? There is a mild suggestion of mild free-loving, the kind of thing that many people at that time indulged in without making speeches or forming groups. There must have been something more. But as usual, we are not given details.

In *The Light and the Dark,* 1947 it appears that the Old Gang are on the way out, but in fact it is the Old Old Gang: there is not much relief for the Passants. The class that is on the way up is typified by Rosalind, whose social categoricals will be as rigid as any that went before. Lady Boscastle knows that her day is done. Her class should have disappeared in 1914 but it managed to hang on; it can hardly be expected to perform the same miracle twice.

---

1. It is interesting to note that the word "protegees' is spelt in the female form, though Passant could not possibly have distinguished it in speech.

It will take someone much stronger than they are to live as
they've been bred to live. It takes a very strong man nowadays
to live according to his pleasure.

Lady Muriel, a tougher nut, kept her resistance right up to the end.
During the war she officiated at a refugee centre every day and was
slapped on the back by cheery women helpers. But at home by night
she was more snobbish than ever. 'It was her defence, her retort, to
those who kept saying that the day of her kind was gone for ever.'
Her daughter Joan had little social awareness but the snobbery used
to irritate her. The younger Marches *(Conscience of the Rich)* had
gone left-wing. Joan never approached this but she felt a passionate,
undirected rebellion.

Lewis feels the suggestion of new social forms coming into existence
when he goes to Germany and dines with a Nazi minister. (Again
one feels the ambience is blurred, there is none of the sharpness of
impression that makes Isherwood's *Goodbye to Berlin* such a land-
mark.) He notices how obsequious the don Ammatter is to Schäder.
This marked a real difference in tradition. In England there was a
closer connection between the academic and official worlds[1], far less
respect was shown to politicians and civil servants. Lewis is
immensely impressed by the idea that this man wielded power: 'he had
come into more power than the rest of us had ever dreamed of. I
might not meet again anyone who possessed such power.'

In *The New Men*, 1954 (a slightly embarrassing title, for they have
more the appearance of old men with new tricks) the atomic bomb is
seen to have changed the rules of the game. The situation had become
too dangerous to permit chivalry or impartial attitudes. You had to
fight the enemy with every means at your disposal, but there is no
longer agreement about who the real enemy is. The 'relics of liberal
humanism' have no place in the new order, says Martin, but Lewis
disagrees. Snow rarely makes apocalyptic statements, or even allows
his characters to make them, but he puts one into the mouth of
Hankins—it is characteristic of what liberal journalists were saying.
'The party's nearly over. The party for our kind of people, for dear
old western man—it's been a good party, but the host's getting
impatient and it's nearly time to go. And there are lots of people
waiting for our blood in the square outside'. As a statement it seems
to have strayed from *New Lives For Old*. Hankins is not a convincing

1. In his essay on Winston Churchill in *Varieties of Men,* 1966, Snow says
that England is a country 'where the high officials and the academics are
interlinked, and more powerful than in any other.'

spokesman. Although Snow likes to straddle the culture barrier there is little doubt which side he would think it best to fall on. It wouldn't be Hankins's, and if Hankins says anything worth listening to he says it more by luck than by intention. Times are changing but he doesn't really understand why.

But if the scientists were coming into their own, they still found it difficult to adjust. The engineers gave no trouble in any country—they were usually conservatives, only interested in making their machines work[1] But the physicists had spent their lives seeking new truths, and they couldn't turn off the current when they looked at society. It was the scientists who produced the heretics, the fore-runners, martyrs and traitors. The old ideas of patriotic feelings for a particular country were beginning to wither. The new patriotism was not for a country but for an idea. The traditional patriots saw communism as an enemy but they accepted the Russian alliance because Britain was being threatened by Germany, not Russia. Sawbridge, the traitor, believed that his duty to the Soviet Union overrode, or included, all others; national terms only confused the issue.

The social criticism which is latent in so much of Snow's work but so tantalisingly withheld receives a more positive presentation in *Homecomings*, 1956. The successful civil servant, Rose, is contrasted with the big industrialist, Lufkin. Rose is not to be despised but he is the champion of a decadent society which deliberately made safe appointments. He was fonder of the secondrate than he should have been because it caused less trouble to him and the machine. Nevertheless, Eliot is compelled to respect such people because of their moral certainties and a 'conforming indignation which never made them put a foot out of step.' This is the soft under-belly of Eliot's personality, for he persists in scrutinising society as if it lay on the other side of the zoological cages. Lufkin could not accept such complacency. In fact, there were not enough men for the top jobs—the top jobs were increasing as society became more complex but the number of competent men had not increased. Rewards weren't enough, it would be necessary to deal out a few perks. No-one actually admits it, but there is the occasional implication that many suitable candidates were being blocked because they were not

1. "Engineers—more uniform in attitude than one would expect a pro-fessional class to be—tend to be technically bold and advanced but at the same time to accept totally any society into which they may have happened to be born". *Science and Government*, Godkin Lectures at Harvard University, 1960.

sufficiently conformist. The lofty view that the necessary governing skills are in short supply is depressingly familiar. Everyone knew in 1917 that the Soviet Government would be unable to maintain itself because the governing quality was not there—and it was exactly the same with the new states in Africa and Asia after the second World War.

One would have expected the old class divisions to dissolve but, on the contrary, they were codifying.

> In our forties we had to recognize that English society had become more rigid, not less, since our youth. Its forms were crystalizing under our eyes into an elaborate and codified Byzantinism, decent enough, tolerable to live in, but not blown through by the winds of scepticism or individual protest or sense of outrage which were our native air. And those forms were not only too cut-and-dried for us: they would have seemed altogether too rigid for nineteenth century Englishmen.

Snow makes Lewis Eliot and his colleagues sound like a gang of desperate conspirators ('sense of outrage'!); it's rather like the old man who looks back on a blameless life and murmurs, 'What a dog was I!' At the most he had snatched a kiss on Southend pier. But he was not really discussing society, he was admiring the nuts and bolts that held the enormous edifice together. The honours list, for example— it had ceased to be corrupt and unpredictable but was now systematized by Civil Service checks and balances.

> Just as the men of affairs had fractionated themselves into a group with its own rules and its own New Year's Day rewards, just as the arts were, without knowing it, drifting into invisible academies, so the aristocrats, as they lost their power and turned into ornaments, shut themselves up and exaggerated their distinguishing marks in a way that to old Bevill, who was grander than any of them, seemed rank bad manners, and what was worse, impolitic.

The Sleep of Reason, 1968, is in many ways a very fine achievement. It stands out in a sequence that is of extremely uneven quality. In this novel Snow seems to be emotionally involved rather than a dispassionate onlooker who at times appears to be propounding a thesis. Not that there is no element of thesis in this novel (one of the weaknesses of the sequence is that it appears to be deliberately pummelled into shape to suit the convenience of the hour—or day) but at least it keeps away from the dreadful snob areas Snow has so ingenuously made his own. And the presentation of the Pateman family is beyond criticism. For my purpose of social discussion it is absorbing.

At a new university four undergraduates are being disciplined for being found sleeping together: two couples, nothing terribly exotic. Arnold Shaw, the Vice Chancellor, is determined to send them down. Lewis Eliot tries to explain that there has been a change in the moral climate and most members of the Court regard such a punishment as too extreme these days. 'He must admit, I said, that most of the people we knew—probably most people in the whole society—didn't really regard fornication as a serious offence. In secret they didn't regard it as an offence at all.' Shaw challenges Eliot by asking him what would have happened in his own time if four undergrads had been found in such circumstances. Eliot admits that they would have been sent down but reminds Shaw that that was thirty years ago. That the environment had changed, including the moral climate, was obvious in many ways. Eliot walks round his old town, sees West Indians talking on the pavements, cars outside houses in mean streets. He meets his old friend, George Passant, who feels he has been excluded by his enemies. They won, he said. But in another sense it was he who had won.

> All those passionate arguments for *freedom*—which meant sexual freedom. The young George in this town, poor, unknown, feeling himself outside society, raising the great voice I had just heard. 'Freedom from their damned homes, and their damned parents, and their damned lives'. Well, he had won: or rather, all those like him, all the forces they spoke for (since he was, as someone had said during one of his ordeals, a 'child of his time') had won.

Walking round the town with Maxwell, the head of the local CID, he went up streets where every third or fourth face seemed to be coloured. He remarked that when he was a boy it was an oddity to see a dark skin in the town. The town was more prosperous. He ate well at an Italian restaurant. When he was a boy he could not have eaten like that, not only because there wasn't the money but also because that type of restaurant hadn't existed. There are several references to well dressed, vigorous middle class women.

But something has gone wrong. Eliot's mother used to say, when something unpleasant threatened, 'After all, it's the twentieth century' —meaning, it couldn't happen. But others, like Austin Davidson (Eliot's second father-in-law) called it 'the dreadful century'. Lewis's brother Martin says, 'I have seen freedom. And it rots.' For excessive freedom has meant full play for our worst impulses.

The new permissiveness had produced a family like the Patemans, each of whom (except the mother, who barely communicated, and was clearly puzzled) insisted that everyone's hand was raised against them and that something must be done to help them. Mr Pateman had never been able to make a go of anything. Dick had been sent down from university for sexual misconduct, Kitty was on trial for a gruesome murder, with her friend, Cora Ross. Dick expresses the family grievance.

> 'They' were to blame, 'the whole wretched set-up', the racket, the establishment, society itself. We should have to break it up, said Dick. Look what they had done to his father. Look at what they were doing to him. His discontent was getting violent (I gathered that he was having more trouble with examinations at his new university). Kitty would be happy in a decent society. There was nothing wrong with her. As for Cora Ross, if she'd 'done anything', that was their fault: no-one had looked after her, she'd never been properly educated, she'd never been found a place.

The lack of precision, the sledge-hammer effect of this kind of talk is splendidly reproduced. Permissiveness was one leg of the enemy; the other was something that called itself 'revolutionary' sentiment, but was in fact a kind of emotional wallowing.

Since Snow finished his sequence and got rid of Lewis Eliot (surely a relief!) he has published two novels which, while not tracing a new ground, certainly create a very well-worn path through the old ground. 1970 is the terminal date of my main concern with these novelists. *The Malcontents*, 1972, and *In Their Wisdom*, 1974, open a new chapter in Snow's literary progress. They are extremely depressing— in fact, the main theme of the later book might well be referred to as 'there ain't no justice'. Cosmic justice is intended, for the human variety is necessarily faulty. The chances are loaded against people in an entirely irrational way and very little can be done to alleviate the suffering. The first centres round the activities of a group of seven students, coming from very different homes and possessing very different attitudes to life. Superficially they have drawn together but at the first sign of tension the solidarity cracks. It seems impossible that the discontented working class intellectual will ever come to terms with the cultured bourgeois. The nearest any of these people can get to a faith is the wiping out of race as a distinction. The parents are helpless, supporters of lost causes, and when they profess a faith the children declare it a sham. The working class mothers are equally at odds with their children, for when they express a desire that their sons should have 'nice' friends it is clear they mean rich ones. In this vein Snow's work is complementary to that of Angus Wilson, who has mapped so clearly the dilemma of the bourgeois intellectual. Snow's people do not belong so obviously to the *New Statesman* belt of well-intentioned fatuity; well-to-do liberals, they are neither so dogmatic nor so cocky, but they are equally bewildered. One feels, while reading this novel, that class feeling is becoming more and not less rigid, in Snow's view of our society. The major animosity he describes occurs when two of the students (golden youths) enter a lorry drivers' caff. The atmosphere sparks with hatred.

In Their Wisdom could have been a fine novel but it is damaged by Snow's insistence on talking round his characters and his theme instead of allowing them to display themselves. He is always at his best when he is describing a dramatic contest whose outcome is uncertain, but this is less surely handled than *The Masters,* 1951 or *The Affair,* 1960. The atmosphere is thick with gloom. What is really the matter? Jenny, a dispossessed heiress, is drawn to Lorimer, an impoverished peer who does a little part-time teaching to eke out. They stroll through the streets of London, past the striptease posters, the pornographic bookshops. It used to be better. Now it was horribly sleazy. 'They each had what Lorimer as a boy had been taught to call a code, and their codes were very much the same. One hadn't to go far in central London that night to feel that such a code—like the class who formed it, whether they kept to it or not—had gone for ever.'

Privilege

'In the past, privilege may have exercised good influences in many directions, but during our lifetime its shortcomings have been increasingly obvious. Today it seems to be falling into disfavour all over the world', writes T.H. Pear in *English Social Differences,* 1955. The latter statement seems to me highly dubious—in fact, in many modern societies privilege has replaced wealth. However, Pear's view is shared by one of Snow's academics. Crawford, the Master of the College, is an old-fashioned radical who refuses to budge an inch in matters of etiquette. He presides over a dinner at which the men wear white ties and tails. 'Speaking as the oldest round this table by a good few years', he says, 'I have seen the disappearance of a remarkable amount of privilege' (*The Affair*,). The one thing all serious people were agreed upon, he said, was that privilege must be done away with. It had been steadily whittled away ever since he was a young man. All attempts to stop this process had failed just as, by and large, reaction always failed. People were no longer prepared to see others enjoying privilege because they had a different coloured skin or spoke in a different tone or were born into families that had done well for themselves. 'The disappearance of privilege—if you want something that gives you the direction of time's arrow, that's as good as anything I know.' The argument is satisfactory if you accept its selective basis. If, however, you recognize that position in a bureaucracy or a party has replaced the earlier criteria, the argument becomes unacceptable.

Crawford, speaking from his closed academic keep, is no doubt sincere. He still enjoys one of the small remaining areas of ancient privilege and is unaware of the new areas that have been opened up. We can see the old-type privilege in operation in *The Masters*, where ritual wine-drinking (wine-kultur as distinct from viniculture) is an integral part of the action. The drama of the election of the new Master is played out against a background of port and sherry, madeira and claret. The wine circulates in the accepted manner. Brown is the connoisseur—all discussions take place over a bottle of specially chosen wine. At the beginning of each June he held a claret party. 'I should be lucky if I had the chance to drink wine so good again', thinks Eliot. Brown had been trained by Pilbrow. 'He fixed one of us with a lively brown eye and asked what we noticed at each sip—at the beginning, middle and end of each sip. The old man rang all the changes possible with ten bottles of claret. When we were half-way through he said with extreme firmness: "I don't think any of you would ever be quite first-class. I give our host the benefit of the doubt. . . ." ' Each man had ten glasses in front of him, labelled to match the decanters. Crawford says it's difficult, in such circumstances, to believe what's going on in the world outside.

In *The Sleep of Reason* the decline of privilege (that is, of traditional privilege which people have been trained to discern, while the new privilege is still obscured by euphemism) is replaced by attack. The Patemans represent this trend, each member of the family convinced that he has been cheated, and that the frauds have been perpetrated by those who wield privilege. Bosanquet, the prosecuting counsel, is one of the 'new men' who by definition oppose old-type privilege. He was irritated by the psychiatrist, Cornford, who reminded Eliot of his father-in-law, Davidson. 'They were clever, they were privileged, to outsiders it seemed that they had found life too easy: they were too sure of their own enlightenment. Bosanquet hadn't found life at all easy: despite his name,[1] his family was poor, he had been to a north-country grammar school. He wasn't sure of his enlightenment, or anyone else's, after living in the criminal courts for thirty years.'

The subject is touched again in *Last Things*. Gordon Bestwick, a bright student of proletarian origins (though, typically, his brightness is not apparent to the reader), visits Guy Grenfell's rooms. (Grenfell is from the top drawer.) The room they were in was handsome but very cold. Before the war there would have been a coalfire but now the college had installed central heating, and it was turned off for the Easter term. Eliot remarks to Bestwick that 'privileged living had become increasingly unprivileged' ever since he was a young man. But one kind of privilege still works. Arthur Brown says of Eliot's son Charles: 'It did occur to me that we might manage to construct a vacancy for him here'. This would have been at the expense of Bestwick.

Oddly enough, Snow is the most hierarchical of all my novelists. The greater part of his writing is about privileged groups and he accepts their right to privilege. There is an aristocratic disdain and an unspoken contempt for the multitude, which is expressed largely by ignoring them. Once again (in *The Sleep of Reason*) the university is virtually without students—the only four we not only meet but even hear about, are on the carpet and can be dealt with. The leaders are represented admiringly as Narcissists. They are always expressing their moral doubts, never conscious of their self-importance. Lewis Eliot is the Student's Representative on the University Court—elected, presumably, by a conference of student ghosts.

The Generation Gap

The Gap and the War have become news since the second World War. Snow was aware of it before the war (he was a bit before his

1. Snow loves the irony of surnames. In the late novel, *The Malcontents,* 1972, one of the poorest students bears the most aristocrat name, St. John. Immigrants change their names to something more agreeable, especially Jews. And the wine connoisseur, acquiring one of the aristocracy's major arts, is named Brown. Even in his latest novel (at the time of writing), *In Their Wisdom,* 1974, we are told that back in 1820 Pemberton had changed his name to his wife's, as Englishman on the make never needed much persuasion to do.

time in this, as was Rosamund Lehmann) but in later years tended to fight shy of it. He was unable to ignore it but he was certainly baffled by it, and at times irritated. There is an element of the old buffer in some of his later works, a feeling that the young men are not quite up to the mark, not like we were, what?

The most angry protagonist for the Angry Young Men was Tom Orbell in *The Affair,* but Orbell's ideas get their first airing in Snow's first novel, *Death Under Sail.* They actually provide the major theme of his second novel. This is to say that he was concerned with the conflict of the generations at the two most likely moments in his own life: when he was young, and impatient with the prevarications of older men, and when he himself was no longer young, and became aware of how the mind reacts to aging.

In *Death Under Sail* William attacks the older generation. He is a man with a history something like Snow's own—self-made, a rising scientist. Finbow says he has been thinking about the situation in China, whereas the youthful Christopher says his own life interests him a lot more than any number of Chinese. When they get older their attitude will change, says Finbow. William breaks in:

> Nonsense. Your generation exhausted England's supply of social conscience. You were all damned keen on the future of the world; and look what you did with it! Look at Christopher and me. Our first real memories are of war-time hysteria, nerves, foolery of all sorts. We were adolescent in the post-war years, the silliest years that have ever been, I should think. And now just as we've got our lives more or less arranged, we get a financial crisis that may upset everything. It's a legacy of your generation, Finbow, and your damned social consciences.

The unusual thing about this passage is that it is the older man who is being accused of being idealistic—but his idealism has been phoney, it has led to mass suffering and international idiocy. The youthful revolt is not against idealism but against falsity.

New Lives For Old is concerned with a technique of rejuvenation by which thirty years can be added to a normal life. One of the two scientists responsible is young and despises the old—they learn nothing and merely cling to the follies of youth. Professor Pilgrim says excitedly to Callan, 'Do you realize what it may mean, my boy? Do you see what we may be able to do?' Callan's reply is curt. 'It was annoying of the old, he thought, not to grasp that one could see a point as quickly as they could. Or usually more quickly.' This aspect of the generation relationship is obscured in the later work, but is brought out again in the last novel of the sequence, but by now the shoe is on the other foot. The author is no longer young, and his sympathies are not quite so clear-cut. The young Charles is patient and tolerant with his father, Lewis Eliot, who has serious doubts about youthful intransigence.

The principle result of the rejuvenation process was the return of vital energy. Shaw's notion that an older population would be wiser is not realized. In fact, the logical aim of modern youth would be to cut the life-span. Young men who invent rejuvenation processes are creating more old men and not behaving very intelligently. But in Snow's novel it is the sex aspect that is stressed almost to the total exclusion of all others, except in the last section where a revolution occurs as a bye-product of the new situation. All the old men take young mistresses, and vice versa. Without the benefits of rejuvenation Kittigrew, the prime minister, illustrates the degeneration that comes with age. As a young man he had been enthusiastic and sincere in his devotion to Socialism in Our Time. Later he did more than any one man to destroy that cause and to become the complacent mouthpiece of the Right Wing. Callan is appalled by the possibilities and rather late in the day tries to block the new discovery. 'If we let it out, the old will get young. It's revolting. The thought makes me sick.' Callan is Snow's first portrait of the culturally naive scientist who has no idea of the wider implications of his work, conceived before the Two Cultures controversy made headlines.

At his trial George Passant made a statement which brought the subject into prominence again, and represents a consistent undertone of rebelliousness in the early novels of the sequence. 'I believe that while people are young they have a chance to become themselves only if they're preserved from all the conspiracy that crushes them down.' The conspiracy is that of age and the clogging of the spiritual as well as the physical arteries that accompanies it. Passant's moderate statement anticipates Tom Orbell's tirades against old men in *The Affair*. One has a certain amount of sympathy with Orbell, despite his wildness, when one considers the position of Gay, who is encountered in both *The Masters* and *The Affair*. He is the supreme example of the doddering old geezer who not only holds a place of power but uses it. In fact he does no damage but his capacity for damage, if the situation were ripe, was enormous.

A very large part of the drama in *The Affair* is represented as a phase in the war between the generations. Orbell's point of view is expressed thus: 'The good young middle-aged had got caught up trying to keep the country afloat. The generation coming up had got

to fight some other battles, had got to smash "the awful old men" '.
Orbell is one of Snow's most successfully observed characters. He is
always at his best in portraying twilight characters, men and women
(but usually men) who are a credible mixture of one fairly sound idea
and a lot of hot air. Mr Pateman is another. Compared with these
parti coloured personalities, the positive men, those 'outlined with
firm, deft strokes' as I fear some of our reviewers would call them, are
hard to take. Of course, the starkness of some people is real, not the
invention of an author. Laura Howard, the wife of the scientist who
has lost his Fellowship on a charge of fraud, has a *Simpliste* view of
life in which there are good men and bad men, the bad men are
reactionaries, and the reactionaries are usually old men. These people
exist, especially in politics. When Howard is reinstated Orbell is not
satisfied: he wants payment in full and the period of deprivation added
on to the original time of expiry. When the Eliots and Getliffe refuse
to support this he jeers at them for playing safe with the old men.
'I'm beginning to think the real menace is the Establishment behind
the Establishment.' These contain the middle-aged who wish to appear
liberal but in reality are guided by personal interest.

The Sleep of Reason, with its greater involvement in the diurnal
world, manages to keep the generation conflict in perspective, though
not always successfully. Lester Ince is a recognizable figure; he had
been a vague Angry and had married a rich American woman. Ince
switches from one role to another without any noticeable transition.
No exception can be taken to this, he is a character who illustrates
the difficulty of making valid judgments on the young. He had had
a reputation for holding advanced opinions. As soon as a chink of
opportunity opened, he and the woman both got divorces and started
looking for a historic country house. 'A very suitable end for an angry
young man', said Martin. He appears insincere. If the rich marriage
had not presented itself he might have remained angry and become
sincere. Who knows? But where Eliot's son Charles is concerned,
Snow's touch is less sure. It is, admittedly, a much closer and more
subtle relationship than the one between Ince and Eliot, in that case
a colleague and observer, not a father. The relationship seems muted,
and so it is for Eliot is half afraid of his son—not afraid of being hurt
but of hurting. They are too fond of each other, and Charles is too
understanding, much too adult for his years. Before he was seventeen
he went off on a European tour by himself. It would have been
unimaginable among Lewis and his young friends, they would have
had neither the money nor the confidence.

Eliot is beginning to find the young irritating. He attends a dinner party at Brown's Hotel with a group of eminent scientists. Most of these men, when younger, had tried to warn people against Hitler; they had been prepared for war and immersed themselves in it when it came. Most of them had risked unpopularity and had paid a price. But however true this may be of any group of men, it is nearly always associated with a complacent sense of moral superiority. 'There was scientific ability about, comparable with theirs, but either the younger professionals didn't take their public risks, or there was something in the climate which didn't let such rough-hewn characters emerge.'

All these strands accumulate and together form a very important factor in *Last Things,* which is very markedly a summing-up. Eliot is now treating his son as a member of a different species, and with some reason, for his own generation is seen to be increasingly pompous and fossilized. Snow gives a remarkable picture of a man who knows all the text-book stuff about spiritual arteries becoming hardened as well as the physical ones, and yet insists in his heart that although no-one may have a monopoly of virtue yet he has the greater part of what's going. Outwardly he is not as crude as this description suggests. He seems to try very hard to understand, but at times it seems to be little more than gesture-making:

> They were friendly, both with an older generation and each other. They didn't drink as much as my friends used to at their age: there were all the signs that they took sex much more easily. Certainly there didn't seem to be many tormented love-affairs about . . . I sometimes wondered how much different was the way they lived their lives from their parents' way: was the gap bigger than other such gaps had been?

Charles agrees that their manners were different from his—'but they think yours are as obsolete as Jane Austen's.' Eliot wondered: 'Are these really our successors? Will they ever be able to take over?' This betrays the same kind of lack of imagination that had formerly caused the oldies to think that Eliot's generation were hopeless—and what was the evidence? Nothing significant, and mainly on the level of long hair and not addressing envelopes properly. Eliot Senior's virtues were plain for all to see.

Yet when Eliot returns to his college he meets some of the younger scientists, and Getliffe tells him they represent a change for the better. They were much more genuine academics than their predecessors, most of them were doing good research. But they provided fewer examples of free personality than the earlier crowd, and at times one felt that some of the latter had often practised eccentricity as an art. Eliot also discovered that Charles and his friends were more serious than he had thought; their politics might be utopian but they were at least their own. They were more genuinely international than his own crowd had been; they were not so much concerned with Europe as with the world. Eliot gives the impression of being always haunted by George Passant—which means, perhaps, that while writing this novel Snow was haunted by Ian Brady. Brady and Passant are by no means identifiable, but a link can be traced. Eliot was impressed by the sexual freedom of the young, though his comments are sparing. What else might there be at the heart of all this unrest, rebellion and alienation? It was happening all round the world; there was also the queer suspicion that the whole thing was being helped by commercialism, with which the movement had basically so little in common. There was no ideology or mass base, that was what worried Eliot.

My distaste for Snow's work (I might as well admit it for I have been unable to disguise it) probably relates, not to his lack of imagination but to his pose as the scientist who, unlike the majority of his colleagues, possesses imagination. In fact, his approach to character is clinical, the approach of the scientist and not that of the empathic novelist. No-one can doubt his good intentions but his capacities do not seem equal to the task he has set himself. Eliot frequently admits his inadequacies, for which we must respect him. He cannot simply be dismissed as a frump. But the fact remains that even if he is honestly struggling to understand, the general tone is one of disapproval. If we ask why, the answer seems to be no more rewarding than that the young were adopting new methods and outlooks (no ideology, no mass political base). Presumably the older methods and outlooks had been 'hilariously successful', as Huxley remarked on an occasion when he was rebuked for his pessimism. There used to be a much-quoted folk tale about a goose that thought it was a swan. Snow will get the point if I suggest that a man may wish to be a Bradman and turn out to be a Luckhurst. It is important to note that no-one has the right to scoff at such a failing. It is also important to note that ideology is dying, if not already dead, and that the young with unimpaired vision, recognize the corpse immediately. Lewis Eliot's vision was notoriously faulty. Snow made so much of this we must assume it is to be regarded as a symbol, even if an awkwardly planted one.

Power and the Ruling Class

Snow's human interest is in the groups who have assumed power in the twentieth century and make the decisions necessary for civilized life: mainly lawyers, scientists, academics and administrators. If decisions were left to the man with a classical or literary education, solutions would probably go begging and would devolve upon the politician and soldier. The only force that can act as a conscience or brake upon the latter is the scientist, for the politician and soldier depend for their success on what the scientist can discover. The scientist is the new man of conscience; his imaginative powers are analogous to those of the poets in the past, he has replaced the poet as the unacknowledged legislator. Frederick Karl claims that Snow's New Men are politically and socially conscious scientists, dedicated men who have been created by the new world and who, in turn, will help create the still newer world. Snow thinks they should bear the responsibility of decision and become increasingly important in government and public affairs. Recent eruptions of student protest have been against the old-type administrators, men such as Hector Rose (of whom Snow thinks highly). Many of the New Men, especially in the universities (that is, the real universities, not Snow's) appear to support the protests.

But if scientists are to form a kind of advisory panel, the cardinal choices are still to be made by a handful of men in secret. Usually they are men who cannot have a firsthand knowledge of what those choices depend upon or what the results may be. 'No country's governmental science is any "freer" than any other's, nor are its secret scientific choices', Snow said in his Godkin Lectures at Harvard University (published under the title *Science and Government,* 1960). In these lectures Snow, perhaps unwittingly, contrasted two phases of social organization, particularly illustratable through the person of Lindemann (Lord Cherwell). Lindemann was a most unlikely figure to work his way so easily to the higher levels of English society, but this society was a traditional grouping, and 'for generations English Society has been wide open to, defenceless against, rich and determined men.' Lindemann also, by his friendship with Churchill, became a crucial figure in the control of government science, but his influence was disastrous because there was no-one with the knowledge to check his inaccuracies and misjudgments.

Snow's own career has caused him to pass through egalitarianism to a faith in elitism. As a result he holds a rather hybrid view of educational needs, for example. According to an interview with Terry

Coleman of the *Guardian*, Snow has supported comprehensive schools (the egalitarian approach) but insists that a country must make special provision for the education of its leaders (the elitist). He wants to educate separately a very special elite—'not one in a thousand or one in five thousand'. He has come to believe that inherited ability is far more important than environment. 'If you're lucky, God gives you a hand of cards. All education can do is teach you how best to play those cards.' A democracy must come to terms with the facts of life and recognize that people are not created equal in ability. A difference in emphasis, if not in viewpoint, is presented in *The Sleep of Reason*, however. 'There were about ten thousand jobs which really counted in the England of that time. The more I saw, the more I was convinced that you could get rid of the present incumbents, find ten thousand more, and the society would go ticking on with no one (except perhaps the displaced) noting the difference.' This certainly contradicts the usual implications of Snow's work. We see groups of privileged men, plotting together, evaluating each other in the greatest detail, and always taking it for granted that the minor differences of knowledge, temperament, skill and understanding were of first importance. A chance remark might damn a man, and it was right that it should. Snow always gave the impression that he accepted this point of view.

But we must turn to *The Corridors of Power* if we wish to determine what Snow really thinks about the mechanics of government. It is his *vade-mecum* on the subject. In *New Lives For Old* the disappearance of the old ruling class had been prophesied. The new novel was published during the time-scale of the earlier work, and the old ruling class still clings to power. Eliot is at Basset, the home of Diana Skidmore.

> It occurred to me that, a quarter of a century before, I had sat in rich houses, listening to my friends, the heirs, assuming that before we were middle-aged, such houses would exist no more. Well, that hadn't happened. Now Diana's friends were talking as though it never would happen. Perhaps they had some excuse.

We have already seen aristocrats in a Mitford novel gloating over their class's powers of endurance. David Rubin, the American scientist in *Corridors*, is impressed. 'No country's got a ruling class like this. I don't know what they hope for, and they don't know either. But they still feel they're the lords of the world.' Snow attributes their success to their great self-confidence. Rubin says Eliot borrows the confidence from them, without believing anything they believe.

This is scarcely a true account of Eliot, who gives little indication of believing anything. Confidence in itself is not enough—the French aristocrats had plenty. And in this very novel we see the ruling class getting desperate because their power is deserting them. Rich and privileged mediocrities like Sammikins refuse to accept it and behave with an almost Nazi-like determination to drag the world down with them in a glorious last-ditch gesture. Sammikins uses expressions like 'one of us', and says he hoped his sister would have married within the caste, not an outsider. 'He spoke as unselfconsciously as his great-grandfather might have done, saying he thought that his sister might have married a "gentleman" '. He could combine this with hero-worship of his brother-in-law for a while, but in the end the hero-worship broke down.

Hector Rose, the civil servant with the expensive education who hadn't got on as well as he had hoped, knew that Francis Getliffe was as unlikely to betray his country as Lieutenant-General Sir James Brudenell, Bart., C.B., whose portrait looked down on him and Eliot from the wall of the United Services Club. He had been a hero of the Zulu Wars. But what Rose implied in saying this was that the Establishment could not really believe it. It was their country—why should others be loyal to it?

Eliot's early socialist views seem to have worn very thin, although he refers to them briefly on occasion. When he accompanies his down-at-heel friend Porson to a pub he encounters a type of bohemian society he had once known but had long ago left behind. It wasn't a political group at all, but it was not Establishment, and it is the kind of group one still associates with left wing opinion. It was the kind of life one never forgets if one has lived it. On the whole they were people of goodwill, kinder than those he normally worked with and met, but they didn't feel that anything mattered very much. This was a flat rejection of the portentousness that marks all Eliot's normal experience and behaviour. It is odd that even in the novels describing Eliots youth the references to his left wing activities are extremely sparse. It comes almost as a shock to hear (we can scarcely say be reminded), when he is being questioned by a Security officer, that he had spoken at local meetings and had associated with the I.L.P. Perhaps through a final spasm of conscience he tells his interrogator that once the Russians acquire some insight they may produce a 'wonderful society'. It's not enough to hang a man on.

We are made to feel that we are in the presence of an emerging power complex which will remodel society. Where does power reside is a question that exercises the minds of Eliot and his friends considerably. No-one really knew. Douglas Osbaldiston, who lived in suburban unpretentiousness, felt that the wealthy Basset group had a strong effect on government decisions, yet they in their turn had a frightening vision of suburbia as the emergent ruling force. Both the politicians and the scientists were ignorant of the true social forces. All they could do was wait for time to show them which factors counted for most.

It was men like Quaife who still counted. He was in the peculiar position of wishing to run down the nuclear military effort, when such ideas were considered to be the prerogative of the other side. But it had to be him, or someone like him. 'In our kind of society—and I mean America too—the only things that can possibly get done are going to be done by people like me. I don't care what you call me. Liberal Conservative. Bourgeois capitalist. We're the only people who can get a political decision through.' But there was one changed factor, represented by the 'new men'. Quaife recognized the import-ance of the unofficial scientist, men like Getliffe and Luke, whom he put on committees and whose advice he accepted. They were 'committed' to a line of thought and, if possible, action. There was a class of scientist (Astill) who was simple-minded in an old-fashioned way—he simply believed that ministers were likely to be right. But in this he was not behaving particularly like a scientist but like an ordinary unaware member of the general public.

Snow usually links the cynical and the unworldly, which is unusual. Normally it is the worldly who are supposed to be cynical. Snow is right. Those who are innocent of power processes always imagine the worst: they are the progenitors of the various theories of con-spiracy which amateur politicians love to display, and to connect with whatever system they support, whether it be Marxism or Liberalism. Snow says that business gets done in an implicit manner, rarely by intrigue or private deals, or with cut-and-dried arguments. But the effect of reading about all the 'busyness' of these people (there was a tremendous lot of to-and-froing, though the emphasis was rarely political or pointed) is similar to that gained from reading of Gulliver in Lilliput, except that here the effect is not intentional. Snow writes from the angle of a committed Lilliputian. It is his lack of critical appraisal, of satire, that finally appals.

But these aspects of society play scarcely more than a peripheral role in Snow's vision. The essence of it is contained in a passage like this:

> A week after Lufkin's birthday, I was standing in a crowded
> drawing room at the American Ambassador's house, deafened

by the party's surge and swell. Margaret and I had been exchanging a word or two with the wife of J.C. Smith, Collingwood's nephew. I had not met her before. She was a short slender woman, dark, attractive in a muted way, not very talkative. I wondered incuriously why I hadn't seen her husband's name in *Hansard* for so long. She passed away from us. Someone else called out to Margaret, and in the huddle I found myself against David Rubin.

Soon I was shaking my fingers to restore the circulation while he looked at me with sombre-eyed *Schadenfreude*. I had asked for whiskey with plenty of ice, and had got it: the glass was so thin that my hand had become numbed with cold. Just then, one of the embassy counsellors came towards Rubin, looking for him, not drifting in the party's stream. Although he knew me well, his manner was constrained. After a few cordialities, he apologized and took Rubin aside.

For an instant I was left alone in the ruck of the party. Over the heads of the people nearby I could see the flaxen hair of Arthur Plimpton, the young American who was going round with Francis Getliffe's daughter. I caught his eye and beckoned him: but before he could make his way through the crowd, Rubin and the diplomat were back.

This is, sadly, what a lot of life is like and, sadly, what Snow chooses to write about. There is absolutely no enlightenment in this sort of thing and it is hard to believe that one would read it for amusement. It is simply the condition that humanity has slowly, so slowly that we do not notice the change while it happens, waddled into from one of purposeful behaviour. This sort of environment— whose stations are the dinner party, the drinks party and the country house weekend— plays an increasing role in our social structure and is increasingly accepted as a natural development. It is essentially sterile. Of course, Snow has reasons for giving a thumbnail sketch of Mrs Smith and for bumping into Rubin and seeing Plimpton's flaxen hair, but the situation is something like a five-minute ride on the Dodgems. There is neither drama nor significance in this sort of thing, yet Snow takes it seriously. It reinforces Forster's view that the literary uses of eating and drinking are entirely social, but develops it to a farcical extreme.

Enclaves

The secret of Snow's failure to project his society either convincingly or meaningfully can be associated with his best-known work, the one with which he is identified in the public mind: *The Two Cultures,* a printing of his Rede Lecture in 1959, and republished in 1963 with *A Second Look.* He expressed his dilemma in these words: 'Constantly I felt I was moving among two groups—comparable in intelligence, identical in race, not grossly different in social origin, earning about the same incomes, who had almost ceased to communicate at all, who in intellectual, moral and psychological climate had so little in common that instead of going from Burlington House or South Kensington to Chelsea, one might have crossed an ocean.' Snow's thesis was not well received. In my view this was not so much because his critics disagreed with its essential truth but because in his own work he failed so signally to cross the divide. *Strangers and Brothers* is fiction by a scientist. The normal insights of the artist are largely missing.

Snow's argument may be summarized as follows. Scientists are 'inclined to be impatient to see if something can be done' to improve the social condition, in which most of our fellow human beings are underfed and die before their time. This tempts one to think nothing can be done, but scientists are inclined to think that something can be done until proved otherwise. 'That is their real optimism, and it's an optimism that the rest of us need badly.' The nature of our dominant traditional culture is unscientific; in fact, its flavour is often on the point of turning anti-scientific. 'The feelings of one pole become the anti-feelings of the other. If the scientists have the future in their bones, then the traditional culture responds by wishing the future did not exist. It is the traditional culture, to an extent remarkably little diminished by the emergence of the scientific one, which manages the western world.' This cultural divide is sharper in England than elsewhere, due to a fanatical belief in educational specialization and a tendency to let social forms crystallize. 'This tendency appears to get stronger, not weaker, the more we iron out economic inequalities: and this is especially true in education'. Social forces tend to make the cultural divide more rigid, not less. (In *Second Look* he said he thought he had not emphasized this point enough.) But the gap is widening. 'The separation between the scientists and non-scientists is much less bridgeable among the young than it was even thirty years ago. Thirty years ago the cultures had long ceased to speak to each other: but at least they managed a kind of frozen smile across the gulf. Now the politeness has gone and they just make faces.' Young scientists feel their culture is on the rise, the other in retreat. We still have some assets, including our wits, which have served us well in two ways.

We have a good deal of cunning in the arts of getting on among ourselves, and we have been inventive and creative out of proportion to our numbers. In *Second Look* he felt that a third culture was forming: it was a body of opinion, without organization or conscious direction, under the surface of debate. It was being formed from intellectuals in a number of fields: social history, sociology, demography, political science, economics, psychology, medicine and social arts such as architecture. All are concerned with how human beings live or have lived. They do not all agree but in their approach they betray a family resemblance.

It is very easy to shoot holes in this argument, and this has been done to such an extent that most of us are as weary of the debate as we became of the U-non-U craze. Snow's third culture was probably a reaction to the criticism, which led him to admit how much he had left out. The major fault seems to be the solidarity he posits among scientists. In fact, there are as great divides among different scientific disciplines as between scientists in general and artists in general. Many artists have a much more intimate knowledge of natural forms, crystallography and microscopic data than many anatomists; many novelists could run rings round most physicists in formal psychology, yet alone their intuitive insights; I even suspect that some poets are better read in physics than many psychologists. One only has to transfer his reasoning to another field to realize how unreal it is. Think of the gap that divides games-players and intellectuals, for instance—consider how solidly united professional footballers and chess grandmasters are in their opposition to things of the mind. This is not meant to be an argument, certainly not a conclusive one, but it suggests that Snow has succumbed to the enticements of his own exaggerations. But in any case, it is not my concern to support or attack such a theory. I am interested in tracing its reflection in his fiction.

One sees the major reflection, of course, in *The New Men,* but it is also implicit in *The Corridors of Power.* Failure to understand and to communicate is, with full justification, one of Snow's major themes. He is fascinated by men of academic distinction who live in what he later called enclaves. This was merely a reflection of the greater society, although they had cut themselves off from it. Snow's conviction is that intelligence is capable of bridging the gaps between different expertises, though in this he never equalled Waugh's naivety. In *Corridors* there is a mild suggestion that some kind of change is in the air. In this novel it is the politicians who represent one side of the cultural divide, and they are lumped with 'tradition' which includes all forces which pre-date science. (The suggestion might be that they are magicians and wonder-workers, shamans and charlatans.) Eliot was interested in Roger Quaife, the new minister. He, like the others, talked about the chessboard of Parliament as though nothing else existed. 'These people's politics were not my politics. They didn't know the world they were living in, much less the world that was going to come.' Yet Eliot shows little indication that he knows any more or is interested in anything outside the chessboard. He nods his head gravely and discusses politics without ideas. (Universities without students, etc.) Frederick Karl compares the typical Snow hero to the existentialist hero. Despite their great differences, there is a considerable area where they overlap. The existentialist is outside society, whereas even the most peripheral of Snow's characters want to stay in. But in each case there is a lack of communication. Snow's New Men reject traditions and institutions because they are no longer effective; the existentialist sees no value in society.

In his last book of the sequence, *Last Things,* Snow clarifies the situation by introducing the notion of enclaves. Everyone, Lewis Eliot included, is engaged in building an enclave for himself in which he will find some kind of security. It has its attractions as a theory of social development, and even the unfortunate George Passant is accommodated by it. Now Eliot tells his son Charles that he and his friends are doing the same, and Charles doesn't like the imputation.

> All over the advanced world, people seemed to be making enclaves. I thought that wasn't just a fantasy of my own. The rich like Azik and some of our American friends; the professionals everywhere; the apparently rebellious young; they were all drawing the curtains, looking inwards into their own rooms, to an extent that hadn't happened in my own time. The demonstrations (that was the summer when the English young, including Charles's friends, started protesting about Vietnam), the acts of violence, were deceptive. They too came from a kind of enclave. They were part of a world which, though it could be made less comfortable, or more foreboding, no-one could find a way to shake.

No-one would suggest that enclaves do not exist. The idea only becomes significant if it can be shown that they are on the increase. Eliot offers no such proof but is satisfied with the bare assertion— despite the fact that elsewhere he is impressed by the way his son and his friends are much more concerned with the world than previous generations had been. In fact, the enclave theory seems to be a last-minute attempt to save something from the ruins: to provide a principle that will somehow make sense out of all this irritating variety.

VIII

Democracy and Inequality

In the second volume of his autobiography, *Editor,* 1968, Kingsley Martin relates how he visited the Paris Exhibition in 1937, saw the enormous German and Soviet pavilions and then the British one which appeared to be housed in a large packing case.

> When you went in, the first thing you saw was a cardboard Chamberlain fishing in rubber waders and, beyond, an elegant pattern of golf balls, a frieze of tennis rackets, polo sets, riding equipment, natty dinner jackets and, by a pleasant transition, agreeable pottery and textiles, books finely printed and photographs of the English countryside. I stared in bewilderment. Could this be England? If so, it was the England of the cultivated rich or perhaps of the England foreseen by Bernard Shaw when Britain's economy would depend on the export of chocolate creams.

Paris saw England through the medium of pastoral scenes and old churches. No factory chimneys, no hint of empire or proletariat, the twin supports of the good old times. A very nice England, of course, and quite unlike any that had ever existed or ever could. It was the England seen by the guests at a country house party which is, of course, not England but a tiny part of England. And on the whole this is the England illustrated by my six novelists, though they have extended the canvas somewhat to take in a little more of the environment, especially since the war. But 'the cultivated rich' have been well served by fiction.

I do not intend to discuss whether we live in a democratic society or not. I am largely concerned with what kind of society my six authors project and to what extent their picture coincides with the one given in the first chapter, based on descriptive and statistical analysis. I claim that my six novelists represent a good cross-sample of the middle ground. I could, of course, have chosen more eccentric writers but this would have defeated my purpose. It would be possible, by referring to the works of romantic idealists such as Elizabeth Myers, Anthony Thorne, Rachel Ferguson and Norman Davey, to form a picture of society which would be wildly unlike the one discovered here but this would be the natural result of a disparate choice of aim: by and large I believe my six novelists are all concerned to give what they consider a reasonably accurate picture of society as a whole or in part (as opposed to personal comment) whereas the emphasis among the others I have mentioned would be deliberately peripheral.

In Elizabeth Bowen's posthumous collection of writings entitled *Pictures and Conversations*, 1975, there are some 'Notes on Writing a Novel' which, apart from anything else, form one of the most careful descriptions of how a novelist thinks and sets about his work to be published. But here I am concerned with what she has to say about 'pre-assumptions'. She says that these may exist, 'sunk at different depths', in any novelist and determine the appeal that any particular novel will make to its readers at a variety of levels, of which the social is one. She says quite flatly that pre-assumptions are bad, because they cause the novel to act immorally on the reader. As the most clear-cut example of the pre-assumption at work she cites the detective novel, which works on the single and unchallenged notion that an act of violence is anti-social and that the doer must be traced.

One's immediate reaction is that pre-assumptions cannot be bad because we all must have them. It is pointless rejecting a faculty that is common to the whole human race. But Bowen claims that great novelists write without pre-assumption, from outside their own nationality, class or sex, which means that she must have an idea of this faculty beyond the superficially obvious. Does it mean that the great novelist should have no angle or moral viewpoint, she asks, and replies that this is not the case. A moral viewpoint is necessary to maintain conviction and to *light* the characters, for they must necessarily be seen in a moral light.

I am here dealing with good novelists for whom no-one has claimed the stature of a George Eliot or a Thomas Hardy, the latter being an example of a novelist whose moral conviction and power of lighting the character often transcended technically bad writing. In each case my six novelists are at times guilty of letting their pre-assumptions corrode the poetic truth which Bowen claims should be the main concern of the novelist. She claims that what she calls the 'front against pre-assumptions' has its weak point in humour. Almost all English humour shows social pre-assumptions. The employed classes are quaint or funny, aristocrats served by butlers are absurd. And it seems probable that nothing gives fuller rein to the exploitation of pre-assumptions than the resort to satire.

Elizabeth Bowen gives the impression of reluctantly agreeing that there is a serious sickness in our society, but at no time does she write satirically. (It is probably just as well—when another female novelist of our time, who was capable of incisive social criticism in her fiction, Pamela Hansford Johnson, resorted to satire, the results were extremely painful.) The leading satirists of our time (Waugh, Orwell and Huxley) agree that there is something terribly wrong with our society, but they do not agree on what it is that is wrong: Waugh depicts the defeat of civilization by the forces of savagery, stupidity and liberalism; Orwell warns of the corrupting force of power and the evil spread of tyranny; and Huxley portrays the progressive alienation of man from nature and attacks the growth of hedonism. *The Waste Land* was a prototype, particularly for Waugh and Huxley. How do my six respond?

Before summing up (for I have already shown where each of them stands individually) it is necessary to state that a novelist is not necessarily a satirist. There is tremendous disagreement on the validity of satire, Huxley at one point stating that under modern conditions satire is the most valuable creative work the writer can perform, while Snow has frequently shown his contempt for the satiric method. It is possible to disapprove of a society without resorting to satire.[1] But if he does eschew satire and writes straight he may well give the impression of accepting the existing system as does Snow. Is it then possible to make a general statement about the responsibility of a writer in his approach to society?

The prevalence of satire in itself suggests that there is a need for it. It was as strong in the eighteenth century as it is today; the nineteenth century produced little and it is significant that one of the major characteristics of nineteenth century writing was its complacency. Complacency is one of the marks of Snow's work. The nineteenth century believed completely in its own virtue. Looking back from our own vantage point, we feel that there was more virtue to the eighteenth

1. It is in fact Snow's wife, Pamela Hansford Johnson, who does this most satisfactorily.

century. These are very general statements, but they help to establish a critical colouration. On balance, it appears to be a fault for a writer to give the impression that he accepts inferior values. He can still give an undistorted picture. The thorough-going satirist deliberately distorts. There is a danger that the more sober critic will hedge his criticism with so many qualifications he will in the end not be a critic at all but a gentle conscience who stirs nobody.

Satire usually requires a base considerably removed from the target of attack. Straight criticism does not, as it usually consists of the little more attacking the little less (or the other way round). The other base in English society is the pre-industrial order, for although at first sight it has been virtually extinguished in practice it still fights for its existence. The odd thing about our novelists is that two of them choose for much of the time to attack from this diminishing ground: Hartley often, and Bowen now and again. But these areas possess enormous tribal power, as has been well expressed by Ralf Dahrendorf:

> The 'distinctions of rank' in pre-industrial societies of even the eighteenth century rested as much on a myth of tradition, an intricate system of age-old, often codified rights and duties, as on the comparatively crude gradations of property, power and prestige . . . The power of the landlord was not based on his having money, land or prestige, but on his being a landlord as his fathers had been for time immemorial.
>
> (*Class and Class Conflict in Industrial Society*, 1959)

Marx argued that as a society develops to its maturity, the originally divided interests become increasingly united. Applying this to the bourgeoisie, the division is between landownership and capital. Writers such as Waugh and Hartley have resisted this development, in so far as they object to it and do their best to ignore it.

The basic rights common to all citizens have been extended, during the last two centuries, to new spheres of social life. Legal status was the first to lose its differentiating force and was followed by political status. Recent social development is characterized by a tendency to equalize the social position of all citizens with respect to his rights and privileges (a thesis made familiar by T.H. Marshall). Dahrendorf holds that in post-capitalist society industry and society have been dissociated, especially in contrast with capitalist society. The social relations of industry dominate society less than in the past, in so far as the average worker spends less time on his job. Other roles besides occupation have gained in importance. Occupation has been confined to a set place in the individual's life, just as industry has been confined to a set place in society. The ruling class of industry rules over a more limited part of the lives of the workers. Industry now appears as a society within a society. The proportion of the population occupied in industry in modern societies has decreased. This is partly due to the extension of 'tertiary' industries, such as services and administration. As fiction deals overwhelmingly with the leisure lives of its characters, and only to a very limited extent with their working lives, modern conditions have provided the opportunity for the novel to become more realistic. But realism is not merely quantitative.

Not one of our novelists has attempted to portray the industrial aspect of our society, though it accounts for at least eighty per cent of the whole. In their picture, industry is always peripheral, a source of wealth (and even then rarely mentioned) but of nothing else (such as manners or tastes). Their approach has for the most part been pre-industrial, although it could also be seen as post-industrial, as a foretaste of what the novel may become in the future. (Not in style, but in areas of action.) Perhaps the true description is extra-industrial. This is the sphere of Snow's civil servants. The outstanding fact is that they are all middle-class novelists (it would be very difficult to find a single working class novelist of their standing, and contemporary with them—there was Lawrence before and a very few since). The middle-class, even those who can barely pay their way, have always had a hierarchical view of society. It is derived from the notion of a bureaucracy in which everyone has his defined place, both above and below others. One can rise, it is extremely rare and unfortunate to fall, and there is an accepted, institutionalized scale of symbols, titles and status. Where else could one find a better example of this attitude than in Aunt Sarah in the Hilda and Eustace trilogy? Aunt Sarah is so wedded to the idea of hierarchy that she is extremely dubious about the propriety of rising in the world.

William Kornhauser writes in *The Politics of Mass Society*, 1959, that England is exceptional in never having had a mass movement. All the more likelihood, one would have thought, of a solid corpus of writing about working individuals, as traditional fiction does not take kindly to the handling of human masses. In fact potential mass movements have always broken down before reaching fruition, despite the high degree of urbanism which is usually associated with mass movements. 'Actions taken for economic interests tend to be moderate', writes Kornhauser, 'whereas mass actions tend to be extremist.' Mass actions usually grow out of envy, resentment and alienation. Fear of mass action underlies the attitudes, whether stated or implied, of nearly all our novelists, and especially of the class to which they belong, however much they may feel to be misfits. They appear to be reactionary and unenlightened because they set their faces against irreversible processes. The growing equality of condition is one of the irreversible processes, suggests Kornhauser; Hartley, Mitford and Lehmann feel that their personal security is being threatened. Large-scale organization and consequent alienation are also irreversible. But modern trends provide escape hatches at the same time as they seal up some of the traditional openings: greater social alienation is accompanied by enhanced opportunities for new forms of association; the destruction of small enterprises is accompanied by conditions of abundance freeing people for new ways of life; traditional social groups are atomised but there is also a variety of contacts and experiences that broadens the range of social participation. A bargain could be struck but it is not one to be accepted by my novelists, with one major and one minor exception. Isherwood is prepared to use the escape hatches. Bowen may not use them but she recognizes their existence.

Eighteenth century fiction probably gave a fairly accurate picture of eighteenth century society. Nineteenth century fiction was less successful, undervaluing industrialism and ignoring sex. Twentieth century fiction, despite its growing freedom, resembles Restoration drama in giving a picture of its time which could scarcely be recognized by those concerned. The reasons are similar. Restoration drama sees life through the eyes of a dissolute aristocracy. The fiction of my six, which I repeat is fairly representative of their generation (the generation which produced their first fiction between 1920 and 1935), sees life through the eyes of a middle class soured by loss of privilege. Apart from romantic idealists and other exotics, one expects a novel to reflect the life and society of its own time.

Snow certainly has made more pronouncements on society than any of the others, although much of it has been in his speeches and critical writings. In *The Two Cultures* he claimed that what he calls the Scientific Revolution (as distinct from the older and familiar Industrial Revolution) was the result of the application of real science to industry, instead of the hit-or-miss methods of the old inventors. He would not date this earlier than thirty or forty years ago, 'the time when atomic particles were first made industrial use of.' In other words, 1920-30, when most of the novelists in this study were beginning their careers. But which of them seemed aware of this and, if he had been aware, cared? This development, which Snow obviously feels to be the most important one of our time, has virtually been ignored by each of my six and loathed by some of them. It is hard to recall, offhand, a single novelist beyond Snow who introduced a scientist into his work.

At this point it is instructive to compare Snow with Waugh because they polarize the two main currents of our society.[1] There must have been very few issues on which the two were in agreement. Sherriff, in Snow's early work, *The Search*, 1934, fumes about modern civilization in a way that would have been inconceivable to Waugh:

> We're (scientists) getting the power, and that's making our civilisation the first stable one there's been. It's because it's the first civilisation that has got hold of science—not enough yet, but enough to give it power. Call it plumbing if you like, but it's making us unique. And as well as that, we've got scientists: the first collection of people in the world who've been trained to be honest and detached about the things they see.

Waugh would have regarded such a declaration as ridiculously naive. He would have agreed entirely about the statement, 'call it plumbing, if you like'—but he would have added that no worthwhile or even stable civilization can be built on plumbing. The basis must be the circulation of accepted ideas, not of water. In the same novel Miles used to keep a special notebook which recorded the progress of his work, which clearly excites him. He wants to work and he does. None of Waugh's characters want to work. Work is something they regard as being in the nature of a necessary penance. When they are compelled to work they do it grudgingly and it is often trivial (as in *Vile Bodies*) or would-be glamorous (as in *Handful of Dust*). The workpeople are either servile or vulgar. The attitude is that of the schoolboy to the swot. Work is degrading, and one's aim should be to reach a situation where it is no longer necessary. There is a similar discrepancy in the attitude to money. As Miles's work progressed he had fewer fears for the future or security and began to enjoy luxuries. He says one has to be poor to enjoy spending. His friends were often astonished by this trait, which he called 'exulting over the vulgarities of luxury'. Constantine, the son of a Devonshire squire, now living in poverty, used to shake his head over such behaviour. Waugh would not have given a pin for either of them—for Constantine because he considered the enjoyment of luxury as a vulgarity that a refined

1. Although Waugh is not one of my selected novelists, I refer to him when it is appropriate in this chapter because he expressed a certain outlook more forcefully than anyone else. His views are, however, comparable with those of Hartley and Mitford.

person should avoid, and for Miles simply because he took the trouble to regard it as a vulgarity at all.

These are fundamental matters, and go far beyond social structure. They belong to the personality, and common ground between Waugh and Snow is inconceivable. If we turn to a more mundane matter, one which affected everybody and which required a deliberate act of will to acknowledge or ignore, the differences may be even more remarkable. This is the coming of war. Towards the end of the thirties every intelligent person except Lord Beaverbrook (if we are to believe him and his editors) knew that war was coming. Even Waugh ended *Vile Bodies* with a disastrous vision of the future. The probability scarcely troubled the surface of writers such as Bowen or Hartley, although the former at least has a social conscience. Even the flippant Miss Mitford was worried. Isherwood's concern was virtually the subject of his writing.

When we look to novelists for a picture of what is happening in society, we do not expect them to give solutions. (There is a type of reviewer who thinks his business is done when he says Mr So-and-So describes the problem but fails to come up with the solution, but we can ignore such puerility.) The modern writer who has stated most clearly what the writer can do is not one of my six, but he was once engaged in a correspondence with one of them which has been published. *Why Do I Write?* is an exchange of views between Elizabeth Bowen, Graham Greene and V.S. Pritchett. Pritchett wrote the Preface and in it he said that an author's use may be to show the inconvenience of human nature. My six do this admirably. One could not imagine them agreeing about anything that involved valuation. But what is even more interesting is that they do not always agree about the physical aspect of modern life, what one might call the statistical, which should not allow variation. Pritchett says that a contemporary cliché of a particularly unhelpful kind is this: 'This is a time of crisis, an age of revolution, transition, despair, etc.' It assumes in advance a positive social reaction of a definite kind, that the author will support this or that, oppose that or the other. Pritchett believed that the contributors to the symposium did at least agree on one thing, that we must turn away from the social situation with its pre-fabricated demands. Beyond that it would be unwise to go. In a letter to Bowen he said he hoped that there was inside every imaginative writer 'an imperialist, expansionist group, urging him to expand beyond the native frontiers of his knowledge and capacity', but he hoped this merely because he didn't like to think he was the only one! 'What fools writers make of themselves in public life', he adds, and when one considers the list, ranging shall we say from Sir Herbert Read to John Braine, most of them well-intentioned, but myopic in areas where you would expect them to be myopic, one has to agree.

The real weakness of the modern novelist is the weakness of everybody else—he is conditioned by his personal past. This is middle-class and relatively comfortable, which disqualifies him when he tries to discuss the social condition. Orwell once reviewed a book by a cotton operative who had undergone long periods of unemployment and poverty (*Caliban Shrieks,* by Jack Hilton, 1935). He made the point that such books are exceedingly rare. 'They are the voices of a normally silent multitude. All over England, in every industrial town, there are men by scores of thousands whose attitude to life, if only they could express it, would be very much what Mr Hilton's is.' Most of these people have no idea of how to get their thoughts on paper. The reason Orwell was so greatly intrigued by Miller's *Tropic of Cancer* was that it did partly bridge the tremendous gap which exists in fiction between the intellectual and the man-in-the-street. 'English fiction on its higher levels is for the most part written by literary gents about literary gents for literary gents . . .' This takes us to the hub of the matter. Orwell goes on to say that there is fiction on the lower levels but it is the most putrid escape stuff—'old maids' fantasies about Ian Hay male virgins, or little fat men's visions of themselves as Chicago gangsters.' We are still familiar with this—postmen in the Midlands finding fulfilment in a fantasy Wild West, for example. Even Maclaren-Ross did not really break through. He had the good fortune to be writing when a natural anarchist's delight in social mockery was enabled to make contact with the working man's delight in sending up the bosses.

A casual observer in Britain could see the middle classes but on the whole did not encounter the others. This is less true now than it was, but it still holds. Talk to any American tourist who thinks he has seen the country. Cole and Postgate, in their valuable *The Common People,* 1956, say that despite the poverty of the working classes in 1939, it didn't show much. The salary-earning class numbered about three million, and many of them did not earn much more than the better paid manual workers, but they spent their earnings differently and the results showed more. Most of my six belonged to this sector and the effect on their vision is indisputable. Wage-earners in industry, the commercial proletariat of shop assistants and warehouse workers, workers in personal service and agricultural labourers numbered seventeen million. The salariat lived along the by-pass roads, they crowded more into the shopping centres, they thronged theatres and shows in the middle of the great towns much more than the wage-earners. They were above all visible in London; and their very obtrusiveness led easily to an over-impression of prevailing prosperity. Again, all over the country the richer a man was the more room he took, and the more he *showed*. The undiminished wealth of the British upper classes was very plain everywhere. It could be seen with the naked eye, whereas the precariousness of its foundations could not.

The authors claim that the nine years of the 'National' Government were more disastrous than any nine years since the Restoration.

Some of the best writing from my six is to be found in descriptions of the places in which people live: their houses, the new estates, the rambling old country houses, the desolate streets of run-down towns. Some of this I have already quoted. Place is, one feels, the most important thing in life to the British novelist and the class from which he comes. Along with the bricks and mortar, which could be portrayed by a photograph or an estate agent's report (discounting the dishonest claims), there is something extra which is the natural contribution of the creative writer—a sense of belonging, or involvement, or of alienation. The spirit is excitingly alive or it is drearily moribund.

The really big social event of my period, the thing all my novelists noticed to varying degrees, even if they missed or ignored unemployment and poverty and even some of the major aspects of war, has been Subtopia, a term that first came into use after they had all established themselves. But they saw it and nowhere has it been better described than in *The Dog Beneath the Skin,* in the Chorus introduction to Act III, words written (presumably) by W.H. Auden, but underwritten by Christopher Isherwood. A man and a dog are entering a city. They approach a centre of culture.

> First the suburban dormitories spreading over fields,
> Villas on vegetation like saxifrage on stone,
> Isolated from each other like cases of fever
> And uniform in design, uniform as nurses.
> To each a lean-to shed, containing a well-oiled engine of escape.
> Section these dwellings: expose the life of a people
> Living by law and the length of a reference . . .

An Impending Disaster

One oddity that arises from a study of these writers is that, although in some ways they appear to be myopic, they all share a sense of things going wrong. It is possible that some of them do not write about certain dominant social trends not merely because they do not have first-hand knowledge of them but because they would find it depressing. The giving of pleasure ranks high in the works of most artists—even Wordsworth and Eliot stressed this point—and those writers who are notably gloomy often turn out to be spiritual masochists.

Elizabeth Bowen frequently expresses a sense of unease. It is a very subtle undercurrent in her work, rarely expressed so baldly as in *The House in Paris,* 1935, when Karen tells her aunt she would like the Revolution to come soon: 'I should like to start fresh while I am still young, with everything that I had to depend on gone.' Max says that nowadays the world is 'in bad taste; it is no longer "history in the making", or keeps rules or falls in with nice ideas. Things will soon be much more than embarrassing . . .' Thirty years later Hartley(*The Betrayal,* 1966) is convinced that the change has already come. His reaction is disgust, a complete lack of hope. The mood is repeated by Isherwood in *The World in the Evening,* 1954. During the thirties he felt and expressed the mood explicitly, but in this novel there is a character named Elizabeth Rydal (one feels at times it could be Elizabeth Bowen) who feels it in the very air she breathes. She is not political but she mentions her fears in a letter to a friend. She is describing a sumptuous banquet on a raft on a lake in Austria. She says to her husband:

> What a marvellous first act for a play! Only, you know, I have an unpleasant feeling that this isn't a comedy. Not even a satirical one. Don't you see something hovering over it all? It frightens me, somehow. I'm afraid it isn't by Shaw. It might even be Ibsen.

Isherwood will always be associated with the period when Fascism triumphed. He described the process. His work is valuable not because he warned us what was happening (dozens of foreign correspondents were able to do that quite adequately) but because he showed how insidiously Fascism could creep into the minds of ordinary apparently decent people. He was able to understand how certain aspects of Fascist ideology might attract people of the calibre of Lawrence and Yeats, so that the unthinking would see that in them and nothing else. He knew, from his own self-knowledge, how it could happen to him.

When he was an undergraduate he did not concern himself much with politics, nor for a few years afterwards— yet when he came to write *Lions and Shadows* in 1938 he was able to understand much of the political complex that was always hidden from most of his contemporaries, including the other novelists in this study, if we are to judge by their writings. If Snow was aware of Fascist psychology and appeals that could be made in its name and the responses it welcomed, he kept it out of his published work.[1]

While Isherwood was evolving his cult of the public school and his daydreams of 'The Test', imagining himself in roles of austere heroism, chastising moral rottenness, repressing feelings, triumphing over obstacles, furtively reading boys' adventure books and exercising with a chest expander, he was preparing himself for the Fascist ideal. 'It is so very easy, in the mature calm of a library, to sneer at all this homosexual romanticism. But the rulers of Fascist states do not sneer—they profoundly understand and make use of just these fantasies and longings.' And he wonders how he would have reacted if an English Fascist had served up his message in the right form for him at that time. Compared with Hitler, Mosley adopted a relatively intellectual approach in his policy.

The thirties were a period when a number of people were dragged into politics by the scruff of the neck. The unpolitical Linda in Miss Mitford's *Pursuit of Love* went to France to help Spanish refugees. Dinah in Miss Lehmann's *The Echoing Grove* took an organizing job in London on behalf of the Spanish Republic—'unpaid, it meant real poverty, but that was nothing.' Neither girl had shown much social conscience previously, yet both married active Left-wingers: Linda's Christian went with her to France, Dinah's Jo was killed in the International Brigade.

But this is overt, explicit politics, an important part of the general atmosphere of breakdown, but not the whole of it. The kind of change sensed by writers like Bowen and Hartley is cultural, something much more deeply interfused with the normal processes of life. Snow had his own alternative sense of things changing. But there was naturally overlapping—many of his New Men, primarily scientists, were also fellow-travellers or even Party members. (In this context the Party is always the Communist Party, which is odd considering its insignificance.) 'It seemed self-evident that the war was being won or lost on Russian land', Snow writes, and he meant more than the miltary war.

1. Except for the early and anonymous *New Lives for Old*. In the latest list of Snow's work this is omitted.

Despite the abuses of socialism to be found in Russia, that was where the hope appeared to lie. Waugh was certain that it could not be won in such company, civilization had been betrayed. Lewis Eliot and Luke and Getliffe used to ask themselves who they would support, Hitler or communism, if there were no alternative. There was no doubt: 'the communists had done ill that good might come.' For Waugh there simply had to be an alternative, which was to oppose both. Thus *Strangers and Brothers* is describing a society that is trying to adapt itself and even making qualified progress.[1]

Before the war nearly all the younger and more thoughtful writers seemed to accept the case against capitalism and to be, with varying qualifications, socialist in outlook. Since the war doubts have been increasingly expressed about the validity of the socialist ideal, and many who used to call themselves socialist now speak of a 'mixed economy' or don't speak at all. There is an air of bafflement. Certainly it is painful to set aside the strongly held convictions of one's youth. As early as 1944 F.A. Hayek was making this point in an important if neglected book, *The Road to Serfdom*.

> It is now often said that democracy will not tolerate 'capitalism'. If 'capitalism' means here a competitive system based on free disposal over private property, it is far more important to realize that only within this system is democracy possible. When it becomes dominated by a collectivist creed, democracy will inevitably destroy itself.

One finds instinctive recognition and acceptance of this view in Mitford, Hartley and Bowen. (What one cannot be sure of, however, is how much real concern these writers have for democracy.) Lehmann and Isherwood have shown a progressive realization of this view while Snow reserves judgment. The interesting point is that while in their youth Isherwood and Snow called themselves socialists, Mitford called herself one with little realization of what it meant, and Lehmann felt herself to be one, it is doubtful if any of them deserve the name now.

Why has this happened? It is in response to the peculiar cultural, social and political climate that has characterized these years. Nothing has turned out quite as expected. It may be objected that historical development is always like that but I doubt if there has ever been a comparable period in recent centuries when all the prophets have been

---

1. It is interesting to compare with another sequence, running parallel to Snow's—Anthony Powell's *Music of Time* which is about social break-up.

wrong. The main factor is that the younger generation just have not behaved as they were expected to do. It is a cliché that youth is always rebellious, but in fact all previous rebellions have been in concert with a more mature group. The words of an English headmaster, Mr John Elam of Colchester Royal Grammar School, made on retirement are particularly perceptive in this respect.

> The teenagers are worried, very worried, to some extent because they are more informed. Essentially they are worried about the affluent materialistic society. But whereas in the twenties and thirties there were directions in which they could channel their feelings—in the direction of social democracy, for example—so much of this has been achieved, and they feel social democracy has been turned into materialism. And how right they are!

Not only the teenagers have reacted in this way. The only one of my six who appears to be largely satisfied with contemporary society, or with the direction it is taking, is Isherwood. And this is because he himself has suffered a change in direction. England is more socialistic now than it was before the war but that is not the main reason he is pleased. What delights him is the element that horrifies Hartley and Mitford, the increased permissiveness of our society. Snow is also alarmed by it, but his misgivings are caused by one aspect which is surely not a necessary part of permissiveness: violence. He stands on a middle ground which approves of the material advances but not of the atmosphere that has accompanied them. Each of my six novelists is a traditional writer, but it is Snow who has been most identified with an attack on literary experiment, which some of my writers would probably regard as a concomitant of unpleasing social behaviour. It is impossible at this stage to discover organic relationships between literary experiment and social permissiveness, but there is a tendency among human beings to relate positively events that coincide in time.

Snow uses the expression Man-in-Society in describing what he sets out to do in his sequence, in an effort to stress the relatedness of all men with each other. His friend William Cooper uses the same term in his essay, 'Reflections on Some Aspects of the Experimental Novel', which appeared in *International Library Annual*, No. 2, ed. John Wain, 1959. During the war he and a 'literary comrade-in-arms' (Snow) decided to assault Experimental Writing, which in their view was about Man-Alone. They intended to write about Man-in-Society *as well*—Cooper stressed the importance of those two words. The novel had been getting emptier and emptier. Anxious, despairing intellectuals saw a general degradation in contemporary industrialized society and a loss of scope for expressing individuality. But this was false . . .

> . . . because in the first place it is not general; since for the few people who, through loss of privilege, have less scope than formerly, there are great numbers who, through longer education and a more comfortable way of living, get *more* scope than they would have got in pre-industrialized society. Though they may only be switching on television, that represents, for them, a step forward, a gain. In the second place, recognizing this general degradation of personality when it is not there makes it easier for the people whose purposes it would suit to introduce it. This is why these particular anxious, suspicious, despairing intellectuals are really on the side of totalitarianism. You see, their response towards degradation of personality is acquiescence; in their novels it is taken 150% for granted.

It should not be deduced from this, however, that despair is the prerogative of the experimentalist intellectual. Waugh's last work was brimming with despair; Hartley's is by no means lacking; it colours Mitford's later work, and may have been partly responsible for her forsaking the novel. And in the case of Snow himself, we have to ask whether the absence of despair may not be the obverse of lowering his sights.

Youthful Protest

As I have said, friction between the generations is nothing new, but the manner of the contemporary friction is. There are naturally several instances of the traditional type friction in the work of my novelists. It had become so commonplace it was frequently treated as a joke. Albert Gates, in Nancy Mitford's *Highland Fling,* speaks contemptuously of the men who made and fought the war. Buggins reproves him.

> Everybody knows—you are at no pains to conceal it—that the young people of today despise and dislike the men and women of my age. I suppose that never since the world began have two generations been so much at variance. You think us superficial, narrow-minded, tasteless and sterile, and you are right . . .

And the famous Uncle Matthew in the later and more famous novels hated the young reciprocally. It was a routine generation reaction of an intensely conservative man who distrusted anything new and unfamiliar. What he did not realize was that the attitudes he loathed were not new and unfamiliar. The special feature of the post-war hatred of the young for the old is that in many cases they do have a new angle on life.

But we today do tend to think that this kind of essential difference is entirely new. We have a sense of breakthrough, and this is because the younger generation are better informed and better educated, and have acquired a new vocabulary with roots in disciplines such as Zen and life-spheres such as pop-music. But there are passages in Rosamund Lehmann's *Weather in the Streets*, 1936, which could describe the contemporary situation, except that the writing is obviously pre-war. For example, Olivia goes to a party and feels old. Although the young are in a minority they seem to have taken over. 'I'm renouncing parties', says Adrian. 'I'm thirty-three. It's time to think of one's dignity.' He says the young are extraordinarily self-centred, entirely wrapped up in themselves. Olivia thinks the new lot are happier, more vigorous and confident than her lot. Adrian says, 'I loathe the young. Selfish, silly little beasts. I'm damned if I see why they should make one feel inferior.'

Isherwood gives the picture from the other end in his *Down There on a Visit*, 1962.

> As far as I was concerned, everyone over forty belonged, with a mere handful of honourable exceptions, to an alien tribe; hostile by definition but in practice ridiculous rather than formidable. The majority of them I saw as utter grotesques, sententious and gaga, to be regarded with indifference. It was only people of my own age who seemed to me better than half alive.

This point of view had not been expressed in his earlier works; it was a kind of grafting on to his past in the light of later events. In this phase it was merely an emotion but since the war the antagonism has hotted up and has even entered a political phase (as Snow realizes). In the same novel Isherwood looks in a mirror, and sees his twenty-three year-old face looking back at him reproachfully. He felt that it was such a pretty little face it should have been blown up and used as a poster on behalf of the World's Young: 'The Old hate us because we're so cute. Won't *you* help?' As an older man he recognizes and even appreciates the point of view, but cannot resist treating it satirically. One form this attitude has taken has been the debunking of those who used to be regarded as great, or leaders. Kingsley Amis revels in it. One could not imagine L.P. Hartley subjecting Jane Austen to the kind of treatment Amis has given her.

The Amis approach has more in it that is akin to sadism than to
criticism. He cannot hurt Miss Austen but one feels he delights in
knocking her reputation. Isherwood has something of this in him, and
it is strange because he belongs to an earlier generation. 'I knew, with
sudden intense force', he writes, 'just how awful the Odyssey and the
voyage of the *Pequod* must have been; and that I would have sooner
or later jumped overboard rather than listen to either of those ghastly
sea-bores, Ulysses and Ahab.' But it is not the stories he would have
resented, it was their age, which affronted him like a bad smell. He
describes in the same novel how Paul registered as a CO (in America)
and went before a draft-board which 'included some really malevolent
old men who wanted to put the entire younger generation into uniform
just because they *were* young.' Perhaps it was this happening a second
time which changed an emotion into an emotional stance.

There are natural contrasts which jump to the mind while considering these writers. Waugh must be contrasted with Snow and equally
Isherwood with Hartley. Isherwood welcomes the new society and
even seems prepared to accept the violence that is part of it. This is
a familiar act, like accepting William Saroyan's sentimentality with
his marvellous vitality or Walter de la Mare's coyness with his
perceptiveness. And it is Hartley who is in retreat! Despite his dislike
of modern frankness, casualness and the 'sophistication' of the
unpolished, Hartley appears to be surrendering occasionally to their
temptation in his later work. To introduce homosexual scenes in a
public lavatory (as he does in *My Sister's Keeper*) is as shocking as
the moral decline in *Nostromo*. But the process had started before, at
least as early as 1961 in the stories entitled *Two For the River,* where
we see the whores on their beat in 'The Face' and the knife blade
pointing at the vitals of the female figure made out of cotton-wool
in 'The Corner Cupboard'. Hartley's acceptance seems uneasy.
Bowen, on the other hand, has come to terms with the new spirit far
more smoothly, as is evident from *Eva Trout,* a magnificent achievement. But it is Hartley who expresses the change that has been taking
place most economically and tellingly back in 1953, in what may be
his best novel, *The Go-Between,* which was set in the Boer War
period: 'Young men in those days didn't try to look young, they
aped the appearance of maturity.' In other words, it is a matter of
confidence. There is a bitter undertone to the whole novel, which
accounts for its peculiar quality. Along with the sense of personal
betrayal there are references to the new century dawning and the
glory it would bring. With his love of symbolism (in this novel
capably handled) this comment intensifies the feeling.

But there is a considerable difference between a change in atmosphere and the explosive situation that had arisen by 1968. To what extent did any of these novelists foresee the social sundering that came to a climax in that year, following on the mods and rockers, the wildcat strikes, bureaucratic hardening and the decline of political democracy? The answer is surely very little. The character of the new movement was so different from what had gone before, my six novelists had had no training in the prediction of this sort of thing. Diana Trilling, who belongs to their generation, put the matter succinctly in an article, 'Celebrating With Dr Leary', that appeared in *Encounter,* June 1967.

> We too, at their age, had pointed to the violence of those in power. My contemporaries, too, had set themselves to make a revolution in consciousness, which would make us 'free'.[1] But our means had been social and political, and now the very concept of society was inoperative. But if ours had been an ideology of social involvement, not of withdrawal, this could now be no boast—it had led to a blockage of hope which could perhaps never be, certainly had not been, surmounted by a succeeding generation.

Such honest admission of failure is rare in public statement. But compare the thoughtfulness of this statement with poor bewildered Miss Mitford, who became a socialist because she could not bear social injustice and withdrew horrorstruck when a new generation decided to follow their own way to utopia, or nirvana, or whatever the vogue word might be. Her 'French Revolution Diary' was published in the *Spectator* and a sad, trivial document it turned out to be. She seemed to be impatient with the students who were demonstrating around her (she was in the thick of it, in Paris) not so much because their slogans were democratic or progressive but because of their youth and their attack on age—anyone over thirty. 'It now seems they think that everybody over thirty ought to be dead. Marie Antoinette, when she became Queen, said she didn't know how people over thirty dared show their faces at court. She called them *les siècles*. Poor dear, she was soon over thirty herself and didn't end too well.' On her way home from a park two boys on a motor-cycle pretended they were going to kill her and followed her on to the footpath,

1. This is doubtful, a kind of rationalisation after the event. The only group who thought in terms of a 'revolution in consciousness' before the war were the surrealists, always a small minority group. (Footnote added)

but it ended in laughs and friendly waves. 'I do hope the over-thirties are going to be killed mercifully and quickly and not starved to death in camps.' She listened to a BBC programme, which said nothing of the 'demographic aspect of the revolt: the young against the old.'

Underneath the rather nervous gaiety there seems to lie a core of humourlessness. The students are not morons (when charges are made against their intelligence they come out of irritation) and they know quite well that they themselves will all too soon be over thirty. What it amounts to is a sensational, and typically French political, way of putting a point—that the older generations have lost their idealism and made a mess of things. This is true and there should be no need to spell it out. The method is symbolical and a creative writer might be expected to grasp the point. I am reminded of one of the occasions when mods and rockers rioted on a southern beach, and a well-meaning bourgeois family man asked one of them why he was doing it. The boy snapped back, 'So I won't grow up like you'. To the school-trained, pap-fed mind this is illogical. To the free intelligence it says all that is necessary.

Bowen makes an interesting statement in the 1949 Preface to the re-issue of her first book, *Encounters,* a collection of stories first published in 1923. 'I know that I had a snobbery with regard to age. For my generation (possibly the last of which this was true) grown-ups were the ruling class.' She was always afraid she might fail to attain grown-up status. A writer and a grown-up had to be synonymous. 'As far as I can see (more from these stories, re-read, than from my memory) I was anxious at once to approximate to the grown-ups and to demolish them'. The demolition project is interesting as being a very early instance of what was to prevail.

Is it surprising? In a lecture Ralf Dahrendorf mentioned a 'profound and justified sense of frustration with a society which has promised so much more than any other society in history, but which has so far not kept its promise.' What remains to be decided is the nature of the failure. Is it that the odds were too great or that the progressives did not fully understand the implications of their policies, as Hayek would have us believe? In fact, a failure not in policy but in intelligence.

> We are ready to accept almost any explanation of the present crisis of our civilization except one: that the present state of the world may be the result of genuine error on our own part, and that the pursuit of some of our most cherished ideals have apparently produced results utterly different from those which we expected. (F.A. Hayek, *The Road to Serfdom,* 1944).

Hayek believes that socialist theory and propaganda, backed up by socialist experiments, often by well-meaning people, have caused social and economic crisis. Against this we have the views of Lord Snow, an active agent in the implementation of the new policies, who suggests in *The Sleep of Reason* that all might have been well had not a cloud of permissiveness blackened the social sky. And so we come back to views on the permissive society, which tend to be circular. One of the outstanding points about English society is its inegalitarianism. I hasten to add that there is nothing unusual about this—writers who suggest that England is exceptionally inegalitarian must be unforgivably naive and insular. But the fact is there, staring you in the face, and it is possibly the major characteristic noted by my six novelists. I say 'possibly' because it would take a committee of seven statisticians seven full working years to measure it and the effort would not be worth it.

As I have said, all my authors come from the middle class, but the range within the class is fairly wide. In fact, the distance between Snow and Mitford, in origin and in current attitude, is immense. What use are we? is a question occasionally asked by the rich men in Snow's fiction, borrowing conscience from their creator. No Waugh aristocrat would ask such a question, but a Mitford one would. If the question were put to the Waughmen, and they felt bound to make a reply, it would be that they supplied a way of life, rural and hierarchical, that was superior to any other. Waugh took the line that the aristocracy ought to be accepted because there was no better alternative. But accepted for what? The only valid justification is for governing, and aristocrats do not govern any more. When they did they governed sufficiently badly to cause the population to demand a change. What Waugh really meant was that the aristocracy should be social leaders, a brave idea that on examination turns out to be entirely nebulous and unnecessary. Society does not require leaders as society has no policy. Beau Brummell and Lady Docker are historic freaks.

The concept of aristocracy is based on the idea of natural leadership. There is no viable idea of this kind as applied to a class. There are natural leaders within each class, but leadership by a class (which is a valid concept) depends on functional criteria, normally concerned with ownership of the means of production. Only deliberate blindness can accept that a class can be selected for leadership without a term. But as many people are blind, deliberately or through thoughtless surrender to tradition, it is possible for a class to go on exerting the role of leadership long after its functional powers have declined. A true aristocrat, like Miss Mitford, is likely to acknowledge this, for he admits that his privileged position is almost certainly based on robbery, chicanery or violence at some time in the past. Hartley makes this quite clear in the case of Denys Aspin *(The Betrayal)*. The ancestor won his position, the descendant inherits the prize. Grace Allingham's father, for instance, in Mitford's *The Blessing,* tells her that luck is the basis of life. (Thus Chesterton's defence of the House of Lords: institutionalized luck.) A belief in luck can be supported by rival groups. It can maintain an aristocracy or, as luck must in the long run be shared out equally, there will be a levelling out over the generations.

Considerations such as these presumably occur now and again to those who inherit wealth. The best example in my material is Charles March, the son of a very rich man, in Snow's *The Conscience of the Rich.* He becomes a doctor because he wishes to live a useful life and his father disinherits him because he is denying wealth (and therefore rejecting his father). Charles finds his new circumstances enjoyable, despite the financial pinch. He says to Lewis Eliot, 'Last month I made over eighty pounds—if they all pay me. You've no idea how pleasant it is to earn your own living. It's a pleasure you can only really appreciate if you've been supported in luxury every since you were born.' No Waugh character would regard it as a pleasure. But Waugh characters were the creations of a man who envied wealth from a severely middle-class background. Charles's friends often felt that his new life of abnegation suited him badly, and they looked back with regret to the days when they remembered him as 'gay,[1] malicious, idle, brilliant'—in other words, a Waughman.

The outward and visible sign of inequality in society is privilege. In my chapter on Snow I drew attention to the claim made by one of his characters that privilege has declined. This, as I said, is doubtful because the nature of privilege has changed. Certainly one type of privilege has virtually disappeared for good. This is the abject, automatic respect that used to be extended by the worker to his boss, often described by journalists as 'forelock touching'. Faint memories of it are to be encountered in some of these novels—for example, in Bowen's *The Death of the Heart,* 1938, an old-fashioned couple from Shropshire, the Peppinghams, still expected, it: '*instinctive* respect. That means so much to the people working for us.' The notion that it was the worker or servant who demanded the right to offer such respect used to be strongly held—native servants could never with-

1. This was written before the homosexuals confiscated, with no-one's authority, the word 'gay' and perverted its historic meaning.

hold their tears when the sahibs left for good. When the old-fashioned ideas about correct behaviour began to crumble, it was always the younger generation who suffered first—if suffer is the correct word. In the same novel, when Portia went to live with her brother Thomas and his wife Anna, she had to dine downstairs. This surprised, even shocked the old family retainer, whose ideas of propriety dated from a time when 'the young ladies, with bows on flowing horsetails of hair, supped upstairs with their governess . . . In the house of today there is no place for the miss.'

This may at first sight seem to have little to do with privilege but in fact it was a brick in the house of hierarchy. One can regard it as the outer defence works; the real strength of privilege still lay untouched. Boys from the right families would continue to get preferential treatment. In one of Rosamund Lehmann's stories, 'Wonderful Holidays' (*The Gypsy's Baby and Other Stories,* 1946), Mrs Ritchie is greatly taken by eighteen-year old Roger, who is so attractive and talented. It is wartime. 'He would go into the Army, and be drilled and do fatigues and go on courses, and be sent to his O.C.T.U. and get his commission . . .' Not quite so effortless as a Waugh hero's progress, but there was no reasonable doubt about what the future held. One can find innumerable examples of this sort of thing in these novels. Mitford's Linda marries Tony Kroesig, the banker's son, they have their honeymoon, he starts work in his father's bank 'and prepared to step into a safe Conservative seat in the House of Commons, an ambition which was very soon realized.'

Snow explains why the privilege implicit in these relationships decayed and had to decay with the development of the kind of society that is now becoming worldwide. His famous *Two Cultures* was republished in 1963 with an addendum called 'A Second Look', which contained this passage.

> With singular unanimity the unprivileged have elected for societies where they are as far away as possible from the Captain-Sam situation (i.e., Master-Man)—which, of course, highly articulated societies are. Trade unions, collective dealing, the entire apparatus of modern industry—they may be maddening to those who have never had the experience of the poor, but they stand like barbed wire against the immediate assertion of the individual will. And, as soon as the poor began to escape from their helplessness, the assertion of the individual will was the first thing they refused to take.

This is a lesson about the development of working class power which was only obvious to those who had thought long and hard about the actual implications of such development. There have been well-meaning people who imagined they would welcome the justice of increased economic freedom and a degree of socialist practice, only to recoil angrily when they discovered what these things meant in pragmatic terms. Among my novelists Mitford is clearly one of these. At heart a generous soul, she wanted the lower classes to improve their lot. When it happened she found that the new situation impinged on privileges she had taken for granted, and she reacted angrily.

The spread of privilege (and to a lesser extent, its redistribution) had been foreseen by Thorstein Veblen as early as 1899 when *Theory of the Leisure Class* appeared. At that time leisure and extravagance were the hallmarks of the upper class, visible proof that they could remain aloof from sordid industry. By the time Anthony Sampson wrote *Anatomy of Britain*, 1962, the change was well advanced. 'Today the aristocratic prerogative has spread downwards, and all England is putting on style'. This is a shadow-statement of what Snow had already said. Mitford drew attention to the process in *Don't Tell Alfred*, 1960, when Fanny asks Basil if he is giving up the Foreign Service to run tours abroad. 'Now listen, Mother dear', says Basil, 'the Foreign Service has had its day—enjoyable while it lasted, no doubt, but over now. The privileged being of the future is the travel agent. He lives free, travels soft— don't think he shares the sufferings of his people, he has a firstclass sleeper, the best room in the hotel.'

Basil draws attention to a social truth that tends to be ignored by more static commentators. The latter speak of 'the spread of privilege', but this is a situation that cannot endure for long. Eventually the privilege finds a new home. It floats about, like existentialist thistle-down, and finally alights on a new terrain. Note that the travel agent is not sharing privilege with the old established classes. He is replacing them, in thoroughly up-to-date terms. On his package tour there will probably be at least one person of aristocratic or erstwhile upper-class connection. But the agent is the new magnate, the posh hotel his castle, the servants and stewardesses his staff, the tourists his duty-paying peasants. This is a minor example of what is happening on a much bigger scale. The recent growth of monopoly is largely the result of a deliberate collaboration of organized capital and organized labour where the privilege groups of labour share in the monopoly profits at the expense of the community and particularly at the expense of the poorest, those employed in the less well organized industries, and the unemployed. One striking result of this situation is that many middle class people, who have been brought up to regard themselves as superior to the working class population, now earn far less money than, and live in greatly inferior style to, large groups of workers.

But the change may still not be as great as might appear. It may yet consist more of a swapping of personnel rather than a change in the way of life. Put briefly, it could result in little more than a change in the domestic origin of boys going to public schools. The lower classes and their spokesmen deride the public schools until they are in a position to send their offspring to them. I am certainly not denying that a major change in way of life is taking place in this country, but this is a technological matter and would happen anyway, and is happening everywhere. But in human terms it may not amount to much more than a shuffling of the classes.

Class inequality is based on a money structure, and much of social behaviour is concerned with its concealment. No-one expresses this fact so subtly as Elizabethan Bowen. In *The Hotel* Mrs Kerr tells her son Ronald how pleased she is that he has come from Germany to see her. She hopes it didn't cost a lot. Ronald looks embarrassed for she has broken one of the unmentioned rules: she had referred to money. She covers the slip hastily. 'I meant in *development*. Pictures. Music.' She translates money into commodities; despite their artistic affiliations, they are still commodities. The Victorians, of whom Mrs Kerr is the heir, made a commodity of everything, even including sex. (See Steven Marcus.)

The most remarkable statement on this fundamental lubrication of the English social structure, money, is to be found in Hartley's work, especially the Eustace and Hilda trilogy, and especially *The Shrimp and the Anemone*. In this novel concern for money reaches the intensity of obsession in a way that cannot be found elsewhere. The English novel, like any other novel, is greatly concerned with money and would be false if it were not, but nowhere else will we find anything approaching Hartley's unremitting concern. Money and the problems it poses fill the minds of Eustace and many of the other Hartley characters. It cuts Eustace off from those who possess it like a fence. Think of any other novel which appears to be about the acquisition of wealth, and the difference becomes obvious. *Great Expectations* is about money, but it is about money's corrupting power, and in any case the money was not deliberately sought after. *Vanity Fair* is about social ambition, but at no time do Becky and Rawdon see money itself as their target—in fact, one famous chapter describes how they are perfectly happy to live on Nothing a Year providing they can pursue their pleasures. In novels of social-climbing of the *Tono-Bungay* type the leading characters are always concerned with values which are distinct from money; Uncle Ponderevo was like a machine which had been set in motion and thought as much or as little about ultimate aims as does a machine, while the narrator's concern is entirely for his scientific research. In all of these money is important and is certainly desired, but it is still regarded as the agent, not the principal. Eustace sets his mind on money and even his fantasies are concerned with its acquisition and the terrors that its lack may evoke. Perhaps the novel that comes closest to it in its obsessive power is Orwell's *Keep the Aspidistra Flying,* but it is greatly inferior because the money theme is poorly integrated with the rest.

The money obsession is less in Snow but he acknowledges its existence, sufficiently indeed to provide one of those lectures which constantly impair his fiction. Not only were people becoming increasingly concerned with money but they were becoming more prudish about it. (He draws a parallel with the Victorians and their approach to sex, which they did not like to discuss but by which they were hag-ridden.) Letters to the press, parliamentary debates, the major concerns of public life, all focussed on money. This was a developing trend and had become paramount by 1974, when *In Their Wisdom* was published. (It was set in 1972.) A visitor from another civilization would have concluded pretty quickly that most men thought about money more than they admitted, and badly wanted it. 'The only thing they wanted more, perhaps, was that other men shouldn't have more money than themselves: or ideally should have less.' The pursuit of money became a condition of daily life—Snow compared it with fear in a cholera epidemic—but there was also enjoyment, for the pursuit engendered excitement. It was even possible that those who did not experience the excitement would not have felt fear in an epidemic.

Now we can return to Elizabeth Bowen and her Mrs Kerr, for they have not finished. They are conducting a typically subtle joke. Ronald is in fact in Germany to study economic problems. Pictures and music are in fact secondary matters, so Mrs Kerr corrects herself and says, 'I *mean:* the Rentenmark'. So money is to be mentioned after all, but it is someone else's money, viewed not as a measure of one's wealth and standing (which would be vulgar, and would therefore be regarded as a serious criticism) but as an academic exercise. Once again, money is a commodity, this time a college course.

Among Bowen's characters there are some who are seriously short of money, and this occasionally results in a Hartleyan concern for money. It is never the result of straightforward poverty but of hotel-living, which is the poverty of the rich. The most interesting victim of this situation is Portia in *The Death of the Heart*. She goes to stay with Mrs Heccomb while her brother Thomas and his wife Anna go to the continent. Mrs Heccomb was previously Anna's governess. Portia invites Eddie down and then worries about the expense. 'Having lived in hotels where one's bills wait weekly at the foot of the stairs, and no "extra" is ever overlooked, she had had it borne in on her that wherever anyone is they are costing somebody something, and that the cost must be met.' This is a typical Eustace emotion. In such a situation his nervous intelligence would have quickly created a fantasy in which he would be working for the rest of his life (perhaps in a blacking factory) to cover Eddie's expenses.

The authors of *The Affluent Worker in the Class Structure*[1], research carried out in three Luton plants, found that the strongest tendency among the affluent workers was to regard the class system 'as being primarily a matter of money; or, to be more precise, of differences in the incomes, wealth and material living standards of individual groups.' I doubt if there have ever been working class communities which have thought differently, with the possible exception of those that have been temporarily over-influenced by employers' propaganda. The well-to-do middle classes, on the other hand, have liked to maintain the notion that class distinctions are based on personal qualities of moral leadership, intelligence, foresight and so on. It is only when a member of this class finds himself perilously near the line that divides him from those below that a measure of social realism begins to colour his thinking. There is a remarkable story by Bowen called 'The Disinherited' in *The Cat Jumps*, 1934, in which she seems to concentrate all her normally unexpressed feelings about class failure and social collapse. All the characters feel that they have been let down by society. The story ends with Davina, a sprig of the aristocracy, walking up a hill, clicking her thumb and finger, and thinking: 'If I had money . . .' Eustace needed money to enter the wonderful world of the aristocrats. Davina knew that if you were in that world and lost your money you might get squeezed out. (In fact, as I have stated earlier, this is by no means certain, as the upper reaches of society have a tremendous tradition of loyalty to the less fortunate members. Drop-outs can

1. *The Affluent Worker in the Class Structure,* by John Goldthorpe, David Lockwood, Frank Bechhofer and Jennifer Platt. Cambridge University Press, 1970.

cause great damage.) In the same volume of stories there is a girl named Maria (in the story of that name) who consciously enjoys the idea of her family's wealth. She is a typical Bowen child without parents, but an aunt who dumps her with different families from time to time. When she is taken to stay with people she likes to know how much they think she is worth. In her well-bred way she is a little whore.

Each stratum of middle class society has its peculiar way of coming to terms with the ogre-magician, Money. The Waughmen regard it as their right. Bowen's slightly impoverished aristocrats would like to regard it as their right but acknowledge that an odd thing has happened—at times they find it rather short. This leads to the occasional embarrassed comment—'it's cheaper here' thinks Antonia (*A World of Love*) who doesn't enjoy being at Montefort and would much rather be back in London or, better still, abroad. She elaborates: 'If it weren't for money, we could get off to Spain.' Hartley's characters come from a lower social stratum. Money has never been their birthright, they have had to work for it, but they do not want to give the impression of having worked for it. They know, from observation of their betters, that they should never talk about money; the result is that they think about it endlessly. This attitude, of pretending that one is above such a mundane thing as money, filters through to the lower reaches of the middle class, but their defences are meagre. They will be cavalier about money when there is a reasonable chance of their possessing it, but if they see it withdrawing they are ready to pounce. It is not so easy to write about social matters as it used to be because the study of society, or sociology, has become institutionalized. Once that happens rules and regulations are drawn up; they may or may not be useful. But at least they give direction. Today it is direction that is most obviously lacking, as the academics who now act as the College of Sociological Cardinals simply fail to agree. One often longs for the influence of a thinker and writer who is not half gagged by the universities, another Herbert Spencer perhaps, or someone like Peter Drucker, to assert itself. Meanwhile the sociological world is a foggy one, made all the more dangerous by a series of mantraps which ought to be cleared (would be cleared if it were any other discipline) but are deliberately left in position to cause inconvenience to fellow-workers. These admittedly rambling observations come to mind whenever one tries to make a positive statement—about alienation, for instance. One lot of sociologists thinks alienation is a major aspect of our culture, another lot derides such an idea. The latter certainly come from the world of my six novelists, who give scarcely any impression of what is meant by the concept. If we are prepared to broaden it to dimensions that make it practically worthless for purposes of enquiry, we will find many examples of man at odds with his environment. But this is not what is meant. In the modern meaning of the term, man is not alienated in these novels. In a more traditional one he is alienated all the time, for alienation is a seed of conflict and without conflict there is no art of fiction. If any of my six seems at times to straddle the two worlds, it is L.P. Hartley. The frustrations of his characters are not merely personal irritations; they are the product of social forces which the individual resents and resists.

There is no point in asking whether my novelists reflect satisfaction or dissatisfaction with their world. Responses vary too much, even on the part of a single writer. But it is interesting and even instructive to ask whether they have noticed any discernible improvement in the human condition. Lewis Eliot in *Last Things,* looking back over his past life, said that one of the things he had wanted had been a better world. Now he felt that this sounded priggish, even innocent. He does not explain this reaction, and it is not easy to understand why one should feel ashamed of such a hope. As for the innocence, that lies in assuming that the world is worse today than it was forty years ago. This is a familiar fate of the young idealist, who learns by the hard way that improvement is never as simple a matter as it seems. This in turn acts as a self-accusation, for one stands exposed as naif. On balance I feel that the world today is a better place and a more hopeful place than it was fifty years ago, when the first of my six began writing. Isherwood feels the same about England, and does not suffer from a sense of unreality. On the other hand, the world is a far more dangerous place than it was fifty years ago.

Perhaps Snow's judgment (or mis-judgment, as I feel it to be) illustrates the lack of balance that lies at the heart of his sequence, and which becomes more obvious as it develops. As the work is very self-consciously projected as a balanced survey of our time it serves to demonstrate the difficulty, if not impossibility, of creating literature entirely with one's rational faculty. And this is how I must leave my subject: the craziest vision (Waugh's) produces the truest perceptions, and the most controlled approach (Snow's) goes most seriously astray.

INDEX

INDEX

(of non-fictional persons and publications by the six writers under review.)